MORE PR

LEWIS MUMFORD AND THE FOOD FIGHTERS

"Part Appalachian tall tale, part thoughtful critique of the global systems that feed us, Turner weaves an engaging story about people working together to create a new way to eat that is better for land, community, and the planet."

— Laura Lengnick, author of Resilient Agriculture: Cultivating Food Systems for a Changing Climate.

"Warmer climate means two things: floods and drought... When that happens, crops fail. And when that starts to happen on a global scale mass migration becomes a strategic problem. There will be food shortages. There will be border wars. There will be water scarcity and countries will fight over water. Countries will fight over the fact that migrants are going from one country to another."

— Mike McConnell, former United States Director of National Intelligence

DISCLAIMER

This book describes the author's experience with farming and the industrialized food system and reflects his opinions relating to those experiences. Some names and identifying details of individuals mentioned in the book have been changed to protect their privacy.

CONTENTS

CHAPTER ONE

THE SCHOOL OF POSTMODERN ACTIVITIES

One time I had to kill a guy.

In a clandestine hideout on a dark and snaky road deep in the woods of Appalachia, a grungy group of men made a terrible, fateful decision.

"We have to kill El Tigre," said Butch in a cold, angry voice.

'El Tigre', as he was known in parts of Central and South America, deserved to die for all the trouble that he started. I figured we'd be doing the world a favor.

El Tigre had a first name—it was Tony. That's right, Tony the Tiger, and he came out of New York, the creation of an advertising man from the corporate underbelly of Manhattan. Sure, he was a cartoon character and a brand mascot, but that didn't make killing him any easier.

When I last saw 'El Tigre' on television, I couldn't help but notice that he was looking bigger and stronger than I remembered him, like he had been working out, and I wondered if I could still take him. But I knew even then it was all just a false rendering of the truth and part of a sinister deflection and propaganda campaign, one that was designed to convince children that it's alright to eat lots of sugar. Just get a little exercise and you'll be fine, they said. Tony even wore a shiny coach's whistle around his neck. He's a dead man.

I was heading down a precarious path when I found myself in this meeting with a disorganized gang of revolutionary insurgents bent on disrupting the industrialized food system as we know it. I would eventually come to lead them for a brief time, haphazardly, with both feet slipping precariously on the greasy, slimy floor of a darkly lit Brazilian meat factory. International Corporate Kingpins had taken over the food supply, with all the stench of rotting waste and filth and corruption, and someone had to stop them.

For my cover, I was a manager of a small, experimental farm and I read research papers. I also wore reading glasses. After a decade undercover I decided that the modern, industrialized food system was not sustainable. It was heavily dependent on fossil fuels, seriously damaging to the environment, and a major contributor to climate change. But I could see something else much more ominous on the horizon: the complete and total collapse of the corn belt economy, resulting in millions of acres going fallow and economic devastation in the Heartland. Midwestern rural America was headed for a train wreck, and no one saw it coming.

So me and a bunch of oddball fuckups were going to try to do something about it. My neighbor Lewis Mumford was there to pull us back from the brink.

The School of Postmodern Activities, as it came to call itself, is not a school. It's a subversive, covert organization dedicated to dismantling the corporate control of our food supply.

Located fifteen miles outside of Asheville, North Carolina,

it's hidden in a tiny, one-room schoolhouse that was built in 1920, with asbestos shake siding painted brightly red, and tucked away nicely on a twisting mountain road deep in the green woods of the Pisgah National Forest. I'm talking about Western North Carolina, the heart of Appalachia, where the spine of the Blue Ridge mountains cut the eastern United States in half. The road dead-ends just a few miles past the old wood schoolhouse where the mountain gets too steep and says, 'go no further.' The school was the perfect hide-out for a clandestine operation, with lots of tree cover, and almost impossible to find or spot from a helicopter.

A small path behind the schoolhouse vanished into the trees as an easy escape route. If you knew the way through the nearby Pisgah Forest, you could make it to the Appalachian Trail in about ten miles, and from there flee all the way to Southern Georgia or Northern Maine, depending on which way you turned when you got to the dirt footpath, and you would never have to leave the woods. Bring food and water.

The organization is made up of various misfits, farmers, hippies, artists, petty criminals, poets and other beatniks, pranksters, and rebellious types. A couple rich people fill out the group to finance operations, but they didn't often attend the meetings. We listened mostly to the scientists, but we recruited as many guitar players and tree huggers as we could because we needed boots on the ground. They would become our food fighters, and as it turned out, they would do just fine.

In the artist group, many were bohemian by nature, because they believed first in freedom, (meaning never holding a real, full-time job, and a 48-hour workweek was laughable to them), free love when they could get it, and avant-garde art when they could create it from scrap materials laying around. Some lived in the Asheville art district down by the river, in old, dilapidated warehouse buildings converted into art studios along the French Broad. Many of these artist-types slept on a couch, or a cot, or in a sleeping bag on the floor of their shabby little studio because they couldn't afford to pay rent anywhere else. The threat of fire was always present in these dirty, run-down warehouses by the river, especially with so many old kilns set up for glassblowing or pottery and just sitting there, waiting to torch the place.

The farmers and growers were salt of the earth types; hippy environmentalists who sometimes wore shoes or muddy boots, but not always. More women than men, they were small scale, organic farmers and not like the large-scale industrial farmers of the Midwest. Most of them scratched out a living, or at least supplemented their income, growing on three acres or less on the hill tops or in the valleys of these mountains. They sold their goods at the farmers market or in a community support-ed agriculture (CSA) program, and they spent their days toil-ing in the soil and the hot sun trying to grow food in a more just and sustainable manner. The mountains here set the limits and boundaries for the size of a farm and determine the mind-set of what and how food should be grown.

I have a great respect for people who farm the land. They have deeper roots, more patience, and stronger values than most people I know in other occupations. They are the rock upon which our whole movement stands.

A couple poets and writers were recruited from another subversive entity in town; a bookstore on the west side of Asheville called Firestorm Books. West Asheville was a side of town that I didn't frequent very often, until recently, when I needed to start recruiting. It's mostly made up of small coffee shops, funky bars, hole-in-the wall restaurants serving vegan food, artists and musicians, the unemployed (by choice) and the unemployable (by all appearances). It's very bohemian and a little scary, much as I imagine some streets in Paris were like in the 1920's. Creative types and heavy drinkers.

West Asheville is a strange neighborhood in a weird town. A good example of the crazy people that we attract to this part of Western North Carolina comes from a local news story. A giant sinkhole opened in the parking lot of a small strip mall, the result of a fractured culvert pipe that ran under the lot. You could stand close and look over the jagged edge of broken asphalt into a twenty-foot diameter hole that went deep beneath the surface. It was cavernous. When a local media company asked its readers what they wanted done with the giant sinkhole, about one-third of respondents said they wanted to turn the sinkhole into a new subterranean bar and supper club.

One respondent to the survey suggested that we let it grow to become the Grand Canyon of the East and another fine tourist attraction. All the interesting layers of fill dirt would illustrate the history of the parking lot. "Think of all we can learn!" he said.

While I like the geological and deep time angle of his idea, a nail salon and a yoga studio still needed the parking, and science and understanding must always take a back seat to progress. But I must say—What the heck is wrong with these people?

It might be the climate and the natural beauty of the surrounding Blue Ridge Mountains that attracts them, but only a culture steeped in counterculture would suggest building a subterranean bar inside a giant sinkhole. My point is that Asheville has attracted a lot of free-spirited, unhinged people over the years. It was the perfect spot to start a little revolution.

And there were plenty of places to start recruiting people for a movement like this, like lots of crystal shops and wholistic herbal medicine stores, Zen Buddhism retreats, meditation centers, vegan restaurants and craft beer breweries, farmers markets and food co-op markets, the American Museum of the House Cat, the nearby Coon Dog Festival, and the Bigfoot Festival. The last three on the list because we needed people who can think outside the box (and sometimes outside the known universe).

I first heard about Firestorm Books, my main recruitment center for radical types, from a farmer girl named Anna who helped out on our farm and never wore shoes. She told me that she was in the bookstore and was surprised to stumble upon a copy of my recently published book, *Carrots Don't Grow on Trees: Building Sustainable and Resilient Communities*. That surprised me too, partly because someone actually carried the book, but mostly because I had never heard of that bookstore. My first thought was, "What kind of a sink-hole-in-the-wall bookstore is this?"

Later that day I googled the name Firestorm Books, and before I even clicked on the first link, I could read the first few lines on their website. It read; "We are a collectively-owned radical bookstore and community event space in Asheville, North Carolina." They used the word radical on the web site, and I scooched my chair a little closer to the computer screen. My google search then brought up a Wikipedia page that described the business this way: "Firestorm Books & Coffee is a worker-owned and self-managed anti-capitalist business located in the West Asheville section of Asheville, North Carolina, USA." Perfect. The sign out front could have said "Recruitment Center" as far as I was concerned.

The next day I walked into what was, surprisingly, a quaint little shop, brightly lit with a coffee bar on one side, and old, wood bookshelves scattered throughout full of colorful books. I expected something a little darker and more mysterious. A young girl named Audrey was at the front counter, and I asked her if she could help me find my book. She knew right where it was, God bless her, on a side wall close to the counter. She had three copies of the book on the shelf, and I told her that I was the author and I asked her if she'd like me to sign them. I don't know if that helps sell books or not, but it makes me feel important, so I asked.

"Yes, that would be great. We love having author signed copies," said this little flower-child working in this anti-capitalist bookstore.

As I signed the copies, and she placed stickers on the cover, I asked her about the business.

"Your web site says this is an anti-capitalist, collectively owned, radical bookstore. What does that mean?"

"We don't make profit, or any profit that we make goes back into the community through the support we give to others," she answered. "As for radical, go look at some of the titles." She smiled.

"But it takes capital to buy and stock all of these books. And what about paying the workers?"

"There are three owner-workers here, and I'm not one of them yet, but I'm working toward becoming one also. We don't make much money working here. The owners agreed to work for minimum wage years ago, but just recently bumped it up to $10 an hour so it could be closer to a living wage, which really, it isn't. But they're happy to put any profits over that back into the community in any way that they can, after paying rent and for book inventory, of course."

Just then a young man with long, blond dreadlocks and likely unemployed, who was sitting at a store computer accessing free internet, jumped into the conversation, and said, "Dude, this store is awesome."

That was my guy, I thought. I need that guy. That's the kind of guy who could get arrested, and I could bail him out, and he wouldn't lose a job or anything over it. Besides, he'd get three squares a day while he's incarcerated.

I decided then that I would need to stake out this place to find recruits. But for now, I would just walk the aisles and look for books related to starting a radical movement, and there were plenty. Entire shelving units full of books with titles like *How To Make Trouble and Influence People*. The book cover had a photo of a guy in a bear suit (it could have been some kind of rodent suit) getting arrested, hand cuffs around his furry paws, and being led away by London police—Bobbies in their funny hats. The poor quality of the photograph on the cover was convincing; this was a picture captured in the moment and this really happened.

There were other books by culture-jammers, like *The Revolution Will Not Be Funded*, and *D.I.Y. Resistance: 36 Ways to Fight Back!* There was also *Rules for Radicals* and another I liked, *Direct Action Manuel*. For those unfamiliar with the term, Direct Action is a form of protest where you actually do something, like Occupy Wall Street or chain yourself to a tree—fun stuff like that.

I purchased three books to get myself started down this path toward revolution. The titles were *How We Win—A Guide to Nonviolent Direct-Action Campaigning*; *This Is An Uprising*; and *Full Spectrum Resistance*. There was no turning back now—I spent money. I needed to learn about some of the pranks, protests, and political mischief making that worked for other nefarious, immoral, despicable, and reprehensible groups, like mine.

On the way back from Firestorm Books, I stopped by my neighbor's home just down Avery Creek Road. I found the sage of Appalachia, Lewis Mumford, out spreading compost in his garden. Mumford was a big reader and collector of books, and I thought he might like to take a look at the titles I had just purchased.

"You spend more time prepping your garden beds than anyone I know," I said as I approached the large vegetable garden in his front yard. "Just plant the damn seeds, Mumford!"

He looked up and smiled, and said, "Healthy soil makes healthy plants, which feeds all the animals, including me. I'm an animal."

He stopped working and rested his arms on top of the shovel, and said,

"Ya' know Robert, I was just thinking. I was reading a story in Progressive Farmer this morning, and what many commercial farmers are doing to our soil borders unethical and immoral behavior—they're destroying the soil that everything above ground depends on to gain short term profits. And they're doing it on such a massive scale. It's not prudent behavior. Soil health is so important to life on this planet."

He pulled a handkerchief from his back pocket and wiped his brow, and then continued,

"There are evolutionary biological principles that govern the life of entire systems on earth, starting with the smallest microbes in the soil, and we're either a part of that or not."

Lewis Mumford was a self-taught scientist of the first order. He read and researched everything related to the natural sciences and was an expert on soil health, among other things.

"Since we began agriculture about 10,000 years ago," he said, "and really since the 1950's, we've become completely disconnected from the earth. We've transcended it, technologically. We really don't belong here anymore."

With those words he glanced over at me and feigned a smile and then continued raking the compost into his garden. "What'd you bring me?" he said.

We really don't belong here anymore. See, that's the kind of talk that starts a revolution.

I've played a few different roles in my life, including big-shot businessman, journalist, and farmer. It was time in my life that I played a more serious role, the role of radical revolutionary.

I decided that belonging to an anti-establishment organization could be my way of sticking it to the man, and perhaps make up for some of my own transgressions in my previous life. It would become my own path toward redemption.

I am reminded of an old TV commercial where a crotchety, rich guy, sitting in his mansion in front of a giant fireplace, says, "It's just my way of sticking it to the man."

His butler replies, "But, you are the man, Sir."

The old, rich guy says, "I know" with a weird smile.

I'm that old, rich dude, and I appreciate the irony of it all. I spent a career in business sourcing products from around the world and capitalizing on cheap labor in far off places. I would travel all over China, India, Southeast Asia, Europe, and Central America looking to save a few nickels. Now I'm trying to stop all that—at least when it comes to food anyway.

Why would I do that? Because cheap, taxpayer-subsidized corn and soybeans have enabled agribusiness to build up vast, monopoly power over farmers and our food system and to reap massive profits while leaving farmers broke and dependent on the subsidies. Meanwhile, large multinationals are outsourcing the rest of food production to foreign nations and far-away places, including meat and vegetables, which is seriously eroding our food security and food sovereignty as a nation. That seemed like a pretty good reason to drop whatever it was that I was doing and join a renegade band of food fighters.

The word 'school' in the name School of Postmodern Activities is just a layer of cover for this organization dedicated to anti-establishmentarianism. And in case you didn't catch it, I just used one of the longest words in the English dictionary. I'll use shorter words from now on. The Oxford definition of this word is, "a political philosophy that views a nation's or society's power structure as corrupt, repressive, exploitative, or unjust."

Please allow me to digress on this word anti-establishmentarianism for a moment. Take a stroll through a bookstore like Firestorm and you will not likely find another book with a longer word, except maybe the dictionary. Not many of your friends have ever read a book with a longer word, and that simple fact puts you in the upper echelons of the intellectual elite. We'll go downhill from here. But if you're going to follow me on this journey into radicalism, you have to learn a few of the terms and definitions, and most importantly, you have to learn the truth, because fighting lies and bullshit is like fighting weeds in a garden. They keep sprouting up and you're always a little behind, and sometimes they take over.

The School of Postmodern Activities is not really an 'institute of learning' of any kind. It's more like a movement or a way of thinking. It's really more like a friendly mob. In a normal mob, one guy yells, "Let's get him?" and another guy yells, "Get who?!" and the first guy yells, "I don't know, but Let's Go!" and they all run down the street. In the mob I'll be describing, it's a more passive, laid back, we'll get him tomorrow kind of attitude. The good thing about our group is that concepts like anti-establishmentarianism can be discussed over beer, and you don't go running around when you're drinking beer. Someone could get hurt.

The sign out front of the old schoolhouse is yet another layer of cover, and it reads "The Creekside Farm Education Center." One of our more radical members wanted to take a paint brush to the sign and graffiti it to read "Re-Education Center", but I stopped him. No sense in sending up a flag with the authorities.

I realized that we were a subversive organization at our first official meeting in the old schoolhouse when Butch made the opening statement, "We have to kill El Tigre!"

We were supposed to be there to discuss the concentration of power in the food industry, and right off I started to wonder if it was a good idea to even allow beer at these meetings and if I had invited the right group of people to attend.

Butch continued in an angry tone.

"And that goofy Cocoa Puffs bird, we need to kill him too, and that whole cartel of bunnies and elves. We need to wipe 'em all out!"

He took a swig from his beer bottle and then added,

"Ya' know, they kicked that frickin' tiger out of Chile, and Peru doesn't want him either. We just need to kill him. If we kill him, what's left? Just a cardboard box with a boring picture of some sugary dehydrated corn flakes on it, and it's over!"

I later found out that in preparation for the meeting, Butch read Bee Wilson's book *The Way We Eat Now* and it radicalized him. It's not really a radical book, but in the hands of the wrong person, well, any book could be, like this one in your hands. Butch was now ready to wipe out every cartoon character on every box of fruit loops and sugar smacks on the planet. I knew that if he got riled up enough, he would end up getting caught drawing graffiti on cereal boxes in the grocery store, or worse, and then he'd get arrested, and then we'd be without a secretary. Things can spiral out of control like that quickly in any subversive organization.

Butch told me privately, in fact, about this very idea just after the meeting. He wanted to use social media to get a couple hundred people, maybe more, to go into grocery stores and graffiti boxes of Kellogg's corn flakes. I put my hand on his shoulder and said, "Good idea Butch, but it's a little risky, don't you think? You're too important to this movement. If you go to jail, what good does that do us when we need you. I like the spirit though," and I patted him on the shoulder and we both smiled at each other.

I regret it now. Was I a chicken-shit or what? Why didn't I just say, "Go for it." I could see it happening, Butch getting pulled out of Ingles grocery store in hand cuffs for defacing boxes of Frosted Flakes because he drew a little mustache on Tony with a black magic-marker, and little devils' ears, and maybe a pointed tail. Then he'd write something stupid across the front like, "They'rrre Poison!" Besides, someone could bail him out the same day. No big deal.

That's a pretty harmless act of semi-passive resistance, and no one would get hurt. Why did I try to stop him? Was I just some beatnik quasi-intellectual afraid to go out and actually do something? Never again. I needed to get into the game here. I could organize rallies and email campaigns, and I could write books and articles and letters to congressman, but why would I stop someone from taking direct action, no matter how stupid it was?

Butch was right about Chile. Chile and other countries in South America had recently outlawed "El Tigre" and other cartoon characters on sugary cereals in a dramatic move to combat the significant rise in childhood obesity rates in those countries. This of course came with serious legal opposition from the cereal manufacturers like Kellogg's and General Mills, but they did it anyway. That took guts.

Butch wanted to be David, and Kellogg's, for the moment, was his Goliath. That's because Butch knew that Kellogg's was one of the ten most powerful multinational food corporations in the world that control most of the food that we buy in grocery stores. These ten companies control over 60 % of the brands and foods that we all know, and they own the center isles of the supermarket. About 140 people sit on the boards of those companies and decide what we'll all be having for dinner tonight. Suffice it to say that they all likely come from similar educational and socio-economic circles.[1]

They are the evil nemesis against which we will take our fight. They are the enemy. Every resistance movement needs a target. That was lesson number one from my radical book library. And yet I tried to stop Butch from an act that meant something to him. I wouldn't do that again.

Because this is the story of the everyday man fighting against all odds. An underdog story in a fight against injustice and the massive multinational corporations who control more and more of our daily lives, and not just food, but technology, energy, the media and just about everything else. It's the story of regular people (and I use that term very loosely here) just trying to do the right thing in a messed-up world. We were going to take back control of our food and give it to the people.

How could it all get so messed up, from the very beginning, at the very first meeting? The guys over at Kellogg's probably weren't drinking beer at their meetings. We were going to get crushed, and I knew it.

"Now slow down a minute Butch," I said, "we need to set an agenda for these meetings. You can't just blurt out bullshit like that."

"OK," said Butch, "but I just have to ask, has anybody seen the news that the USDA is paying out over $100 million to buy pork from the Brazil-owned JBS corporation, using taxpayer funds that were intended to help U.S. farmers in the trade war with China? Can you believe that shit! JBS is notorious for their role in the burning of the Amazon rain forest so they can set up more livestock farms, and they've been nailed for offering bribes to government officials about 2000 times! And how about this, the two largest pork producers in America are now owned by foreign companies, and JBS is one of them, and some Chinese company that bought Smithfield is the other. It's frickin crazy!"

This was typical Butch. He jumps around on subjects like that when he gets excited or drinks beer.

"Butch, we need to set an agenda for discussion before you go off on a rant like that," I said.

"What are you saying about killing Tony the Tiger?" someone asked. A few chuckles came out from the group.

"Yea Butch, that's my childhood you're talking about," said another member. "I loved Frosted Flakes as a kid."

"Of course you did!" replied Butch. "Because it got you all juiced up on sugar! You were probably bouncing off the walls and driving your mother nuts. Don't you guys pay attention to what's going on, man. Chile just outlawed 'El Tigre' on cereal boxes. He's gone, man. Now we need to kill him off. We don't need him pushing his sugar crack on our kids any longer. Radical change is coming, boys. There's got to be a war. And Big Brother isn't going to give up easy."

Any anti-establishment organization, such as this one, needed guys like Butch. But still, I was concerned about the way this whole thing was getting started. "Please sit down, Butch," I said.

"OK, you guys just go on being good little consumers," Butch said. "Don't make any waves. We wouldn't want to hurt anybody's feelings."

He dangled his beer bottle between two fingers, and waved it back and forth, and said in a soft, drawn-out voice as if trying to hypnotize the room, "Just drink and forget…Drink and forget…"

"Butch, how many beers have you had already?" I asked. "Don't get your feelings hurt, we're all in this together, but we just need a little structure and organization to these meetings, so let's begin, everyone. We need to come up with some language for a ransom note tonight."

Butch wasn't a bad person. In fact, he was a good guy with a big heart. He just tended to rub people the wrong way when he got riled up. Anyone can understand why a person like Butch could become angry and even radicalized, particularly when something involves children. Butch had kids of his own, although they were mostly grown now.

In many respects, he was dead right to be angry. The Center for Disease Control and Prevention (CDC) recently released a report saying that forty percent (40%) of our children in the United States will likely face type 2 diabetes in their lifetime. For children of color, it's 50%—that's half.[2] We are facing a health care crisis of epic proportions in the decades to come, and it's all related to unhealthy diets of high sugar, high fat, high calorie processed foods. Who's going to try to stop that?

What the future may hold for many of these children is blindness, the amputation of limbs, heart disease and shorter lives. Diabetes also happens to be a very expensive disease to treat, and we'll all pay dearly in skyrocketing health care and insurance costs and an economy weakened by illness and lost work, reduced output and absenteeism. The illness will affect everyone under the burden of rising national debt as we try to cover those health care costs through Medicare and Medicaid.

The coming crisis is clear, but we fail to recognize it or really deal with the root causes. The CDC also reports that 20% of our kids are clinically obese, not just overweight, but obese; 40% of our kids are seriously overweight. The same is now true for kids in Central and South America, and in China, as their snacking and junk food diets have followed our lead. 70% of American adults are overweight and that number continues to rise, meaning less than one-third of the adult population is living at a healthy weight.

This is a recent phenomenon that started in the 1950's with the corporate take-over of our food system and the dramatic increase in processed foods, easy carbs, sugars and soda pop. And it's gotten much worse since then as the food industry consolidated and concentrated power. Butch was mostly angry at large, multinational food corporations because of the power they now wield over our lives. Maybe this is what it takes to create change in a world entrenched by big money and powerful corporations. No more pussyfooting around. Grab your magic markers and Let's Go!

I have come to view it this way. There are two opposing forces that operate in our society—one works toward mass-consumption and mass-concentration, where everyone shops at the same places, and eats the same foods from the same fast-food joints all around the world; and the other force is driven by a group of people trying to stop all that by taking back some control in their lives—first by taking back some control of their own food. Fuck it, I'm with them.

I've invested millions of dollars in agriculture only to find out that we need a better way to feed people. There's just too much pressure on the earth's life support systems, and the concentration of power and environmental degradation threatens our long-term health and well-being. What are we going to do about it? What's the big solution? I kept waiting for some big 'Aha' moment that would give me some answers. What I do know is that capitalism is a game with winners and losers, which is OK until someone tries to stack the deck. I think we need to level the playing field so that the little guy has a chance to compete. And I believe that there are tools within capitalism to help solve our problems, because we can all vote with our wallets.

The globalization of food has reached the point of insanity. We currently import about 20% of our food in the US, but this average doesn't describe the whole picture—which tells a more troubling story. Still, that's one out of every five bites that you take. The U.S. imports about 35% of its vegetables, over 50% of fruits, and 90% of seafood.[3]

Of all the food grown and produced in this country, one state, California, produces 90% or more of our fresh produce, most of our homegrown fruits and nuts, and 40% of our dairy supply.[4] This kind of concentration in food production is unwise under any circumstances, but it is especially foolish given the extreme and growing drought risks in that region, which I'll describe later.

When it comes to our food security and food sovereignty, it's very risky business to become dependent on foreign nations and far-away places for our food supply. We'll hear more about this later from a guy who should know, former United States Director of National Intelligence Mike McConnel. But I believe it is in our own best interest, in the interest of our national security, to reduce our imports of food. Not all of it, we can keep the bananas and pineapple, and coffee, of course. What are we going to do—not have coffee? That's crazy talk.

As the owner of a small farm, I understand how local food strengthens a supply chain that creates jobs and food sovereignty in our community. The recent Covid-19 pandemic and then Russian hackers in our oil and beef supply created food shortages and higher prices that revealed the weak links in our globalized food system. Locally produced food is like an insurance policy, a buffer, for when things like that happen. And they will continue to happen.

As I write this, the meat processor JBS was just hacked by the Russian mob, which followed on the heels of a hack on the Colonial Pipeline that supplies gas along the East Coast. And that hack came soon after a hack at Solar Winds that uncovered security threats in several branches of the US government and at hundreds of companies. This was just a warning. A hack on our electrical grid would be far more devastating. Fresh food, like meat, produce and dairy, spoil quickly without refrigeration, and food deliveries stop without warehouse lights, communications, and computers.

JBS is the largest meat processor in the world with six

massive meat processing facilities in the United States, and it's a Brazilian owned company that has been mired in legal battles for corruption and bribery in both the US and Brazil. The meat supply dropped 25% when processors shut down for a brief period during the Covid-19 pandemic which created shortages at grocery stores and higher prices.[5] Meat prices went up again after the hacking at JBS.

Food shortages and price increases from the Covid-19 pandemic exposed the risks and fragility of a globalized food system that promotes itself as a source of plenty for all but actually creates monopolies for wealthy corporations and inequalities and food insecurity for the rest of us. And the impact on low-income households, and for people of color, was disproportionate and unfair.

Food sovereignty at the national level, and also at the community level, is critical to our health and security. Food sovereignty includes the control over all means of food production and processing, including land, soil, seeds, and the knowledge and skills to produce our own food. I believe that retaining the ability to produce some of your own food locally and regionally is, if nothing else, a necessary insurance policy, just in case.

It's also better for the environment and a buffer against climate change. Making our peace with the biosphere and reducing the impacts of climate change will require building closer relationships between sustainable food sources and local communities—relationships that build and sustain human life and the life of the ecosystem on which we depend. We must not forget that everything comes from nature. Everything. Even a Twinkie.

Most local, small farmers that I know in my region use the best agricultural practices that include protecting the microbial life and health of the soil, and they grow a diversity of plants in an organic and regenerative system. Not just because the food tastes better, but because it protects and preserves our food producing capacity and the healthy soil which we depend on. But our global, monocropping industrialized system works in the opposite direction and is decimating our soils, leading us all down a dangerous path. This is what Mumford was talking about.

Local farms represent biological and cultural assets that we need to preserve. Farming is a big part of our cultural heritage in this Asheville region where I live, and we need to protect that. But it's also true that every community in every country around the world needs to protect and preserve some capacity to grow some of their own food. That creates food security—for when shit happens.

Food is national security. The short of the problem is this—we are outsourcing our food production to foreign countries at an alarming and increasing rate. We'll continue growing way too much corn and soybeans here in the U.S., but we'll be turning over the rest of our diet to people in far-away places, including meat production in South America. Here's just one interesting fact related to global food that might surprise you—one in four pigs living in the United States is owned by a Chinese company.[6]

According to a recent report from the USDA, by the year 2027, over 75% of our fruits and half of our vegetables will come from a foreign nation. Currently it's about half our fruits and one-third of our vegetables, but the rate is increasing quickly.[7] In California, the current source of over half of our vegetables grown in this nation, severe droughts are quickening the pace of dependency on foreign food.[8]

The average person in the U.S. eats ten pounds of meat per

year from a foreign country, without even knowing it.[9] That's because the law doesn't require country of origin labeling on meat products.[10] It's more than enough meat to eat a quarter pounder every day for a month, and you have no idea what country it came from. It just amazes me that everything we buy must have a country-of-origin label on it except for the important stuff that we put into our bodies. You can thank big brother for that—and the man behind the curtain pulling the strings.

The food system in the United States is a complex, global supply chain that circles the planet. It's complicated, and I've spent years trying to figure it out. The most difficult question for me is this: How do we create a just and fair regional food system that pays farmers and farm workers a livable wage, and still keep food affordable?

Here is a truism about farming in this global food system: if a multinational food corporation can grow a pepper cheaper in Mexico or Peru, then that's what they're going to do. It's just business. The average wage for a farm worker in Mexico is $8 per day.[11] Not per hour—per day. As a small farmer here in Western North Carolina, I don't know how to compete with that. And that's why, very soon, over 75% of our fruits and half our vegetables will come from a foreign nation, even in the summer months.

We can't fully understand or control how this global food system affects people in other developing countries, like how powerful drug cartels have taken over lucrative avocado production in Mexico by way of kidnappings and extortion. In developing nations, where there is money to be made, even in avocados, there is often corruption[12].

The organic food trend helped to establish a stronger local food movement here in the Asheville region, but local food still only represents a small percentage of the total food consumed in Buncombe County. Organic farmers here are competing with massive organic factory farms in California, Mexico, and Brazil, and those factory farms are setting the consumer price expectations that people are willing to pay in this crazy, risky race to the bottom. Farmers across the US are feeling the pinch in this globalized food system. They're getting squeezed by rising costs for inputs and lower prices for their produce.

Migrant workers and other farm laborers on U.S. farms are paid very low wages for all the hard work that they do feeding the rest of us. The average hourly wages for migrant workers in 2020 was $13.68, with an average of $14.62 for all farm workers.[13] This is just half (51%) of the average hourly wage for all workers in the U.S. in 2020, which stands at $28.78 per hour.[14] So, it's not like farms in the US are paying great wages while other countries don't.

The US farmer's percentage of the retail dollar keeps shrinking as processors, wholesalers, distributors and retailers grab a bigger slice of the pie. Here are just two examples from a recent study: For an eleven-pound Butterball turkey that retails for $16.39, the farmer got .66 cents; for one pound of tomatoes retailing for $3.39, the farmer received .33 cents. On average, the US farmer receives less than .14 cents on the retail food dollar.[15] This means of course that farm workers, families and the surrounding rural community are also getting a smaller piece of the pie.

I don't really know what the answer is. Maybe we need to pay a little more for our food so that farmers can actually make a living at it. Most farmers work a second job off the farm just to get by. The truth is, we pay a lot less than our grandparents did for food as a percentage of income, about half.[16] (We spend a lot more of our income on bigger homes, cars, and gadgets than they did.) And we pay a lot less for food than people in Europe do, as a percentage of income (about 9% vs 16%, on average.)

Breaking up the largest monopolies in the food system, those large corporations that are putting the squeeze on farmers and consumers, will help. But are people in the United States willing to pay more for food in order to improve our own food sovereignty and food security in this country? It's a tricky question.

Localization in our food supply can offset the pressures from concentration and globalization that we've been seeing in the food system. Localization, or 'regionalism', is the alternative to global corporate control of the food system. It doesn't mean eliminating trade or absolute self-reliance. It's simply about creating a more sustainable and resilient economy by producing and consuming goods closer to home.

Localization means shortening the distance between producer and consumer. It is a leveling of the economic playing field that currently favors large, transnational corporations and banks. It means reducing our dependence on import and export markets in favor of production for local needs. And in that way, we can keep a closer eye on things, like the health of the soil beneath our feet and the ecosystem that supports it all.

That may come with a price tag that includes higher wages for farm labor. And maybe part of the problem is that some people find it easier purchasing a $400 smoothie machine than paying a little more for the ingredients that go into it. Like I said, it's complicated.

We just don't grow food anymore; we manufacture food. Corporations have taken over and in their zeal for efficiency they stripped the land and subjugated the farmer. I have come to believe that by taking control of the food system, taking it out of the hands of multinationals and putting it back into the hands of farmers and the local and regional community, is the only way we're going to be able to survive long term on this planet. As resources like topsoil deplete to a certain point where profits dry up, the corporations will fold or move on to other businesses anyway, and food production will go back to the people in a much-diminished state.

I was frustrated, and about to give up. The problems were too big, and most people were complacent about it. I knew that many of the world's great civilizations collapsed because of environmental degradation, mostly related to the depletion of the soil, from the Maya to Easter Island to Angkor Wat to the Romans to the Vikings in Greenland. The fertile crescent, the birthplace of civilization, was once fertile and now it's a desert. Environmental collapse, and the collapse of agriculture, took out the ancient Babylonians, the Phoenicians, and the Macedonians.[17] Why should we be any different, except that we're looking at environmental collapse on a global scale?

The low point for me came when I learned that we had already killed off half the insects and a third of the birds in North America, largely due to the overuse of deadly pesticides. Then a United Nations report came out that suggested we had enough topsoil left worldwide for about 60 years—that means 60 harvests.[18] Would my kids and grandkids have to live with desertification, water wars and the turmoil of mass migration on a scale that we can't even imagine, with millions, even billions of people on the move?

Then Lewis Mumford started teaching me about regenerative agriculture and its ability to rebuild the soil and pull carbon from the atmosphere at the same time, and that gave me hope. Regenerative agriculture, Mumford told me, could solve climate change, reverse desertification, increase yields for a growing population, and reduce the need for hazardous chemicals.[19] Corporate led industrial agriculture was destroying the soil and the environment, but regenerative farming could reverse all that. That was a turning point for me; it was a life changing moment. Something shifted in me, in my head. I spent years looking at how bad things were getting in the food system, and struggling on my own farm, and suddenly my eyes were opened. It wasn't about sustaining, or sustainability, it was something bigger. We could actually regenerate the land and build up the soil faster than we ever thought possible. That was worth fighting for. That became my 'why', and that's when I joined a quirky band of rebel food fighters.

CHAPTER TWO

THE FAR-DISTANCE COMPANY

"That just don't make no sense," Butch said as he stoked the fire with a stick. "It's that kind of senselessness that worries me."

On a warm and calm July evening, we were sitting around a campfire on a small hill at the farm, looking out at black hills against the nighttime sky, drinking beer. Lights from homes on the high hills twinkled like the stars just above them. Butch took another bite from his chicken leg and tossed it into the fire, then licked his fingers and wiped them on his pants. He stood up, grabbed the pint bottle of whiskey, and took a swig, passed it on to Mumford, and then sat down again.

"It makes no sense, and it's been going on for so long, and gettin' bigger all the time," Butch said. "And the more you read or hear about it, the more you know, and it just makes less sense. And you begin to question people in general and if they're just going to get what they deserve. I just get so mad at the government for letting it go on, even encouraging it."

"I don't have a lot of respect for the government right now," Butch added. "The politicians got all the big money corporations in their pocket to keep 'em getting elected. They don't care about fellas like us."

"Those farmers got to look out for their own families," Butch said. "They just get trapped between the prices they get and what they have to pay for seeds and supplies. Maybe they're scared, so they get mad. But they don't really know who to get mad at."

His eyes grew wider and reflected the red embers from the fire. "Those farmers who are strugglin'… I'm going to stand with those folks."

Butch and Mumford had lived on Avery Creek Road for most of their lives. Mumford lived in an old farmhouse so close that he could walk to my farm in about ten minutes, and he often did. Butch lived up the mountain a little further, in an old wood house built in 1930, with a front porch, and on it, a couple old wood chairs that he made himself. Both homes were kept up nicely, painted white, with the lawns mowed regularly. I considered them good neighbors.

"We have to start thinkin' about doing stuff that means something," Butch said as he stoked the fire again.

"But what kind of stuff can people like us do?" he added. He leaned over and grabbed another beer from the cooler. "We 'aint got the kind of money it takes to go up against those lawyers and corporate bigwigs. And the law 'aint necessarily on our side."

"We don't really need to go up against anybody," Mumford said. "We just need to get people to come around, to understand what's going on, and maybe give them some other options, that's all."

"We need an army of those folks to make a difference," said Butch. "It wouldn't make no difference if it was just us and the few other people around here."

His southern accent, his wonderful Appalachian drawl, seemed more pronounced now that he was drinking beer. Maybe the alcohol vapor in his breath distorted the sound waves ever so slightly as they meandered at a slower and irregular pace across the air between us, raising and lowering the pitch. Maybe it was just the alcohol in my own brain that made his voice sound so musical, so I just didn't say anything and hoped he kept talking.

Butch leaned forward and spoke to the fire and the distant hillside.

"How we goin' to wake them up in the first place? How we goin' to get their attention to make them understand? How we goin' to make them see the freight train that's barreling down on us all? The headlight on that train is dimmer than that porch light way off at Curt Lowe's place across the valley. How we goin' to make them see that and know what's coming? Most people can't see or think that far off, or maybe they just choose not to."

"I'm afraid to say it," Mumford replied, "but maybe it's going to take a serious drought or natural disaster of some kind, something that stops the food trucks in their tracks and wakes people up. Hopefully it won't be something really bad, but just enough to wake people up a little."

That little campfire burned in the summer of 2019, before the pandemic hit, and before the serious droughts hit California in the summer of 2021.

Butch said, "Maybe it'll be some kind of civil unrest or a labor strike that spreads across Central and South America, and we run out of some vegetables for a while. Then people might realize we 'aint so self-sufficient and safe as we think we are.

"What if farm workers in Central America got tired of making eight dollars a day and just said the heck with it and went on strike? Who'd grow the food then?" added Butch.

A squeal of protest came from the pig pen in the distance as one of the hogs jostled for a middle position and another objected. All three of us looked over toward the pen.

"What if the pigs went on strike? No more bacon!" Butch said with a chuckle as that last shot kicked in and his mood suddenly changed. "That would be funny. We should do that. Make up some signs that say, 'On Strike' and put them in the pasture. Tell the media, 'No food until our demands are met.'"

"Not one chicken egg!" he added with a snort. "They'd come out for something like that, wouldn't they?"

We were all smiling now.

"It reminds me of a running joke that was in the media a while back," I said. "Someone started a hoax called 'The Society for the Decency of Naked Animals' or something like that. This made-up organization had rallies and slogans in the media to push for the clothing of naked animals, including pets, barnyard animals, and bigger wildlife like deer and bears. They had slogans like, 'A nude horse is a rude horse.' What a riot!"

We all laughed.

"What about chipmunks and squirrels?" Mumford snickered.

"I think they had a policy or limit on the size of animal that was morally acceptable to be naked, like four inches tall," I said.

We all laughed again and washed it down with another swig of beer.

"They did it just for fun. But humor has a way at getting at the truth and making it stick. We should try to use that somehow," I said.

"How about we hold a pig hostage," said Butch, "and we send out a ransom note to the media that says something like 'Fulfill our demands, or the pig gets it!' I think the press might come out for something like that, don't you? Especially if we add a picture of a cute little piglet, like Albert over there. They'd probably come out just to see him and take a picture."

"OK then," I said as I smiled and reached for the cooler and another beer, "What are our demands?"

As I sobered up the next morning, I came to realize that stupid acts of resistance can only take you so far, and sometimes you get sidetracked, like we never got around to writing that ransom note at the first meeting at the School of Postmodern Activities a few days later. But we were starting to formulate a plan.

We were going to stand up to the man and the concentration of power that he has accumulated. That's called resistance. And it started, for me, with a few guys sitting around a campfire drinking beer in the back woods of Western North Carolina, and I think that's appropriate, because I think that's how a lot of important stuff gets started anyway. Beer is so important. In fact, local beer from small, micro-breweries really started a much larger resistance movement. Someone had the balls to go after Anheuser-Bush. Someone early in the craft beer industry said, "I can make a better beer with more body and flavor than this piss-water we're all drinking. I'm going to make my own beer and sell it."

That took elephant balls.

Early Spice Traders

Corporate control of the food system is not really a new thing. It all started about 400 years ago.

In the year 1602, early spice traders gave us the first example of a powerful, multi-national food corporation, and it began with a small business enterprise called The Far-Distance Company, which eventually grew and consolidated into The

Dutch East India Company.[20] The Far-Distance Company is a very stylish name for a business, I might add.

The company's maiden voyage to Indonesia and the Spice Islands took two years, and the ships returned with a belly full of nutmeg, pepper, cinnamon, and other spices that made the original investors very rich men. Plenty of other men got in line to invest in this dot com explosion of the age.

The Dutch East India Company was the first multinational food corporation in the world, dealing mainly in high value spices and tea from far-away places. It was also the first publicly traded stock corporation in the world; the first corporation to be listed on any official stock exchange where an average citizen could buy stock and invest in a company. It was the first corporate-led global corporation and at one point the most valuable corporation ever formed. It was the Google or Microsoft of its day, only much bigger. The company's might and power in corporate history dwarfed any corporate entity that we know of today. The company was all-powerful.

The company came heavily armed and with a fleet of military ships. In the search for high value spices, some worth their weight in gold, many native groups were relocated or simply wiped out and replaced with slave labor. The company was also known to burn or destroy trees and crops on islands that were not under their control to reduce or eliminate supply to a potential competitor.

The Dutch government gave the Dutch East India Company a monopoly on the spice trade, and it opened the door for globalization as we know it. It's corporate logo, using the letters VOC (from the Dutch language and spelling of United East India Company) became the first recognizable world-wide company brand and logo. The corporate logo was seen and immediately recognized by peoples around the world, much like an apple with a bite out of it.

But it was much more than just a brand identity. It represented power. In foreign ports and colonies, the company possessed quasi-governmental powers, including the ability to wage war, negotiate treaties with foreign states and kings, imprison, hold trials, and execute convicts, mint its own money and coins, and establish colonies or take-over existing colonies by force from its competitors. Most of these hostile corporate take-overs were aimed at established Portuguese ports in Africa and Asia, but hostilities were also directed toward other competitors from France and England.

The Company benefitted from a new class of citizen investors that gave them the capital to build ships, hire crews and labor, purchase trade goods, and launch a military conquest. The capital investment helped the company finance the "Spice Wars" which began in 1602 and that lasted another 60 years. To the company, war was just a cost of doing business, and it was investor financing and corporate capital that allowed the company to capture and take control of the important ports of India and the East Indies and eventually dominate the spice trade.

With its increasing importance and growing number of foreign posts and offices, the company became what many consider the world's first true transnational corporation based on the importing, processing and distribution of food products, and the company wielded more power and military might than most other nations at the time.

Arab traders first dominated the spice trade between Europe and southeast Asia and carefully guarded the secret sources of the spices they sold for hundreds of years. To protect their business and market share, and to discourage competitors, they spread fantastic tales of dangerous and far-away places where the spices came from. Stories were told of mythical beasts, strange human-like creatures of enormous size, man-eating tribes of cannibals, and tribes of warrior 'Amazon' women that existed in these far-off distant lands. The spice Cassia, stories told, grew in shallow lakes guarded by winged dragons, and cinnamon grew in deep glens infested with gigantic, deadly poisonous snakes. Horrible sea monsters waited for unsuspecting sailors in the Arabian sea, the route to India. These sea monsters made their way onto many of the old maps at the time.

When the ships finally returned to Amsterdam after a voyage that could last two or three years, or longer, investors in the Company became wealthy men. Enthusiastic investment grew as many more people purchased stock in the new corporation hoping to get rich quickly themselves. The atrocities of war and conquest, the subjugation of people, the decimation of entire cultures, and the lives of sailors, were not accounted for on the corporate balance sheet. It all went sight unseen to the investor buying stock. The management of the corporation was held accountable only to its shareholders and no one else, and its performance was judged solely by profit and loss.

The Dutch East India Company set the stage for an empire in the food industry. Like most multi-national corporations today, the Company took advantage of opportunities and became involved in other lucrative ventures like the silk and porcelain trade, but its primary business was always food additives and flavorings. This was the humble beginnings of the multinational food corporation, and the 400-year-old thinking that still exists today.

Mike McConnel

I needed to go deeper on this subject and talk to more people who understood why it's so important to take back control of our food. I needed to talk to people who understood the risks that come from turning our food production over to large corporations, foreign interests and far-away places. I eventually ran into a guy who had some of the answers—the former United States Director of National Intelligence. If anyone could talk about security risks, it was Mike McConnell.

Late in the summer of 2019, I met Mike McConnell, the former Director of National Intelligence under George W. Bush, at a press conference. We eventually had several meetings and conversations in the mountains near our homes in North and South Carolina.

The Director of National Intelligence is the highest-ranking intelligence officer in the country, a cabinet level position that oversees the CIA, the FBI, the NSA and other intelligence organizations. It's a cabinet level position that reports directly to the president, so I never told Mike about any of the subversive shit we were up to at the school.

Mike McConnell has seen and heard some crazy things over his long career in intelligence, first as a security officer in the Navy and reaching the rank of Admiral, then later in government and business related to security and intelligence; and I imagine some of what he's heard and seen would probably scare the crap out of most people. I learned a lot from Mike, and we'll hear more from him later.

Mike and I worked briefly together on a 'resilient communities' project based in the Carolina mountains, where Mike was born and raised, and we first met at a round-table discussion that involved the press and which we were both invited to speak. I had a chance to ask him a few questions before the event began. The round-table discussion was held under a large, wood pavilion on a grassy mountaintop, overlooking the hazy spine of the Blue Ridge mountains that separated North and South Carolina in the distance.

After some small talk, I asked Mike, "What can you tell me about food security and national security?"

"My normal focus when I speak in public is cyber-security," Mike said. "I often talk about our digital dependency and the fact that our infrastructures are all controlled by computers, and they are susceptible to hacking, degradation and destruction by some party that's removed from our local environment."

Who talks like that? I thought. Very smart people talk like that. Good thing I was recording this because I would never have remembered the language. Mike continued.

"While I was Director of NSA under George W. Bush, I spent a lot of time going around speaking to CEO's at large banks and companies trying to convince them of the need to improve their cyber-security.

"Most CEOs had no idea of the level of threat we were under already back then. We had discovered that China and Russia were spending billions of dollars on cyber-security, and our country was spending just millions. We're still not spending enough, but I'm glad to think that I had something to do with raising awareness and trying to do something about it."

This conversation happened before we all became aware of how serious the problem was, before foreign hackers were able to infiltrate the NSA and several other government departments, and before they took data for ransom at several major corporations. Then in May of 2021 the Russian mob held the eastern half of the US hostage by controlling the flow of oil in a pipe that ran from Texas up to New York, and all points in between.

It disturbed me to know that a few hackers and thugs were able take over the oil supply along the East Coast using just a computer and the internet, and how they were able to cause major shortages and long lines at gas stations for millions of people. I would learn from Mike that the ability to see and understand a threat in the future, or some risk on the horizon, is central to resilience and our ability to prepare for it and to bounce back from it. Mike was obviously way ahead of his time. He saw it coming.

"Can you tell me how your work touched the food supply?" I asked.

"We did a study for the United Kingdom, and the question was, what happens if there's cyber penetration and disruption of the transportation industry in the UK?"

I waited, imagining Mike would say there was a bunker of bananas strategically placed under Kensington Palace.

"The conclusion, the bottom line was this", he said, looking at me dead in the eyes, "the UK is just nine meals away from chaos and food riots in the streets."

I felt myself sinking into the chair as Mike said these words. Not nine days—nine meals.

"They import so much of their food that they've got enough on hand for nine meals before it's gone, and chaos sets in. Now I don't think our situation in the US is quite that dramatic, but a lot of our food comes from outside of our borders."

It has been widely reported and is widely believed in Great Britain that just 50% of the food that they eat is imported. But it turns out new research says that the 50% statistic greatly underrepresents the reality of things and has been used by some people pushing for Brexit to calm fears about disruption in the food supply that might result from leaving the European Union.

The new research suggests that 80% of food is imported into the UK. The previously used lower numbers defined food processed in the UK as UK food, even though the ingredients may have been imported. For example, tea is processed in the UK, but they obviously don't grow tea in England because of the climate there — it's all imported. When ingredients are counted as imported, the real figure is much higher and closer 80%. That seems very risky to me, when four out of five bites that you take are dependent on another sovereign nation.

The implications of this information troubled me because even a minor disruption in oil supplies could cause delays and higher food prices for Brits, and that was one thing. But a larger disruption, like sudden turmoil in the Middle East—or some cyber-attack described by Mike— any larger disruption in oil supplies that fuel all those container ships could spell disaster and large-scale panic, even starvation, in the UK. Hack the shipping company's computers or hack the oil pipeline that feeds all those cargo ships and you the control of the food supply in England.

Venezuela is another country that imports over 70% of its food. When a socio-economic crisis hit there, and the country's credit rating went in the toilet, they could no longer buy food on credit and didn't have the cash to buy the imported food that they needed. The average citizen in Venezuela lost over 20 pounds. Hunger and starvation became rampant.

It's risky business to be dependent on foreign nations for food. This theme of food security, food sovereignty and resilience will repeat itself throughout the book. The United States is not immune from this risk by any means. We are importing more of our food at an expanding and alarming rate.

I had my own story to tell Mike.

"When hurricane Katrina came through and took out oil refineries in the Gulf of Mexico," I said, "we were out of gas in just three days up in Asheville." Asheville was about 40 miles as the crow flies from where we were standing in South Carolina at the time.

"We were out of gas for about two weeks," I continued, "and if anyone heard that a gas station in our area received a gas shipment, lines were quickly formed that went for blocks. It would take hours in line, and they'd limit how much you could buy.

"But the scary thing was this, Mike. The grocery stores were already thinning out in just two or three days. Without the regular truck deliveries, it was unnerving to see how barren grocery store shelves can get in such a short period of time, especially when people started hoarding supplies. And if another hurricane followed Katrina, and ripped up the East Coast, taking out refineries and distribution points there, we would have really been in trouble."

"That's right," Mike said. "People think that there is a warehouse full of food in the back of the grocery store. But there's not. All the inventory is on the shelves out front. Shelves are replenished from deliveries every night. If the trucks stop running, shelves thin out quickly.

"That's why I like what you're doing, Bob," Mike added. "Local food production is important to resilience and security. You still owe me a beer up at your farm, by the way. I'd like to see it."

Creekside Farm at Walnut Cove

The U.S. food and farming system contributes nearly $1 trillion to the national economy, or more than 13 percent of the gross domestic product, and it employs 17 percent of the labor force when you consider all the people working across the supply chain, including food-service workers.[21]

My 50-acre organic farm in the mountains of Western North Carolina is called Creekside Farm, and it contributes very little to the national food supply. I saved this old farm from development, but fifty acres is tiny compared to the massive thousand-acre-plus farms in the Midwest. Here the mountains and valleys and the slopes of the hillsides often dictate the size of farms and workable soil. But we do feed about 80 households, or roughly 200 people, a fair portion of their food needs for a good part of the year. Still, from a financial standpoint, this farm was not my smartest business move. I'm pretty sure there are easier ways to make money in this world than organic farming. But there's a bit more to life than what shows up on a diminishing bank statement. I learned that from the radicals.

I wasn't always a non-conformist farmer. Most of my life I'd been focused on business, and I founded a few companies in different industries, and a couple that touched global supply chains. But in my forties, I decided to give all that up, sold the companies and purchased a small farm in the Appalachian Mountains of Western North Carolina. I purchased tractors and implements and attachments and farm animals and built barns and a farmhouse, and I went all in on it.

The mountain farm is adjacent to Pisgah National Forest, and beyond that, hundreds of miles of wilderness and the Smokey Mountain National Park. From my home in Walnut

Cove, surrounded by high hills and mountains, I can see the Blue Ridge Parkway cut along a high ridge in the distance.

Like most vegetable farms in the region, our farm struggles to compete with massive organic farms in California and Central and South America; farms that look just like conventional farms with perfectly straight rows that go on for miles. We compete with them in a way because they set the prices—the prices people see at Whole Foods and elsewhere.

Soon California will have its own reckoning when the minimum wage for farm workers there rises to $15 per hour in 2022, with overtime pay set at time and a half (which they've largely avoided up till now because of farm worker laws put in place decades ago.) With the average pay for farm workers in Mexico at $8 per day and no required overtime pay increase, how will California compete with that?[22]

Organics from mega-farms in California, Mexico and even China are setting the consumer price expectations in what has become a crazy race to the bottom for producers over the past couple of decades. Truthfully, I don't know how most of the small farmers around me still make a living at it. I suspect many don't.

Over the past ten years, I sort of gave up on the idea of making a profit at the farm (although break-even would be nice) and focused on investing in the health of the soil and in the health of our community. We have cows and hogs and chickens and vegetable gardens and hay fields to feed the cows in the winter. We started a community supported agriculture program five years ago, where people buy a share at the beginning of the season and pick up a box of fresh vegetables every week at the farm. We donated food when we could to hunger organizations like MANNA FoodBank. We supported other important local food organizations like

Appalachian Sustainable Agriculture Project (ASAP) and Organic Growers School.

We developed programs to encourage healthy eating habits and found ways to increase the purchasing power for low-income households at the farmers market, which also helped local farmers.

We purchased the old red schoolhouse adjacent to the farm and tried to do more to educate young farmers by hosting educational classes there, like a year-long 'Farm Beginnings' class run by Organic Growers School. And we often offered cooking, gardening and nutrition classes at the old schoolhouse for neighbors in the surrounding community. We hosted fundraisers for non-profits, farm to table meals, and farm tours for kids, and we paid young farmers a living wage while they learned the trade.

As I listened and learned from Mumford, the farm began growing more food organically and sustainably while improving the health of the soil through regenerative practices, like no till and limited till, multi-species cover crops, crop rotation, and lots of composting amendments. We raised animals on green pasture in a humane and healthier environment than the confined animal feed operations where most of the nation's beef comes from. And Mumford showed me how to divide up the pastures and rotate the cattle between them every few days in an intensive, rotational grazing system that greatly improved the health and carrying capacity of the pastures.

I served on a couple land conservation and organic agriculture boards. I wrote articles for regional papers and a regular column for a magazine. I even wrote a book about building sustainable and resilient communities. But it seemed like everything we did just wasn't nearly enough—didn't seem to scratch the surface of the problems we were facing.

It felt like I was wandering the subways of New York City following a map of the London tube. We went in a lot of different directions not really knowing where we were going. Small farmers were still struggling, and many full-time farmers were still living below the federal poverty level. Childhood obesity and rates of diabetes were still climbing, year after year, and got worse in the pandemic. What would it take to change things at scale?

I believed that I had to do something because the food world had changed since I was a kid, and the world that I was leaving my kids wasn't any better. And the real effects of climate change were just about to kick in. They'd see it, for sure. So, in a world of hyper-capitalism, I went looking for a more meaningful way of producing food. I wanted to reconnect to a sense of purpose, like planting some strange seed and not knowing what would come out of the ground. And finding recruits for our cause was my own form of soul searching. What is a 'radical' anyway?

For a long time, I felt that I wasn't really solving any problems in the world, and maybe just trying to solve some problems that existed inside my own head. I wanted some control, some way of determining my own destiny, some way of becoming less dependent on a fractured system. And like most people, I wanted the conveniences of life without the huge carbon footprint that came with it. I wanted to eat ethically and humanely, if I could.

I think most people would like to use their purchasing power to create a better world. No one really wants to intentionally harm the environment. And when people shop for organic, pasture raised, or free-range food, at the farmers market or at Whole Foods, in some way they are trying to purchase their ideals and values—to validate their beliefs by what they

purchase and consume. And like most people, I want convenience and variety with a sense of virtue. We want to purchase
things but also keep some semblance of self-esteem so we can
sleep at night. Self-esteem and self-respect are, in fact, very
important to our happiness. We humans also seek meaning,
even in our purchases and consumption. But the vast web in
the food supply chain that we depend on makes that almost
impossible. Some people have found some answers at the
farmer's market.

I still believed that we could create a system of food production and consumption where both sides of the equation, the
grower and the consumer, can be proud and have faith in the
system. But first we must take control of production at the
regional level, I thought, where it can fall under the watchful eye of the consumer. That means breaking the chains of
a powerful and corrupt food industry, and that's not an easy
thing to do.

So maybe we needed to push the envelope. Maybe we
needed to radicalize—whatever that means. Maybe we
needed to do something big. It might be something really
stupid, but it would have to be big and something that would
catch people's attention, and maybe the stupider the better. I
think this is what Butch was talking about around the campfire that night.

The dictionary might describe a radical as someone looking for complete political or social reform; some change that
affects the fundamental nature of a thing, and it can be far-
reaching. If something is considered extremist or very different from anything that has come before it, you may call it
radical. In everyday language and understanding, a radical
is someone who has very extreme views that deviate from the
accepted norms or status quo, and you might say that their

views are different from the root up. Radical change starts at the root of the problem. An example of radical, for instance, is the change that allowed women to vote, and it had far-reaching ramifications.

When I started to tip-toe around the extreme edges of a radical movement, where change doesn't come fast enough, I began to question my own moral authority, because I was standing on shaky ground. What the hell do I know about radicalism? What do I know about anything? I suppose radical change always comes with some confusion and a little uncertainty. And messing with the food system and large multinational food corporations can be a little intimidating. Here's an example.

The kid with the blond dreadlocks came up to me one day and said,

"I was following this Frito Lay truck today."

I immediately thought, why was he following a Frito Lay truck? Was he going to steal it?

Then what? Was he going to burn it in protest, an effigy to the corporate-capitalist control of our food? Torching a Frito Lay truck would certainly draw some attention from the media, I thought, and it would make for some great video on Channel 7 News. Maybe too much attention…

I asked, nervously, "Why were you following a Frito Lay truck?"

"To take a picture of it," he replied.

A sense of relief came over me, and perhaps a little disappointment. He pulled out his phone and showed me the picture. It was an image of the back of the truck taken through his front windshield as he followed it, with a large Frito Lay logo and the tagline below it that read, "Food for the fun of it!"

"Can you believe that shit," he said. "What they're saying is, let's all just eat for fun. Let's stuff our faces with high carb junk that has absolutely no nutritional value, and let's all get fat, just for fun!"

"Yea, that is a pretty strange slogan, isn't it," I replied. "But what can we do about it?"

A slew of other questions came into my head. How long did you follow the truck? Do you remember the route that it took? Do you think the driver leaves the keys in the truck when he makes his deliveries? Did anyone else see you following the truck?

But I said nothing, and we just looked at each other, and I think to myself—I must be losing it.

The industrial world is pumping over 50 billion metric tons of greenhouse gases into the air every year.[23] World temperatures are projected to increase by two to four degrees Celsius, which is about 4-8 degrees Fahrenheit. And agriculture plays a major role in all that, producing about 25-30% of greenhouse gas (GHG) emissions, mostly from fertilizers, soil erosion, meat production and deforestation.[24] But agriculture, done right, can also be the most cost-effective tool that we have to sequester carbon and store it in the soil, where it belongs. We'll get to this later, but regenerative agriculture is a big part of the climate solution.

One of Mike McConnell's successors, U.S. Director of National Intelligence Avril Haines, has said that climate change is "at the center of the country's national security and foreign policy," and the reason is pretty straight forward. Earth systems—the atmosphere, oceans, soils, and biosphere—are in various phases of collapse, putting nearly one-half of the world's gross domestic product at risk and undermining the planet's ability to support life.

The big question is how are we going to feed ourselves in the future? Large sections of the United States are getting dryer, that is clear, and the underground water table that supports farming on a massive scale in the Midwest and California is rapidly shrinking, and in some cases already tapped out.[25]

The Central Valley in California accounts for less than 1% of U.S. farmland but produces about one quarter of the total food we eat across the United States: more than half of our fruits, nuts and vegetables, but also meat and dairy, and some grains.[26] Severe and recurring drought in California, and the depletion of the underground aquifers there, threaten that food supply.

Big, industrialized agriculture lies at the heart of the crises that we are confronting now across the country and around the world. Decades of effort to scale up industrial agriculture has been undermining the planet's capacity to support life because it causes massive destruction and depletion of our limited topsoil and a collapse of entire ecosystems and the insects, plants and animals that support it.

In the U.S. Corn Belt, around 35 percent of the region has lost almost all of its topsoil from over-tilling the ground and then leaving it bare in the winter months.[27] Most of that topsoil blew away or washed down rivers and streams and eventually made its way into the Gulf of Mexico. According to some recent research, we've lost almost half of the topsoil, on average, across the U.S. corn belt.[28] That leads us back to the report by the United Nations stating that at the current rate of topsoil loss globally, we have less than 60 years of topsoil left. In some places, it will happen much quicker. The dust bowl of the 1930's proved that, when it took less than a decade for the topsoil across vast areas of Oklahoma, Kansas and Texas to simply blow away because of poor farming practices. The farming economy collapsed just as quickly, and people were soon on the move in a mass migration to California and other places because the land was all but infertile and dead.

The droughts in California and soil erosion in the Midwest will continue to get worse with climate change, bringing serious social, ecological and economic disruption. In our industrial food system, we wash down a big bite of diminishing Midwestern topsoil with a big gulp of California's depleted water. It can't go on forever. Something's got to give.

The earth's ecosystems can't support the kind of ecological overload that we've been causing with industrialized agriculture. As one example of that overload, there are 25 million hogs and just 3 million people living in Iowa. The water from the Raccoon River enters the state capital of Des Moines—home to 550,000 people—with nitrates, phosphorus, and bacteria that have escaped from farms and that far exceed all federal safe water drinking standards. So, hog farmers have destroyed the water source for the city, which is just one example of the environmental hazards of large scale, concentrated, industrialized food production.

Many in Iowa, including the governor, have said things like this about large, confined animal feeding operations in the state; "We're creating jobs while we feed the world". But others counter that by saying it doesn't really create that many jobs to raise animals like hogs and chickens in an automated warehouse, and they ask why we should deplete our soils and pollute our drinking water with hazardous chemicals to grow cheaper meat for export to China or anywhere else.

And we've given this gift of industrialized, chemically

dependent agriculture to places like India, where in many regions, they too are unable to drink the water because of the run-off of toxic chemicals sprayed on fields. They are also struggling financially to pay back the loans that they took out to finance equipment and the big transition to industrial farming. An alarming number of Indian farmers are now committing suicide because they can't cope with what they've done to their land and to their financial situation.[29]

Almost a quarter-million Indian farmers have died by suicide since 2000. Some would even argue, like my friend and neighbor, Lewis Mumford, that the wealthy nations maintain power through the creation of debt in poor nations, who then rob their own people and extract from their land to repay the never-ending debt cycle.

In the U.S., farmers and ranchers have a suicide rate that is, on average, 3.5 times that of the general population, one recent study in USA Today found.[30] The terrible stress from crushing debt and plummeting commodity prices were largely to blame.

"US farmers are feeling the squeeze," said Mumford at one of our underground meetings not long before Covid-19 hit, "but so are people all over the world. So many farmers across the planet are now inflamed and hungry, like Mexican corn farmers angry that we're dumping cheap, US taxpayer subsidized corn on their country and killing their agriculture sector. It's all connected. Corporate greed and the concentration of power," said Mumford, "has fall-out across the globe."

I've come to understand that we're going to need to make some big changes down on the farm because the problems are so varied and numerous, and it's not just about the farmers and the environment, it's about the supply lines that feed us all.

What happens if we don't make radical changes? Many

of us recently came to the frightful realization that we are no longer Masters of the Universe (and I place myself right in the middle of that word 'us'). The dependency and globalization of the food system was by design, and it was designed by and for the accumulation of wealth by a few. It was not designed to help the family farm. Then a little bug from nature came along to shut down our economy and bring us to our knees. The humbling experience of the Covid-19 pandemic taught many of us that we are not apart from nature—we're just an incredibly vulnerable part of it.

It wasn't just food shortages and higher food prices that shocked many Americans. People also realized, suddenly and at a critical time, that most of the personal protection equipment (PPE) came from China, and that we were at the mercy of a communist regime for vital supplies, and it became a huge wake-up call. And when we discovered that the pills and drugs in our medicine cabinet came from India, who is in turn dependent on China for the chemicals and raw materials, that was another wake-up call. And people began to ask, what if India decided to keep all of the important drugs, like antibiotics, for themselves during the next global crisis?

In global politics, there is one thing that you can always count on for certain: Nations will always act out of self-interest. Always. You cannot expect otherwise. And so to become dependent on other sovereign nations for important things is not prudent behavior. Multinational corporations may have created the problem and the dependency, but the sad truth is that almost all of us have unknowingly and unwittingly become completely dependent on a global food system, which is very dangerous.

The Coronavirus forced a lot of people to reevaluate what they consider vital and important, and to realize (hopefully) that we will need to invest in protecting those things, like food and drugs. At least this is the lesson we should have learned from COVID. We'll need to rebuild the infrastructure for the things that we are most dependent on for survival, not just at the national level, but at the local and regional level.

Those things that we cannot afford to lose, like food production and food processing centers, must be nearer to the consumer. People must consider critical things like power and water resources, but also those smaller things like mills to grind wheat, bakeries for bread and small, regional slaughterhouses to process a local meat supply. This is the key to resilience. Our food processing facilities have been concentrated into fewer and far-away places because of decision makers at the top, and that has created risk for the rest of us. That needs to change.

As just one example of the serious concentration that has occurred in my lifetime, consider that just four companies control over 85% of the meat supply in the US.[31] Two of them are foreign owned companies, one from China, who owns Smithfield, and JBS from Brazil. The other two are Tyson Foods and Cargill. When coronavirus outbreaks occurred at these consolidated, massive meat processing centers, our meat supply quickly dropped 25% and shortages started happening at grocery stores across the U.S. almost immediately.[32] In the literary world, this occurrence might be called foreshadowing. In the real world, it's often referred to as a wake-up call. It hints at more ominous events that may happen in the future.

The concentration continues across the food chain, with the vast bulk of seeds and ag chemicals controlled by just three companies, Bayer (who now owns Monsanto), Syngenta and Corteva. The corn and soybean trading markets are controlled by Cargill and Archer Daniels Midland.[33] In many parts of the country, dairy farmers have only one company to ship their raw milk to; Dairy Farmers of America. And as these companies have each gotten bigger, they've squeezed profits out of the American farmer, the taxpayer, and the consumer. They wield massive power in Washington through lobbyists and large political campaign contributions, which makes changing the rules of the game that much more difficult.[34] Large multinationals may not tap corporate coffers to pay for an army like the Dutch East India Company did, but they can pay for an army of lawyers and lobbyists.

For our own food security, we can no longer be dependent on food from massive production facilities and far-away places. We need food produced and processed closer to home, closer to where it's consumed, and that means breaking up the global monopolies that control our food, and setting up hundreds of smaller, diversified companies and operations that spread out the risk of disruption. That may come with a higher cost for food.

Ultimately the question is, should we give up some efficiency and cost savings to build a safer and more secure, diversified food supply? Did we learn anything from Covid-19 about becoming dependent on foreign nations? And how do we justify a higher food cost when so many people are already struggling to get by? Is there a way to offset some of this higher cost? Can we gain enough efficiencies in production to mitigate some of this cost?

I believe the answer must be yes. For our own food security, food sovereignty and community resilience, we must create regional food systems, where every community, every state, and every region take the important and necessary steps to feed itself.

What we're talking about is a more diversified portfolio. People will need to invest in infrastructure closer to home and give other people work that is meaningful and important, which we've largely sacrificed in the name of globalization. More investment in local communities and makers is the huge shakeup in thinking that is necessary and inevitable to a sustainable and resilient future.

Many of our political policies, particularly as they relate to food and the environment in America, are corrupted by business interests. It has been my experience that corruption is not uncommon in global business affairs. I've traveled the world for business, and I've witnessed corruption, the mistreatment of employees, the destruction of community and the environment, and the blatant examples of poor leadership in business as well as government, and much of it under the banner of globalization and free trade.

And the truth is, many 'elites' or leaders around the world have established institutions for the sole purpose of extracting labor and profit out of its citizens, with no regard to the health of the people or the environment.[35] This is now happening in our food system. The Amazon is burning to make more room for cattle because a multinational Brazilian company wants to export more meat to the US.[36] And the crime and corruption are mind-boggling.

As I write this, the Ministry of Health in Brazil is under indictment for soliciting bribes from the makers and distributors of Coronavirus vaccine.[37] And drug cartel mafia-types have taken control of ports in Central and South America where a lot of food products are shipped out of.[38] Corruption is rampant in many developing nations, but we still build our food supply chains there because of cheaper labor out in the field and 'friendlies' in high places.

By paying attention to the details around our dinner, we might get jolted out of everyday complacency to see the world as it really is. And we might learn various forms of resistance.

Before I joined a bunch of screw-ups trying to change the system, I came to the stunning realization that the current problems and injustice in our food system were really the result of injustice-by-design. Butch saw it. Mumford knew it. It didn't just happen. That awareness was the beginning of my journey, a journey into radicalism and who knows where.

But let's face it, there are a lot of risks out there that threaten our food security, and we need to take them seriously and try to take back some control at the community and regional level so that we can build some resilience into the system.

This book is about corruption and control. It's about a fight, an epic battle, between the underdog and the powerful; between a group of misfits and a group of wealthy corporate overlords. It's about injustice and sticking it to the man, and burned-out Frito-Lay trucks.

CHAPTER THREE

A SEA OF CORN

A Bug Apocalypse

The modern era was a time of extraordinary intellectual and scientific achievement, and a time of incredible foolishness. It was a time when entire populations of people climbed out of hunger around the world, and a time when we destroyed our ability to feed ourselves at home. The postmodern era is a time for redemption.

I remember as a child driving down the road with my father and counting the number of bugs that hit the windshield. There was a lot of them, in bright greens, reds and yellows splattered across the windshield like a Jackson Pollock painting.

There are very few bugs that hit my windshield as I drive that same stretch of road today, and I wonder where have all the bugs gone?

I realize this observation is not scientific proof of a bug apocalypse. Perhaps I could have conducted a more science-based experiment over the years, had I driven down the same stretch of road at the same speed on the same day at the same time every year, and recorded the number of bugs on my windshield after so many miles. My science friends should be impressed with how I just designed this "bugs on windshield" experiment, but I'm not sure that I could ever get the results published.

However, some recent published research suggests that there are 45% fewer insects in America than there were in the 1960's, before we started spraying DDT and the numerous other toxic chemicals since then.[39] And closely related to that, other research suggests that there are 30% fewer birds flying over our heads than there were in the 1970's.[40]

While the loss of bird species may be partially related to habitat loss and other causes, birds do eat bugs, and if there are less bugs, there's less food. And if you take out the food source at the bottom of the food chain, it isn't long before the ripple effects are felt higher up the chain, including where we're standing.

Renowned Harvard entomologist E.O. Wilson has said that without insects the rest of life, including humanity, "would mostly disappear from the land. And within a few months."[41]

Bees, butterflies, and other beneficial insect populations are declining as industrial agriculture continues to use chemicals known to kill them. Some studies have shown that U.S. agriculture has become almost 50 times more toxic to honeybees over the past 25 years.[42] At least one-third of our fruit and vegetable crops depend on honeybees for pollination. We spray to kill a pest and end up killing something that we depend on. It's like an alien movie where we fire a missile, and it turns around and comes right back at us. And this is just one example of the backlash that we've created in the arrogance of our industrialized food system.[43]

With the spraying of massive amounts of chemical pesticides on farmland, we don't just kill a targeted insect, we kill all the bugs, including predator bugs who eat the bad bugs that eat our crops. In a healthy, natural ecosystem there is a wide variety of plant and animal species, and no one gets to dominate the playing field. Each species has evolved to keep the other in check, whether that's a predator or a competitor. More food means more eaters. The system checks itself.[44]

When we grow vast monocultures of one crop, like corn or soybeans in the Midwest or cotton in the South, it attracts certain pests that are particularly fond of that food source, and they thrive. When we overspray chemicals and eliminate predators and competitors, that one pest species will inevitably gain resistance to the insecticide we're using because there are just so many more of them and more chances of genetic variation that will bring on resistance to the chemicals.

The Peach Aphid has become resistant to everything we've got, over 75 different chemicals in our arsenal, and it's been able to adapt to eat over 50 different plants now. We've given them a whole new salad bar with no natural predators, like lady bugs, to stop them.[45]

As we change the world, eliminate predator bugs, and turn the insect food chain on its head, a few pests that can adapt will come along for the ride with us, and it's like winning the lottery for them. We're giving these few species of bugs the keys to the kingdom.

My windshield is now a very sparce canvas with just a few small blotches of color, and the only remaining similarity to a Jackson Pollock painting is that I still don't really know what it means. And what does it mean if all the splatterings, while fewer in number, are all the same size and color? I must conduct another experiment! Where are my car keys?

As you are undoubtedly aware by now, you are reading a book that will include some rather gloomy and disheartening information about the modern, globalized, concentrated, industrialized food system. But do not become too discouraged. There is hope at the end of it.

And in case you're wondering about me, your guide on this little journey into the food kingdom, I can only tell you a few things without incriminating myself. First, I'm not a long-haired, guitar playing radical. I don't sing songs of revolution, and I can't even play the guitar.

I have always tried to keep a low profile, and I do many things that appear normal to the authorities. I spent the past decade of my life researching sustainable and then bioregenerative agriculture and testing it in the field. Nothing from that could flag me with any government agencies or departments.

Over time, I could see with my own eyes the loss of valuable farmland happening in my neck of the woods and across the country, so I joined the Buncombe County Land Conservation Advisory Board to guide county government on land conservation and protection initiatives. That put me inside government, where I became a mole, and I had my own agenda. I was pulling the strings of power. I was the man behind the curtain. No one had a clue about the deep throat, undercover double-agent shit that I was up to.

I served on the board of directors for Organic Growers School, which probably sounds respectable, but my sinister plot included the re-education of our youth—once I take over. Many of the classes that the school offered were totally anti-establishment, including courses on homesteading and living off the grid, or how to raise and butcher chickens in your own backyard, real nefarious stuff. If you're off the grid, how's the man going to make any money off you? You're of no use to him. You're non-compliant, and that makes you dangerous. I encouraged these classes and sometimes hired the teachers. There was no way to trace it all back to me directly, of course.

The regular column that I write for The Laurel of Asheville magazine is called Eat Your View and it's filled with hidden, subversive messages.[46] The other articles I wrote for other regional papers and magazines usually carried seditious undertones. You can think of me as a weird egghead plotting mass disruption on an unsuspecting corporate world. I like that association, and I may just shave my head. Like I said, no more pussy footing around.

In my spare time, I farm. Our 50-acre farm in Arden, North Carolina grows vegetables for a community supported agriculture (CSA) program that feeds about 200 people, and we sell some vegetables at the Asheville City Farmers Market on Saturdays. We also raise a couple dozen cows, about 100 chickens for eggs, and occasionally some pigs. I've been thinking about raising some sheep. So far, I've invested over $2 million dollars in agricultural related activities. I figure what's a few sheep going to cost? At this point, I'm in so deep, it's just another drop in the bucket.

When I say that I farm, I mean that I manage a farm while others do all the hard work. I'm really like the farm President or CEO, if there is such a thing. Other people do the hard work and I take all the credit. And if someone ever says to me, "Those were some fine tomatoes," I just say, "Thanks, I know."

Sure, I'll get on the tractor and get the ground ready, or bring in the hay, or feed some cows, but it's not like I'm out there squatting in the dirt and the hot sun transplanting vegetables by hand or staking tomatoes. That's what my farm manager does. And I can't understand why the heck he does it. He can't be doing it just for the money because it's really hard

work, and he can probably make more money doing something else that's a lot less labor intensive. But I know that he's
got his own reasons.

We sell free range chicken eggs for $7 dollars a dozen. That's
a pretty bold statement, in itself. Some people think that's too
much, but with the cost of organic feed and the labor, we don't
make any money on chicken eggs. It's still hard to justify that
price when conventional eggs cost less than half that unless
you want to get into a long discussion about the conditions
under which conventional eggs are produced. Then you're
counting on the listener to actually give a shit about a chicken.
There are so many problems with industrial agriculture that go
way beyond the quality of life for a chicken, but you still can't
forget the chicken.

A few years after I purchased the farm, I hired a farm
manager, and we began to grow food for our CSA program
that feeds people in the neighborhood. He also sold the pasture
raised chicken eggs and fresh cut flowers along with his produce
at the local farmers market. We bankrolled the whole operation, including his salary, and I lost my ass in farming for the
first few years. After investing over two million dollars in the
farm and equipment, I lost over $100,000 in the first three
years farming. Some farm President I turned out to be.

We also purchased an old, bright red, one-room schoolhouse built in 1920 that happened to be directly adjacent to
the farm and looked out over the growing fields, and there we
offered cooking and canning classes, gardening and nutrition
classes, and farm to table dinners for our CSA members. It was
all about building community around healthy, local food. We
had plenty of fun events with old time bluegrass music and lots
of beer and wine and all of the food that we served came fresh
from the farm.

We began building our network of farmers and non-profit organizations dedicated to local food and feeding the hungry. We were doing what we could to support local farmers, food security and food sovereignty in our little mountain community but when push came to shove, we really made no impact outside of our community. We needed to somehow bring this to the next level. The system was messed up and controlled by very few people, and farmers were hurting. In other parts of this country, in large swaths of it, people had already lost the ability to feed themselves.

So, while I may not be a real, big-time farmer, or even a farm President with a decent track record, I had been around farming and business long enough to spot a serious problem when I see it coming. That's when I began thinking about how to build resilience into our food system so we can take a hit, wherever that hit may come from, and not shatter into a million pieces. And that means we need to keep an eye out for what's coming down the track and prepare for it.

A Sea of Corn

It would seem to me that massive disruption is ahead for farmers in the heartland, and it's coming from a thousand-mile-long train load of corn that's heading for a train wreck.

General Motors announced not long ago that it will sell only electric vehicles by the year 2035, which came on the heels of President Biden's executive order to transition all federal vehicles to electric.[47] And while that's a good thing, it could be disastrous and bring considerable hardship to farmers in the Corn Belt.

Why? Because forty percent (40%) of the US corn crop

goes into our gas tanks—in the form of ethanol.[48] By federal mandate gasoline must contain 10% ethanol, and that comes from corn. Electric vehicles represent a significant drop in demand for corn, and that could cripple an already hurting agriculture sector. Not many industries can handle a 40% drop in demand without some disruption, chaos, or upheaval.

To get an idea on the scale of things, you must drive through it. Plan on spending a couple days in the corn at 70 miles per hour. Crossing the Midwest, you drive through a sea of corn that stretches for a thousand miles, east to west. It's bigger than a sea; bigger than the Black Sea and the Caspian Sea. It's nearly one and a half times the size of California, and it's more than two and a half times the size of all the Great Lakes, combined. The corn belt is truly 1000 miles wide, from Pittsburgh to Grand Island, Nebraska. North to South it reaches from Minneapolis down to St. Louis, about 500 miles. Its total estimated area is 250,000 square miles of corn. It's a massive thing.

Over 300,000 corn farmers produce roughly 350 million tons of corn every year, roughly one ton per person living in the United States, or 2000 pounds per person.[49] The average person only eats about 1% of that, or 20 pounds of corn, and a lot of that in the form of high fructose corn syrup. Most of the rest goes into our gas tanks and into cows and chickens. Roughly 36% of the U.S. corn crop goes toward livestock feed.[50]

No one really knows what will happen to such a vast area of farmland when electric vehicles finally take over, but like I said, not many industries can handle a 40% drop in demand without turmoil. It's probably best to prepare for it in some way.

A disruption like this can become an important opportunity to retool agriculture toward a more sustainable system of diverse crops that can improve soil health and mitigate climate change. The only other option is to continue to prop up the corn industry with taxpayer subsidies as it begins to fail. We've been propping up the corn business for decades now, so that the price of corn has no real relationship to the actual cost of production.[51]

Perhaps large chunks of the Midwest will turn back into prairie grasslands, like before we started tilling it under for corn, forcing a reshaping of the American Midwest as we know it. Perhaps we'll find another use for corn in the form of biofuels for trucks and airplanes. Whatever the solution, we need to be working on it right now. Farmers will start feeling the pinch in less than a decade.

The powers that be will suggest that we increase exports as the solution for all that corn, but I would strongly argue against that idea for a couple of reasons. We currently export about 13% of the US corn crop, with the stated goal of helping to feed the world.[52] And yes, we can and should help to feed the world. But if we really want to help with issues of hunger in other nations, we would do better to support them to increase their own agricultural output and infrastructure through sustainable, regenerative, and indigenous technologies. All countries want to work toward feeding themselves as a matter of food sovereignty and national security, and many countries are on their way toward doing that. In some cases, developing nations and marginalized peoples just need to be given back their own autonomy and power, like seed sovereignty and the power to determine their own food needs. That kind of food sovereignty probably doesn't sit well with the board of directors at some multinationals.

If we dump cheap, subsidized corn on these developing countries, like we've been doing to Mexico, it harms their farmers and hinders their ability to grow their markets and production capacity at home.[53] And this designed system, for the benefit of corporate power, is damaging our own natural ecosystems and environment in the process—the dumping millions of tons of chemical poisons like glyphosate onto our land and waterways.

Much of the fertilizer that we use to grow all this corn, along with chemical pesticides and herbicides and vast amounts of soil from over tilling, washes into the nation's lakes, rivers and coastal oceans, polluting waters and damaging ecosystems. The massive dead zone in the Gulf of Mexico is the clearest example of this. In the meantime, weeds and pests are developing resistance to glyphosate and other chemicals. New "superweeds" are showing signs of cracks in the system. Is there a better way?

Propping up the US corn system is not the solution. American farmers must be supported to transition away from the current monocropping system and become diverse growers again, with varied crops and animals in a more sustainable and environmentally friendly system. Disruption in the corn belt might be the impetus to bring on that needed change.

I believe that any new agricultural system that we support with taxpayer subsidies should include crop rotation, no-till and limited till methods of cultivation, and regenerative and sustainable farming practices that improve soil health. I believe that we must focus on increasing living microorganisms and organic matter which reduces the need for chemicals and increases the soils water holding capacity—making farmland much more resilient to floods, droughts, and climate change.

Lessons from the Fall of Tobacco

In the mountains of Western North Carolina, where I live and farm, the mid-1990s marked the beginning of the end for tobacco here. After more than 70 years as the dominant cash crop for farmers, in what was known as the "burley belt", production of burley tobacco entered a period of sharp decline.[54]

The drop in demand was devastating to farmers in the region. From 1997 to 2012, the number of burley belt tobacco farms declined by 97%. Tobacco acreage saw a 95% decline. Revenue decreased by 96%. This is what market disruption looks like when you're dependent on a single crop, and it happened over a period of about 15 years. Coincidently, Midwestern corn farmers have less time than that to prepare before General Motors (and likely other car manufacturers) stop making cars with gasoline engine.

Anticipating the impact that the loss of tobacco could have on the region, a group of farmers and community stakeholders met in 1995 to look for solutions to the challenges facing farmers in the region. What came out of it was the Appalachian Sustainable Agriculture Project (ASAP). ASAP launched a local food campaign in 2000 to build a market alternative for other crops, including fruits and vegetables. They focused on connecting people to farms and food, and they began building consumer demand for locally and regionally grown farm products.

The result was that over a 15-year period agriculture shifted from monocropping tobacco to fruits, vegetables, grass fed beef and free-range chicken eggs. Much of that food was grown using organic and regenerative practices that improved soil health and biodiversity, and it was driven by consumer demand for healthier food without all the chemicals.

From 2002 to 2012, the former burley-dependent counties saw a 98% increase in the number of farms growing vegetables, melons, potatoes, and sweet potatoes. The Asheville region of Western North Carolina is now known as a 'foodtopia' and while the region still faces issues around food accessibility and injustice due to systemic issues, this response to the fall of tobacco has greatly increased the viability of a local food scene that draws people to farmers markets and packed restaurants serving locally produced food.

While the size and scale of the problem facing the Midwest is significantly greater, including the need for new markets, labor, food storage, and transportation networks, I believe that with enough time solutions can be found. And the biggest benefit from this transition may relate to climate change. I believe that the Corn Belt solution can and should benefit the health and biodiversity of the environment as much as the financial health and well-being of the farmer. Monocropping corn year after year has been devastating to the soils in the Midwest, and we are just now beginning to realize how important soil health is to our climate future.

The most recent, cutting-edge research suggests that regenerative agriculture may be the most cost-effective tool that we have to sequester carbon from the atmosphere and store it in the soil, where it belongs.[55] We're just now beginning to understand the mechanisms at work in the soil that sequester and store carbon, and it's closely related to a symbiotic relationship between plant roots, bacteria and mycorrhizal fungi that co-evolved together over millions of years. With better land management that enhances the health of our soils, including no till planting, cover crops, reduced chemical applications, and crop rotation, the corn belt could become a giant carbon sink while providing a broader range of food products.[56] It will also become much more resilient to the effects of climate change, including drought and floods, because healthy soils can absorb and store much more water.

Disruption, like the fall of tobacco, can bring about positive change. But it seemed to me that farmers in the corn belt desperately needed support, including educational and financial resources to help them transition to new crops and better, carbon smart growing practices along with new markets and distribution channels for those crops. In several trips into the heart of the corn belt, to small towns like Ottawa, Illinois, I was to learn the size and scope of things.

We probably had 10 years before farmers really started to feel the financial strain from reduced ethanol demand, but we would need all of that just to get started with the infrastructure that would be necessary. It would be a monumental task. Company men had already taken over.

Just ten multinational food corporations control most of the food that you eat or find in the local supermarket.[57] These ten mega-corps, like Kraft and General Mills, own almost all the brands that you recognize and buy in the center aisles of the grocery store.

Twenty percent (20%) of the food that Americans eat now comes from a foreign country.[58] That's one out of every five bites that you take. Food now travels on massive container ships, trucks and airplanes thousands of miles, from all over the world in a global food web, to finally get to your dinner table. The average vegetable in your grocery store traveled

1500 miles to get there. That's the distance from New York City to Dallas. But a lot of it comes from much further away, like asparagus flown in from Argentina, blueberries from Chile, and beef from New Zealand. The food miles associated with one meal can easily equate to 25,000 miles, or the circumference of the earth.

If all the ingredients that really went into your supper were laid out on the table, there would be a hefty bowl of jet fuel and a jug of truck diesel sitting there, and plenty of CO_2 emissions for dessert. A couple cups of pesticides, herbicides, and fertilizers (made from fossil fuels) would also take their place at the table. It all goes sight unseen. We don't even think about it, but it's in there.[59]

The modern, corporate-industrial food complex is like a well-oiled machine, with standardized, mechanized, and controlled inputs and outputs, as well as centralized processing and distribution centers that deliver human beings our daily allowance of protein, carbohydrates, vitamins and minerals. Truckloads and trainloads of corn enter the massive machine at one end, and brightly colored pipes spew food products out the other end, like high-fructose corn syrup, modified corn starch, mono-, di- and triglycerides, xanthan gum, maltodextrin, lecithin and lactic acid. Even the glue used to seal the box that all this stuff goes into can come from corn. We eat and drink bushels of corn without even knowing it. God help us, it's even in the beer.

These easy sugars from corn in our processed foods are major contributing factors to a serious obesity problem in the U.S. and around the world.[60]

Like the clothing industry (and most other industries), the global corporate food industry chases cheap labor around the world, looking for ways to increase scale, reduce costs and improve profits. Capital flows from one region to another, and like migrant workers, capital can be easily picked up and moved to where resources and profit can be more efficiently extracted around the globe.

Your chicken doesn't come from a pretty farm like the one pictured on the packaging. It came from a warehouse-looking structure where it spent eight short weeks growing up. Some chicken is now grown and slaughtered in the United States, then frozen and shipped on container ships to China where it is ground up and processed into chicken nuggets, with a little corn added for flavor and texture, and then sent back to us. These chickens have circled the globe, twice, and have traveled further around the world than most Americans.

Cattle are shipped to massive, confined animal feed operations, or CAFO's, where corn from other parts of the country is trucked in to feed them. Thousands of cows stand closely confined in knee deep mud and manure when it rains in this far away and mysterious land where almost all of our meat comes from. Your hamburger might also come from Argentina or New Zealand, both huge exporters of beef to the United States. Meanwhile, the US ships a lot of our beef to a rapidly growing market in China.[61]

There is one large processor that cleans, processes and packages almost all the spinach grown in California. It may package the spinach with different labels for different brands, but it all flows through this one massive facility. The risk of salmonella or other bacterial contamination at this one plant instantly becomes a national crisis if just one farm ships contaminated product to the facility, because from there, it goes everywhere. And because we've concentrated food processing and production into fewer, larger hands, national outbreaks are becoming more frequent with regular food alerts and recalls in the national news; a recurrent scare for Americans that can involve anything from swine to salads.

The centralization of food processing is a key to efficiencies of scale and reducing costs for food corporations in America. So is the growing of certain food commodities in centralized regions, like corn and soybeans in the Midwest. And while there used to be thousands of mills scattered throughout the US that could simply grind wheat for making bread, now just a few large facilities strategically located around the country grind most of the wheat. Small local and regional food processing centers, like facilities to grind wheat, process beef or make dairy products, have all but disappeared.

Farmers in the fields of the Midwestern states like Illinois and Iowa grow almost nothing but dent corn and soybeans, and as productive as it is, it's a massive food desert.[62] You don't eat dent corn, it must be processed first or fed to animals. And generally, farmers there can't support their families from it, not without taxpayer subsidies.[63] Most farmers in America have working spouses and work other jobs themselves off the farm to pay the bills, and many are up to their eyeballs in debt.[64] And they're getting older. The average age of a farmer in the United States is now 60 years old. Just 5.7 percent of American farmers are under the age of 35, and they face steep challenges accessing land, capital, knowledge, and credit.[65]

Corporate food processors, who do most of the bulk purchasing of farm products, along with the United States Department of Agriculture, started demanding that farmers "get big or get out" back in the 1960's and 70's, and thousands of small farms were swallowed up by larger corporate farms. It became a farm economy of size and scale, with the gathering of farmland into fewer and fewer hands. With the loss of thousands of small family farms, small towns and communities around the country were decimated. Without all the working farmers and families to shop in downtown stores, small towns began boarding up store fronts; a picture of rural, small-town life that we're all accustomed to seeing now.

With the specialization of mono-cropping farms, we abandoned the ancient knowledge, techniques of replenishing the soil and principles of diversity, of plants and animals and crop rotation, and we became a corn and soybean nation highly dependent on fossil fuels to do what the sun and nature used to do.

Our mono-cropping system of agriculture in America depletes the soils to such an extent that we are completely dependent on massive amounts of fertilizers (again made from fossil fuels) to grow anything now. As Wendell Berry first told us, we need oil as much as we need food, must have it in fact even before we can even eat.[66] Food and fossil fuels have become locked in a dance where our nation is dependent on oil for our food. Our dependence on foreign oil fluctuates with domestic production, but short-term forecasts predict the US to become a bigger net importer of oil, increasing our dependence on foreign nations, and because food and oil are so intricately linked, that has further ramifications to our food sovereignty and security.

While I can go without cinnamon, and even coffee for a while (I'd be a bit grumpy about that), I can live without it. But as we've already discussed, our complete and total dependence on a global food web is creating some serious risk if supply chains or distribution channels are ever disrupted. The recent Covid-19 pandemic was just one example of risk in the food supply, and other threats exist that can take out oil refineries or the power grid. Whether that threat is a series of hurricanes, a solar flare, Russian hackers, or terrorists, certain events could be devastating to our national or regional food supply. The Pentagon has been conducting research related to industrialized and concentrated food production, and here's a new word that came out of it, "agri-terrorism". Take a guess what that means.

As we learned with the coronavirus, we may see a threat, but will we prepare for it or react to it in time? Will we adequately prepare for the risks of disruption in the food supply, and will we do what we can to mitigate some of the risks?

Eat Your View

Our goal at Creekside Farm is to help people create and live in a positive new story. A story that we build and grow ourselves.

One hundred years ago a community could feed itself from local farms. With the growth of the industrial food complex, we're just not that self-reliant or resilient anymore when it comes to our food supply and food security as a nation, and much less so at the regional and local level.

We've all become completely disconnected from our food and where it comes from, and that's happened by corporate design. Just as Arab traders kept secret the source of the spice trade, Corporate America doesn't really want you to know where your chicken or your apple juice comes from. It can be a messy business, and many people don't want to know.

Most communities have lost the capacity (the farmland) and the technical know-how to grow and process food locally. But if we can just grow something locally, at least some small part of what we eat, we'll learn how to do it again as a community and retain some of the knowledge and food producing capacity for future generations. We can take back some power and control in our lives, and I believe that improves our psychological health. It creates feelings of independence, freedom, self-reliance and self-esteem in the individuals growing the food and in entire communities sharing the food. We can change, as a community, ever so slightly, from just being consumers to becoming growers and producers again. That, by its very nature, is an act of radical resistance.

We can gain more control in our lives simply by starting a backyard or community garden, purchasing local food at restaurants and the farmer's market, joining Community Supported Agriculture (CSA) programs, and just supporting local farmers in general. It's a way of standing up to the man and becoming less dependent while we build strength at home, locally. If we do nothing, then we accept that we are vulnerable, helpless, dependent, and unable to provide for ourselves and our own basic needs for survival. Many, like Butch, believe that is risky, irresponsible, and short-sighted behavior, and that we need to take more responsibility for feeding ourselves and building our community resilience. Besides all that, it helps preserve and protect some of the pastoral beauty that we like to look at as we drive through the countryside.

What started with the Far-Distance Company has grown into a massive and complex industry that has removed food production from the local hands of the people and made us all vulnerable and dependent for the necessities that support life. It's also made us very unhealthy. An alarming 20% of US children are now considered clinically obese. With diabetes and heart disease on the rise due to our unhealthy diets of processed foods, this is the first time in history that we can predict that our kids can expect a shorter life span than their parents. [67]

Many people around the world are fed up with the globalization of our food supply, and the industrial food complex that controls it all, and this is one big reason for the organic, grow local and farm-to-table movement that is changing the way we eat in this country and around the world. It's also starting to determine where we choose to live.

The Agrihood

Acts of resistance and rebellion in the food system can take many forms, even real estate development, and so I invested a lot of money into a project based on a radical idea—the Agrihood. When you're a weird, rich guy, you can do things like this. I saw it as a way of conducting social experiments on an unsuspecting population, which is cool.

There is a growing trend in the US toward living in what is called an agricultural neighborhood, or 'agrihood'. I built one such neighborhood and wrote a book about it. It's based on the principle of saving farmland and providing a valuable amenity to residents in a new community. It's also about saving food miles. So rather than bringing food to where the people are, save the 1,500 miles and bring the people to where the food is. In fact, plant them right in the middle of it with the tomatoes and onions. Call it "hyper-local." This is where the local food movement intersects with real estate development. Why bring the farm to the table when you can bring the table to the farm?[68]

While community gardens are a popular trend in new housing developments, in *Carrots Don't Grow on Trees: Building Sustainable and Resilient Communities*, I tell the story of my three-year journey through the process of trying to create a new type of agricultural community where an organic farm takes center stage and residents gain a closer connection to food, nature and the environment.[69] I wasn't trying to build some pastoral Utopia; just a community that was a little more connected to food and farming.

I saw it as the natural extension of an already booming 'grow local', farm to table movement going on everywhere around the world. And I saw good reasons for building it and for taking on the financial risk. They were the same reasons people shop at farmers markets, which are directly related to a concern over the current industrial food complex and the desire for long term safe, secure, and healthy food systems. I just didn't know at the time if the concept would work and if people would buy into it and move there. It was a risky business venture to be sure.

The neighborhood is called Creekside Farm at Walnut Cove, and all homesites look out on the growing fields and farm animals in the nearby pasture. In the process of developing this food centric neighborhood, I worked with The Cliffs organization to incorporate it into the larger, and adjacent, Cliff's golf and wellness community so that more homeowners could enjoy the farm and local food amenity. That partnership brought the added benefit of a golf and wellness center which would attract residents to my little neighborhood development, including miles of walking trails.

At first, I liked the idea of creating a somewhat self-sustaining community, where food production was built right into the 'built environment', like the roads, water and power. For me, it relates to self-reliance and something that my father drilled into my head growing up. He was old school, and would say things like, "Men cannot be carefree and irresponsible, we cannot afford that luxury." My dad worked hard to feed and protect his family of seven kids.

Maybe that's why I'm so concerned about the concentration of power and control into fewer hands, and why I feel that becoming dependent on food from far-away places is so risky. To just be 'carefree' and forget about it, and just assume it's always going to be there, doesn't sit well with me. It feels irresponsible.

But the agrihood was really part of a larger experiment for me, and the question was this: Can a community feed itself? Can a community support a farmer, or two farmers? And can a farmer produce food at a price people are willing to pay, given price expectations now set by industrial farms in Central and South America paying far lower wages?

While doing research for this new community I met an extraordinary group of farmers and growers who perfectly illustrate what sustainable living close to the farm looks like. I discovered that the growing, processing and celebration of food creates the connection points that build healthy communities. When people live closer to food production, the community they create becomes immersed in the working organic farm and intimate with the farmers who work there.

I developed twelve home sites on 16 acres of land that looked out over the farm, vegetable gardens and pastures. We developed roughly one-fifth of the farmland and kept four-fifths in farming production and animal pasture. The financial bottom line on it all was that the lots we developed and sold helped to pay for the rest of the farmland that could remain open and productive into the future.

The book was really written for developers and land planners to show them a new model for development, and one that might convince some of them to stop the bulldozer at a certain point and leave the rest of the land open for small scale farming. The farming aspect becomes a valuable amenity that people want and one that will differentiate your 'product' from other developments.

And for people who want to connect to the land and to where their food came from, it's a cool place to live. It allowed people to come home to the farm and to connect to the farming lifestyle without having to do all the work. Our farm manager did all the work. Residents can just walk down to the garden and pick a perfect pepper for dinner.

The community supported agriculture (CSA) program that we developed to feed people in the neighborhood grew to support the vegetable needs of over 80 households in the surrounding community, or about 200 people. We have about 100 chickens for eggs and butcher a grass-fed cow occasionally to supplement the protein needs of the community. Our farm manager also runs down to the farmers market on Saturdays to sell excess produce and donates excess produce to a local food bank. This was the beginning of my deep dive into food production for a community and the business side of farming.

In case you're wondering why I named a book *Carrots Don't Grow on Trees*, I'll give you the short version of the story. Whenever we had school groups out to the farm for a farm tour, I saw it as an opportunity to test the kid's knowledge and mess with their heads. Sometimes I would tie some carrots to a small maple tree by the garden. When we walked by the tree, I'd say, "There it is kids, the carrot tree." Most of the time the kids wouldn't question it. It made perfect sense to them. Why not a carrot tree? Apples grow on trees.

Later in the tour I would pull a carrot out of the ground and watch a bunch of noses start to scrunch up. Some of the kids were a bit alarmed and concerned that food came out of the dirt like that. I think they preferred carrots from trees because it was cleaner. Anyway, the point is that we're all a little disconnected from our food and where it comes from, and especially kid's.

Where we live and how we live can have the greatest impact on our health and life expectancy, and the built environment is just as important as hospitals and modern health care facilities to our national health. We spend trillions on health care costs that keep rising and that are quickly becoming unsustainable for the long term. As the saying goes, an ounce of prevention is worth a pound of cure, and parks, walking trails and walkable communities are more important than a new pill when it comes to our overall national health. Education and access to healthier food is more important than innovations in open heart surgery. We can spend more on prevention through education and the built environment and save trillions in future health care costs.

Farmers markets have sprouted up everywhere over the past two decades. People are beginning to understand the importance of fresh, local food without all the chemicals. Positive change is happening, and maybe we're just relearning the old ways and the ancient ideas that were erased by corporate colonialism.

Gone Fishing with Butch and Mumford

Butch Barron and Lewis Mumford are cousins, but they couldn't be any more different. Mumford was my mentor. Butch my enforcer. Mumford the scientist. Butch the rebel survivalist.

One bright summer day we went fishing together on Mills River about five miles from my farm. The river came out of the trees of the Pisgah National Forest and ran along the adjacent farm of a friend named Jason Davis. The stream was pure and cold, and it traveled by no dwelling or habitat of man as it came down the mountains and popped out of the forest at Jason's farm.

Jason subsidized his income on the farm by running guided fishing tours and other outdoor sports activities, but he let us fish off his land for free. It was a perfect summer Tuesday, sunny and about 75 degrees. It would be a sin to be sitting in an office on this day. Drinking on the river was the place to be, so we all gave up any obligations or responsibilities we might have had and scooted over to the river with a twelve-pack of Stella and some night crawlers.

Mumford is about 60 and has crazy hair. I think he lost his hairbrush in the 1970's and never bothered replacing it. He often wears incongruent things like a long-sleeve plaid flannel shirt over bright red nylon athletic shorts, black socks, sandals, and a weird safari hat. He gives much more thought to gut health and the microbiome than fashion or appearances. He makes crazy concoctions from plants and seeds that I've never heard of and drinks it. He'll juice stuff and drink it in various shades of color and texture, but usually with some sort of weird, green tinge to it. He's got a gadget for everything, and some by his own design. His kitchen looks like a laboratory with so much equipment filling up the counter space: things for mixing, things for purifying, machines for oxidizing. There's so much stuff piled up on his kitchen counters that you can't find a spot to set down an ice tray.

He didn't drink alcohol very often but when he did, he would get pretty loopy after just a couple beers or a glass or two of wine. He tried making his own mead from honey from an ancient Babylonian recipe that he found in some obscure publication. He said it was much healthier than beer if you can get beyond the taste. I never could, but I did get a good buzz off it.

Mumford walked across Japan in his mid-twenties. In his thirties, he spent 10 years in Costa Rica harvesting hardwood, which he regrets. He gave me an old book written around the year 1900 that was about farming practices in China and Japan that went back thousands of years and that were still being used at the time, and in some parts, still are. We call it regenerative agriculture now. The point of the book was that farmers had been pulling food out of the exact same small garden plots of land for centuries without depleting the soil because they kept feeding the soil organic material to keep it alive (and not chemicals).

Mumford knows a lot more than me about soil health, micro-organisms, food production, natural resources, carbon cycles and about a million other subjects. He has the closest thing to a photographic memory of anyone I know. He'll throw out the name of some German scientist who wrote some obscure scientific paper on microbes 40 years ago while discussing a completely unrelated topic, like his mead. Something about microbes in the fermenting process—I don't know. I wasn't listening. He makes my brain hurt sometimes just keeping up with him. But over a lifetime of hanging out together, Mumford had educated his close cousin Butch about a lot of the research he was working on. Butch may have looked like a redneck hillbilly, but he was smart, and he knew what was going on.

Appalachia has a long history of political resistance. Butch is part of that history. The ability and skills to grow food or forage or hunt is power in the hands of the people, and Butch had that power. Chow-chow, shucky beans, pickled corn, and kilt lettuce. Who eats that stuff? Butch does. He grows it and eats it. He hunts for much of his meat supply through the winter. He wears camo pants and t-shirts and often forgets to shave.

I was just getting to know these two neighbors, but after just a few hours fishing and several beers, we were able to summarize the current food system and the root problem of modern society. Our conclusion was this: we had lost control and we were now at the mercy of ruthless men. It came down to a struggle for freedom.

On this fine, beautiful day, Mumford raised his fishing pole and gently tossed out his line, and said,

"You know, with all the corporate consolidation going on and with companies buying each other up and getting bigger all the time, it's scary to think that someday the guys who sell you soda pop and Cheetos will also sell the pill for diabetes and heart disease. They'll get you in the wash and then get ya' in the rinse."

"That day's coming, I'm afraid," I replied with a smile.

"I'm really concerned about how much money the food and pharmaceutical corporations donate to finance political campaigns and pay the lobbyists. It's getting really out of hand," he said a few moments later. Mumford was fishing for a topic of conversation. He was tossing a couple lines out there to see if I would bite on anything.

"It's depressing to think about Mumford," I said with a smile. "Can we just talk about environmental degradation or something else?"

Mumford smiled and gave a tug on his line. "Yeah, well, we've done a pretty good job of hiding and masking environmental problems, that's for sure," said Mumford. "Until it shows up from a satellite image as a massive dead zone in the Gulf of Mexico. Then it's pretty hard to hide."

Butch was more focused on catching a fish than having a conversation, so he wandered up stream and left the two of us. I continued the stream of thought.

"I've seen studies that suggest we've already lost over half the topsoil from the most fertile land in the Midwest," I said. "It was several feet deep when the Indians lived there, but it's now just a few inches deep in some parts. And that's happened just in the last 50 to 60 years of intensive tilling with large equipment."

"I read one study recently," Mumford replied, "by a professor at Iowa State— big ag school—that said for every ton of corn they pull out of an acre in Iowa, they lose a ton of topsoil to erosion. Mostly because no one uses cover crops in the winter to protect the soil from washing away. It equates to about five tons of topsoil per acre, lost, and the average corn yield is about five tons per acre."[70]

"You're kidding," I replied.

"No, I'm not. At first, we destroyed our soils unwittingly, like the dust bowl era of 1930's Oklahoma, but now we know better, and still do it. That is our crime, our sin, our transgression against future generations. Since 1950, we've lost about one-third of our topsoil around the globe."

"Unlike this beautiful clear creek were fishing in," said Mumford, "the Mississippi and its tributaries are brown and loaded with soil, sediment and chemicals from those Midwestern farms. The strange thing, to me, is that if a big company spotted an oil leak in one of their huge food processing machines, they'd be all over it. They'd fix it quickly. Not because of concern over the oil getting into the environment, but because that machine needs to keep running, they can't afford a break down. It represents production capacity.

"But they don't see the connection with our soil flowing into waterways as the loss of future production capacity. It makes no sense that they don't see that or do something about it. You would think companies like Kellogg's and General Mills, who count on the soil for their livelihood, would be more concerned and pushing for ways to conserve topsoil. You'd think they'd be all over that because it affects future capacity, it affects their future inputs. And they're certainly able to force farmers to implement conservation practices, like cover crops, because of their purchasing power. The real, added cost to the finished product would be nothing. Pennies per box."[71]

"What confuses me," Mumford continued, "is that so many large food companies don't see some obvious connections. They are very careful to do regular maintenance and upkeep on factory equipment that they use to process food because that affects capacity. If a machine goes down, they're out of business until it's up and running again. But they don't see the importance of the health and maintenance of the soil, the health and maintenance of farmers in their supply chain who are going broke, and the health and maintenance of their employees and customers. A healthy population means people don't miss work, they make more money, and they can continue to afford to buy your products. Why don't they see that?"

Mumford gave another little tug on his line to keep it off the bottom and away from the brush on the opposite bank.

"This is true in the meat and poultry industry also," I replied. "They should be protecting themselves from the risk of environmental degradation through their purchasing power that they have in the animal feed supply chain. They wield enough power to make farmers grow corn and soy feed in ways that are better for long term production capacity. And I imagine that would cost a couple pennies per pound of hamburger, if that."

"That's right," said Mumford, "I think it's related to the concept of response capacity, or how you see a risk and act on it. Quarterly profit reports and short-term gain may be clouding their vision."

What Mumford was talking about was a recurring theme that I kept running into—the ability to see and act, and the ability to understand cause and effect.

"And they must realize that their products, processed foods I mean, are killing off their customers from diet related disease like obesity and diabetes," Mumford continued.

"I guess maybe they just count on birth rates and new younger customers coming up, or new markets in other parts of the world," I said. "That's a sad thought."

"People aren't as dumb as corporations like to think they are. And social norms change, like we've seen with smoking. Social norms need to change around food, what we consider decent, healthy food, and how we produce it. Food production must be based on what we as a society deem acceptable, not the corporation," Mumford said.

In my head, I think for a moment, Resistance! Dude! Food is what WE say it is!

But I replied, "I'm just glad that we're seeing more people take back control of the growing and distribution system at the local level, with farmers markets and all that."

In my regular magazine column, I often interview and write about these small, local farmers in our region. I have witnessed how these small growers and distributors were improving their own production systems, improving the soil, and improving the biodiversity of the surrounding environment. People are building a new American food system from the ground up. Small communities and local food sheds are places where food production does good for the environment, society, and economy.

Butch interrupted. Suddenly he was back and had something to say.

"To create real change, this whole 'get to know your farmer' thing will only go so far. I think you need to scare the hell out of people to wake them up! Sustainable food systems are a matter of self-protection and self-determination."

"I think you'll move the needle faster," Butch continued, "if you help people understand the threats of the food system to them personally, like the harm to their health from it, or the sky-rocketing cost of health care, or the threats of climate change. Let 'em know how just a few guys control it all, and a lot of these guys live in other countries like China."

Mumford and I stood quietly watching our lines and letting Butch rant a little, happy to have him join the conversation.

"Most people are clueless to the real threats of climate change to food production and distribution. A lot of places we depend on for food are getting hotter and dryer. Look at California for crying out loud! It's turning into a desert, and half our vegetables are grown there.

"Or how about the scarcity of resources like oil, land, and water. We're running out of Phosphate; did you know that? There's enough scientific research out there to scare the hell out of anyone," Butch said.

Mumford agreed, and added, "We need to do more to encourage large farms in the Midwest to grow something other than just corn and soybeans. We need subsidies to encourage cover crops and diversity to improve the soil and reduce erosion—not subsidies just to grow more corn. Anything that can increase biodiversity is a good thing. Crop rotation is a really good thing."

Subsidies come from the massive Farm Bill, which started in the 1930's as part of the New Deal and is renewed every five or six years. It is a massive thing that in the year 2020 accounted for almost 40% of farmer net income.[72]

From my own research, I knew how big US farm subsidies were artificially driving down global crop prices, unfairly undermining small farmers around the world and maintaining poverty in many developing countries. Mumford had a better idea.

"A subsidy should be used to support the adoption of new technologies or practices that are not common with producers, like sustainable growing methods," said Mumford. "And once we've proven to the farmer that these methods are cost effective and profitable, we can stop the subsidies.

"Subsidies should be used to change behavior and solve problems, not as a long-term crutch that can stifle innovation and cause farmers to become less competitive and more dependent on government."

I kept getting my line tangled in some low tree branches and repositioned myself on the other side of Mumford, upstream from him. A frog jumped in the water as I approached the stream bank. At least it wasn't a snake, I thought.

"The problem," continued Mumford, "is subsidies can eliminate any incentive for a farmer to boost efficiency and can shift his focus from better crops to more farming subsidies— let's just plant more corn. They get caught in a rut."

"Subsidies also lead to the overuse of fertilizers and pesticides and negative environmental impacts just to grow more corn," said Mumford. "And to get a bigger government check, many farmers plant more corn on some of their lower quality fields that really shouldn't be farmed at all, marginal lands that have poorer soils and climates and so they must dump a lot more fertilizer and chemicals to grow on it. A lot of this land is on a slope and prone to soil erosion, and they know it. And a lot of this land should be put back into grassland or forest or wetlands. Taxpayers shouldn't be paying to try to grow something on marginal land like that when we know most of the soil and chemicals are going to end up in our waterways."

Mumford reeled in his line to check his worm, tossed it back out again, and continued speaking.

"Crop insurance, a big subsidy item, encourages farmers to grow in flood plains where they know it's very risky and likely to flood, but they figure the government will compensate them if that happens anyway. It encourages riskier behavior. In fact, the farm bill discourages cover crops like rye or clover, which anchor the soil and build up nutrients during the off-season and would protect farmers from the very losses that they end up needing crop insurance to recoup. It's a crazy system," said Mumford.

Agricultural subsidies do undermine efforts to promote efficiency and more sustainable food production, and could, in fact, make many farmers reluctant to invest in sustainability at all, because they know that the American taxpayer has got his back.

Subsidies certainly discourage crop rotation in favor of planting only a subsidized crop, like corn, which in turn leads to increased use of fertilizers in a monocropping system. The boom in corn production over the past several decades, driven by subsidies and the ethanol mandate, is a big cause of the pollution problems and algae blooms in the Mississippi River and Gulf of Mexico. Cause and effect.

Lewis Mumford was well respected in Western North Carolina for his knowledge about soils and farming methods. It is one of the great coincidences of my life that such a man lived down the road from me. I learned a great deal from him.

Butch was suddenly back and jumped into the conversation; "And stopping the direct and indirect federal support of CAFOs would be huge. We need to get cows back on pasture."

The big, confined animal feed operations certainly like the corn and soybean subsidies because it greatly reduces the cost of animal feed, a cost often below the farmers cost of production, at the taxpayers' expense. All the makers of snacks and soda pop benefit too because subsidies greatly reduce their costs for corn derivatives like high fructose corn syrup. Most of the cost savings is taken as profit by the food processors and CAFO operators and meat processors and is rarely shared or passed on to the end consumer with reduced retail prices.

The back and forth continued, and since no fish were biting, we started paying more attention to the conversation and the beer than our fishing poles.

"What we really need," said Mumford, "if we're ever going to take back control of our food, is the local and regional infrastructure to process and distribute food."

It was here, on the banks of Mills River, that Mumford first talked to me about the importance of regional food systems.

"We need a lot more regional or mobile meat processing facilities. We need places just to grind wheat, pasteurize milk and make pasta and bread. That's where our policymakers should focus to improve our own local and regional food security, food sovereignty, and community resilience." Mumford was also the first person to put those three words together for me in a sentence, and I have since used them together hundreds of times.[73]

"We need to be able to control the farm inputs and outputs locally," Mumford added. Then he went on a roll. "We need to reduce and recycle food waste. Farmers need to be diversified and profitable, and we need to attract new, young farmers into this occupation. Small-scale farming needs to become much more efficient. We need technologies to plant and harvest that reduce labor, increase speed, but don't cost millions of dollars, like a combine does. Something that works like a combine but might be the size of a Volkswagen Beetle, now that would be real innovation that could support regional food systems."

"Did you read the book I gave you about soils in China?" Mumford asked with a smile knowing full well that I wouldn't read it cover to cover. I scanned it. "I read that book about 20 years ago," he said. "It's a great story about regenerative agriculture."

I said "Yeah" and hoped this wasn't going to be a test with follow up questions. Fortunately, Mumford went on to describe a local food shed. Butch wandered downstream again.

"I think we need to focus on creating a new food web entirely," he said. "One geared toward local and regional markets. All the inputs, including compost and seed in our production, and all processing of food, should come from local and regional markets. And when we sell our food, only after local markets are satisfied, only then should we sell any excess production outside the region. This might be less efficient from a food production standpoint, but it protects our resources and capacity, our soil and water, uses less energy and reduces waste, and it offers a great deal of food security. The social and economic benefits far outweigh any productivity loss."

The difference between regional, sustainable food systems and the industrial food system is stark when you look at it. Industrial systems focus on the most efficient manner and machinery to extract food from the ground, including tilling methods that contribute to soil erosion and intensive chemical applications. GMO's, synthetic fertilizers, and pesticides all leave their mark on the ground.

Concentration of food types grown in one area, like corn in the Midwest, is a key premise of industrial agriculture. Mass specialization in production and processing is another. Vertical integration and global sourcing are the other principles of industrialization. Highly processed food is usually the result. That is the difference between an industrialized global system and a local, sustainable food shed. One is about the mass extraction of resources, including labor, and the other is about regional food security and sustainability.

Sustainable regional food systems focus on plant and ecosystem diversity to produce most of the needs of the region, including pasture raised livestock which also includes regional processing centers, and it's a focus on fresh seasonal foods grown in close proximity to where it is consumed.[74] Mumford continued, his voice calm and resolute.

"Here's the thing Robert. I choose to provide some of my own food for my family and choose not to be helplessly dependent on the industrial food system," Mumford said. "I will not support it out of laziness or inaction. I believe that a person can change both his life and his surroundings by making himself responsibly free, as best he can."

There it was again. That feeling started to well up in me. Time to Resist! Radicalize! Are we just going to take this laying down! Are we all just a bunch of lazy chicken-shits? We must stand up!

I knew that other people would agree wholeheartedly with Mumford. But there is a serious gap between what some people think or believe and what they do. It's a moral crisis in our culture. There are also other people who don't have much of a choice because of systemic inequities.

There is a collaboration, some call it collusion, between food corporations and government agencies. And the food system is now divided between two kinds of farms, those who have the money, land, and equipment to farm at a large scale, and those who do not. Again, it goes back to the "Get Big or Get Out" philosophy of the USDA in the '70's.

The global food system is designed to exploit labor and natural resources and does not concern itself with the cost to community well-being. It does not look at things at the smaller scale, at the community or regional level. The industrial agricultural complex has benefited from taxpayer subsidies while they continue to degrade the soil, water and air quality, community health and environmental diversity, and these are community and regional assets that they've been messing with under a global banner of 'food for all'. It was all bullshit.

Can you see how a person might become radicalized? Can you understand how a guy like Butch would get riled up? Do you see the political and philosophical roots of anti-establishmentarianism?

And when systems are already stressed, what happens when you add another stressor to the equation, like climate change?

The risk and exposure to climate change varies by regions, but our global food system has already seen some disruption from it, and it's going to get worse. History shows us that when food systems are disrupted, social unrest quickly follows. The French Revolution, say many historians, may have started with a bread shortage after a couple years of poor wheat harvests. And social unrest tied to food shortages has been happening more recently in countries like Venezuela. It always happens.

"What changes do you see in the global food system when it comes to climate change, Mumford? Is anyone even paying attention?" I asked.

"I think there is still some hope, and there are some large food producers who are starting to feel the impacts and they are now assessing the climate related risks. I think some are starting to look closely at the supply of materials for their business, including the quantity, quality, pricing, and variability of those inputs. They are looking closely at water availability, and any other possible disruptions to their distribution or their workforce. That's what I would do if I was CEO of General Mills, anyway.

"The fact is, in our global system, climate related disruptions and food security issues on one side of the planet will affect the price and availability of food on the other side of the planet. A drought in China can affect what we pay for bacon in the US. I think many CEOs get that," said Mumford. He gave a little pull on this line and watched intensely. I stared at the bank, thinking, 'how could they not see this?'

"There is a lot of supply chain volatility and risk in a global system," said Mumford. "But it is the constant pressure of quarterly earnings reports that may prevent many corporate leaders from doing anything about it," he said. "Fixing our soils is a longer process and a distraction from the short-term quarterly earnings report, especially when your bonus is based on that report."

Mumford threw his line out again, it crossed the stream and bounced off a log laying on the opposite bank and then plopped back into the water in a perfect spot, a natural hole of deeper water along the bank where trout like to hang out. "That was lucky" he said with a grin.

Plants perform an incredible service by pulling carbon from the atmosphere, and 40% of the carbon that trees and plants pull from the atmosphere is stored in the ground—pushed down there through the plant roots and creating little pockets of carbon "glue" that feeds micro-organisms in the soil. Microbes in turn help feed the plants by breaking down vital minerals and nutrients into a form that the plant can absorb and use. It's an amazing and important symbiotic relationship that developed between plants and microbes as they evolved together over millions of years. This is the key to long term carbon storage, and one of the answers to climate change.

There are more microbes in a handful of healthy soil than all the people who have ever lived on earth; billions and billions of them.[75] But as we kill the soil with over-tilling and chemicals like glyphosate, we kill the microbes also. We now need to use 3 times the fertilizer to grow the same amount of food as we did 30 years ago.[76] Meanwhile. glyphosate is in the water, and recent studies show that it's also in all of us now—a known carcinogen.[77] The manufacturers of glyphosate, the active ingredient in Roundup, have lost billions of dollars already in lawsuits.[78] The system will change because it must.

Over tilling our soils disrupts the natural water and carbon cycles and is causing the desertification of nearly half the arable land around the world. Nearly 30 million acres of farmable land, roughly the size of England, is lost to soil degradation every year.[79] Over-tilling soil releases so much carbon into the atmosphere that it can be seen in NASA enhanced satellite images as massive clouds of CO_2 during the spring when farmers are tilling the ground in preparation of planting. As crops and vegetation grow and absorb carbon in the summer months, atmospheric carbon drops dramatically, which is clearly visible in time lapse satellite imaging.[80]

Since the industrial revolution, or around 1750, we've pumped roughly one thousand billion tons of carbon into the atmosphere, or 1000 gigatons. Reducing emissions isn't enough. We need to draw down or pull carbon from the atmosphere by growing food a different way. We need to heal our soils to heal our climate, and as Mumford suggests, large food corporations can help us do that. They can become the lynchpin to create change by requiring their suppliers and growers to use regeneration to repair the damage we've already done to our soil, which will allow our soils to draw down even more carbon. But everyone must take part in this healing process. Consumers must demand it from the food corporations.

This is really a book about redemption. My own redemption and that of others. We must redeem ourselves for our past sins against nature and try to fix some of the problems we've created. We must make amends, and find some atonement, some reparation, for all the damage that we've done to our ecosystems over the past couple of generations. This might, just maybe, lead to our salvation from the hazards of a polluted environment and the worst of climate change. It may deliver us from ruin, and in the end, save us from ourselves.

CHAPTER FOUR

LEWIS MUMFORD

If there were any brains in our rebel organization, they belonged to Mumford.

Lewis Mumford purchased books on every subject of natural science that he could find for his library; a library that included stacks of books on shelves and tables and on the floor and stacks on stairways and all over his home.

"I try to collect whatever is rare and valuable in every science," he once told me.

He was fascinated with the terms and the vocabulary used in every subject, the language of the science, and he strove to become fluent in that language. Learning about the natural sciences and the properties that held the universe together gave deeper meaning to his life.

Mumford began keeping notebooks while in college and continued the practice throughout his life. In them he kept records on anything that he thought of interest or worth recording and remembering, and in these notebooks, he displayed his wide-ranging interests.

His notebooks are filled with daily observations on the weather, including temperature and pressure, the progress of his gardens, what grew well and what failed, how much he paid for seeds and supplies; anything and everything. Learning about plant science and botany, along with some physical exercise in the garden, he would say, helped to keep him young in heart and mind.

Mumford grew up in a time when everywhere men and women were making discoveries in the world of natural sciences, on the connectedness of all things, and at the same time new theories were evolving in the science of sustainable agriculture.

"We were opening our eyes and minds to new ways of growing that allowed mother nature to do her thing, and we started working with nature and not against it," he said.

Advances in crop rotation, the varieties of plants that could and should be rotated in a planned farming system, along with no till planting techniques, were lessening the burden of pests and drought and improving yields for sustainable growers like Mumford, who kept a large vegetable and flower garden for most of his adult life. He had great interest in new machines which promised to increase productivity and greatly reduce the labor involved with planting or harvesting or laying mulch on a small-scale farm, like his new BCS walk-behind tractor, which he loved. He was more interested in equipment that could be made smaller and more affordable, and not the size of a diesel freight train engine; something that could be easily maneuvered around a small farm. He believed this was key to developing stronger regional food systems.

Because of his natural inclinations toward curiosity and understanding, Mumford always had several questions about how a machine worked and what it could do, like when he purchased his new BCS two-wheel walk-behind tractor that was made in Italy. He wanted to know what attachments it could take, and what tasks it could handle, and he wouldn't hesitate to call the manufacturer directly. He was always right on the forefront of discovery in a wide variety of scientific interests with technical questions that would sometimes stump the engineers.

Mumford strongly believed that knowledge and education were important aspects of a free society. A wise man or woman can look at things from all sides and is willing and able to think things through to their logical conclusion. They can weigh all the evidence, they don't jump to conclusions, and they are capable of easily changing their mind based on new evidence and learning. That was Mumford.

There are some people, like Mumford, who are naturally fascinated with diverse subject matter and always discovering new things and topics to explore. The character traits of curiosity and creativity should eventually lead a person to wisdom, and I believe a deep, natural curiosity was Lewis Mumford's key character strength that separated him from other men. It defined him.

The world needs people like that, especially a world that now seems filled with science nay-sayers. To truly understand the problems in the natural world around us requires a lot of science, learning and investigation. Given conflicting research and evidence as it relates just to the climate change issue, it's difficult getting at the full truth. It's important that we don't just chalk it up to an abyss of the unknowable and give up entirely, although it can be frustrating. If we're going to do anything to protect the environment and in turn our national health, we must understand what's going on.

Mumford knew a lot about climate change. He read a stack of books over two feet high on the subject; I've seen them stacked together on a table in his home, many with Mumford's hand-written notes in the margins. Although piles of books were scattered all over his house, he at least tried to organize them in stacks by subject area. And it is my opinion that if you read a stack of books two feet high on any given subject, you may consider yourself an expert on the subject. You'll at least know more than 99 percent of the population.

Mumford attended several scientific conferences on climate, and he believed regenerative agriculture was a big part of the solution. As a brilliant self-taught naturalist, he was at the forefront in his understanding of the atmospheric and ocean-ic changes going on in the environment, and he became an outspoken leader for any discussion about climate change.

Mumford believed, at the deepest level, that learning and education are our only protection from tyranny in all its secret and hard to spot forms. Tyranny can come in the form of large corporations bent on the destruction of the environment for their own profit or gain. The will and gain of the few at the cost and suffering of the many is tyranny. Understanding the truth in the natural world, as well as the political, is critical for a nation to endure.

"A lack of education and knowledge will lead people to narrow-mindedness, environmental destruction, intolerance, racism, and prejudice, and ultimately, if left unchecked, war and even genocide." Mumford once said in a group email to our rebel food fighters.

"History shows us that even the best forms of government tended to revert to tyranny over time", and a people needed "to know ambition in all its shapes," he said. "The power of the Big Ag lobby in Washington is just one of many examples of tyranny."

To Lewis Mumford, scientific exploration and knowledge related to soil health and regenerative agriculture was turn-ing the dark recesses of the food system to light, turning back the fear and ignorance, and opening the doors for sustain-able growing operations. Farm incomes were not going to collapse, and we're not all going to starve if we cut back on the chemicals.

"We must start a campaign that educates people, Robert," Mumford said on the way home from our fishing trip. "We must start a movement to disseminate the current knowledge and facts, and the message must come from all points and from lots of people."

"Understanding the facts and promoting those facts is important work for everyone in the environmental movement and the organic, grow local movement," he said. "People want to know the truth."

"For example, the organic tomato grower needs to be a source of information, either through signage at her vegetable stand or blogs on her web site. The hazards of chemical sprays and their impact on beneficial insects, rivers and the ocean, is one example of why people should buy your organic tomatoes."

Mumford continued, "If you own a restaurant and believe that people should know how important it is to support local farmers, show a picture of the farmer and the farm where your tomatoes come from. Everyone in the movement must become a walking repository for science-based facts. We're up against some powerful people with a strong, albeit false, promise of abundance."

Mumford often taught classes during the Organic Growers School Spring Conference. The subjects he taught varied from year to year, from the importance of microbial life in soils to making your own bio-char. He was an excellent teacher and his students and conference attendees loved him.

Lewis Mumford was a larger-than-life celebrity in Asheville, and especially at the school, because of his experiments and experience with sustainable agriculture. At a national conference, he was seen by many as a brilliant philosopher from the still wild frontier of Appalachia, and he often promoted this version of himself. With some tongue in cheek humor, he once wore a coonskin fur hat, like Danial Boone without the tail, to a farm convention. I think he got the idea for that from Benjamin Franklin, who would do the same thing and promoted himself as such.

There were many parties and social engagements that Mumford often attended as an honored backwoods guest. While many scientists and advocates for environmental causes seemed a little socially distant, grumpy and stuffy, Mumford always enjoyed a good party.

When Mumford and Butch went to a regenerative agriculture conference in Raleigh, Mumford enjoyed himself, while Butch paced back and forth and stewed about issues at the conference, and they probably grew on each other's nerves. For a semi-fat, mostly bald guy, Mumford was quite the ladies' man at conferences, and female attendees often surrounded him there. There was nothing fake about him, and he often referred to himself as a simple working man and a farmer. But Mumford had a serious side and could focus his reasoning skills on more diverse interests than just about anyone else at the conference. He was a man of tremendous intelligence with a great love for reading, and the near photographic memory.

Mumford could meet an expert in some scientific field, like agri-chemicals, and hold an in-depth conversation for an hour about the newest discoveries or trends in that field. It was interesting just to watch. But Mumford also had a quirky side. He liked to sit half-naked on his front porch taking what he called an "air bath". He'd wave to people driving by on the road out front, sitting there in his nylon basketball shorts, and nothing else, even though the temperature might be 60 degrees outside. He got the idea from another polymath, Benjamin Franklin.

Don't ask me why I naturally associate that activity, an "air bath," with an environmentalist, I just do. Franklin must have been an environmentalist.

Mumford was always able to do his own research, discover the facts, and base his decisions on a body of his own scientific knowledge, which I believe is what turned him into an environmentalist. He wouldn't simply accept claims as truths, particularly if someone had a financial interest or gain in promoting one opinion or another.

There were many ongoing scientific experiments that he spent days and weeks working on. It was just testimony to his enduring fascination with the natural world and the desire to discover its truths for himself.

A good example of this is his experiments with electricity in the natural world. Mumford was fascinated with the positive and negative charges in plants, animals, the soil, and the atmosphere and how they impacted health. He had an unusual habit of applying an electrical charge to the water he drank in his kitchen laboratory set up for these experiments.

He drank water from his well on the farm, but treated it multiple times through various filters, oxygenators and electrical contraptions spread out on the counters of his kitchen—most of his counter space was taken up just for drinking water. In a side room, he built an electromagnetic machine that he would lay in (naked, of course) to "charge" his system, with special LED lights to give his body the light spectrum he thought he needed at the same time. I'll admit it here: Mumford was out there a little bit, perhaps a little nuts. But sometimes I wonder if he was just way advanced in his thinking.

He might have been a little reckless at times in his desire for knowledge and truth. He didn't strike me as a mad scientist or anything like that, but I do believe he put himself in danger of electric shock with his electromagnetic whatchamacallit machine. Just looking at the thing that he constructed himself, a bed with cords and wiring running all around it, I can only say that I would never have laid down on that thing myself. No way. And while we're at it, many of the things that he juiced were certainly questionable to me.

Mumford believed that every scientific inquiry, and every invention, should benefit mankind in some way. And whether it was a more efficient method of no-till planting or finding ways to improve the micronutrients in the human body, he always strove to discover something useful to benefit others and the world around him. That gave him purpose.

When he traveled, he would often take notice of the things related to local agricultural production to pass the time. He would stop at a farm off the highway, get out of the car and knock on the door or catch the farmer in the barnyard, just to talk about the varieties of seeds he might be planting. He had no qualms about doing that, and usually made a good friend that he'd keep in contact with.

Mumford was also a good mentor and model for young people, and he loved that role. By trying to emulate his thirst for scientific knowledge these young people might discover future solutions to our energy, environmental and food problems someday.

"The problems are so difficult that we need to encourage as many young people as we can," Mumford told me. "We're going to need them."

History clearly shows us that the first thing oppressive and tyrannical governments do is start burning books and imprisoning professors and intellectuals. They try to bury the truth. These forms of government want to limit the exposure to new ideas and dictate thought and action among the people, making up their own facts as needed. Knowledge is a threat to tyrants. Mumford understood that more than anyone.

"It is knowledge and wisdom that will ensure the freedoms and liberty of a people," he said. "That's why you need to join the board at Organic Growers School, Robert. Your business background might help them with their mission."

Mumford was the first person to introduce me to Organic Growers School (OGS) in Asheville. He dragged me to my first Spring Conference a couple years before. We walked onto the campus at Mars Hill College that OGS had taken over for the weekend, and I followed him into a building, down a hall and into a classroom. Before I knew it, a young lady at the head of the classroom started talking about growing hemp, and all of the wonderful attributes and things that could be made from hemp, including medicinal CBD oil. All I knew about hemp at the time was that it was also called cannabis, or marijuana, and you smoked it, and I wondered if this was all legal and if the cops were about to raid the campus—she had samples! It turns out she was just ahead of her time, and the laws were about to change, and lots of people would soon be growing the plant, including Mumford as part of another scientific experiment. Later we attended a class on butchering a cow with Meredith Leigh, and after that a class on resilience with Laura Lengnick, where I first met Laura and was introduced to her deep research on resilience thinking.

Our misfit organization needed Lewis Mumford. If we were going to fight the lies and bullshit, we needed science and facts. But the industrialized food machine, and those with a vested financial interest, would not give up easily, and they would come up with their own facts and spin.

Lee Warren and The Organic Growers School were determined to disarm it through education.

Organic Growers School

Organic Growers School is the best source for education in sustainable growing and mindful living in the Southeast. If you look at their list of classes offered during their annual 'Spring Conference', you'll find lots of classes on farming and growing organically, but also classes on everything from wild mushroom hunting and edible wild plants, to homesteading, solar power and living off the grid.[81] It's not your normal school. But it's based in Asheville, so what do you expect?

They offer year-round courses in sustainable farming and gardening, an apprentice link for young growers wanting to apprentice on a working farm to learn the business, holistic crop management courses, a full course on homesteading, mentor services that hook up experienced farmers with new farmers, coaching and consulting services for large and small farms, and agroecology tours to Cuba, among other things.

At the school you can learn how to raise chickens for income, make your own soap, can or ferment vegetables, sheer a sheep and power your cabin with solar or wind. You can learn about seed saving, growing medicinal herbs and the best way to raise pigs for profit. You can learn ancient Cherokee culture, tradition, food sources, and the wisdom of sustainable living going back a thousand years. You can learn about everything from cultivating mushrooms, to permaculture, to soil amendments, to raising honeybees. There aren't many schools like Organic Growers School, and they've been doing this good work for 30 years. When it comes to learning how to feed yourself and learning a little self-reliance, there's none better.

At Mumford's recommendation, I joined the board at the school.

Lee Warren

Growing Food is Not Canceled. That was the message from Organic Growers School over the difficult year of the COVID-19 pandemic. You could still get out in the garden for some exercise and the psychological benefits that come from working with the soil to produce your own food.

When I first met Lee Warren, she had been the Executive Director of Organic Growers School (OGS) for the previous six years. With dark eyes and jet-black hair, Lee has become my mentor for passive resistance. She is calm, reserved, and extremely intelligent. She coaxed me back from the edges and extremes of angry, radical resistance and taught me patience. There was a calm strength about her that I admired. Besides, anger can be so exhausting.

Lee had a burning purpose that led her to head up this non-profit that encourages people back to the land. She ran a school dedicated to teaching people how to live closer to nature and sustenance. There is a spiritual connection to Mother Earth in everything the school offers. And Lee had the character strength and virtue of a good and true leader. She is the embodiment, the personification, of local resilience.

Late in the fall of 2019, Lee came out to my farm and the Creekside Farm Education Center for an OGS fundraising breakfast. Plenty of staff and volunteers showed up to help set up for the event, so we took a short walk through the gardens to look at what was coming up. It gave me a chance to ask about her philosophy toward food and life.

"What is so powerful about local food to you, personally?" I asked her as we strolled through neat, colorful rows of peppers, tomatoes, and squash on a bright, sunny morning in June.

"It has been my experience that sharing a meal of locally

grown food together with others is one of the greatest joys of life. I find it so satisfying to be able to point to everything on our plates as being touched by people we love. It makes me happy."

"What kind of world do you imagine at OGS?" I asked.

"We want more farmers on the land in a system in which small scale and sustainable farms can flourish. We want a garden, an orchard, and chickens in every yard. Is that too much to ask?" she said with a warm smile.

"We want the average person to populate their daily lives with homegrown food. We want a Democratic, equitable, and just food system."

"Why do you want this world?" I replied.

"I believe that a direct relationship to the soil and to food will keep us alive and can cure all manner of ills. Growing food makes people healthier not only from the increased physical activity and eating fresher food, but also the natural antidepressants in the soil and in nature that contribute to improved health. So many studies have shown that gardening can be as or more effective than pharmaceutical anti-depressants. Growing food and implementing sustainable practices also builds community, which reduces loneliness, violence, and disconnection. It's good for the soul.

"On a larger systems level, I believe that a local food system increases the money that stays in the community and in our farmers pockets, so it's good for the local economy. Local food contributes to land preservation and scenic beauty. It prepares individuals and the collective for the vicissitudes of economic and political upheaval. It contributes to climate resilience because any scale of soil building takes carbon out of the atmosphere and helps cool the planet. And local food is more accessible for all, making the kind of equitable world we all want. Don't you agree?"

"I agree," I said. "What's standing in your way?"

"The truly one big reason—the ubiquity of the corporate industrial model. It has resulted in many ills. Namely global poverty and hunger. The unsafe, high calorie and low-quality food that makes people sick. Did you know that four of the top ten killers in the US are preventable diet-related illnesses like heart disease, cancer, stroke and diabetes? It makes me sad.

"Even with all that we've done to build up local food production, it's still a small percentage of the total food spending in our region. I wish it were much higher. Local food is healthy food."

Lee smiled again as we continued to stroll through the garden. That statement surprised me. We clearly have a lot more work to do. Lee continued talking.

"And maybe most importantly to me is that the model of corporate food has resulted in such a drastic loss of land-based literacy. You know that growing food was not a fringe activity a few decades ago. It's how people sustained their lives and families. Especially here in Appalachia. The first real supermarket, as we know it, appeared on the American landscape in 1946, and that's not very long ago. Until then where was all the food? The food was in homes, gardens, local fields, and forest. It was near kitchens, near tables, near bedsides. It was in the pantry, the cellar and the backyard.

"Over the course of these recent decades we've drastically eliminated farmers from our midst. The ones we have are aging out and will retire soon. And our own literacy about how to sustain our lives through food production and preservation is nearly gone."

Lee is passionate about trying to do something about this loss of our farming knowledge and heritage. And for nearly 30 years, the Organic Growers School has been offering affordable, accessible, hands-on training, workshops, conferences and partnerships that inspire, educate and support people to farm, garden and live organically.

"In the world we imagine," Lee said, "growing food can transform the health crisis and the food insecurity crisis. It can strengthen communities, establish food sovereignty, and prepare us for climate change."

"How can the average person get involved?"

"Grow your own food. Support local farmers. Volunteer at a community garden. Advocate for regenerative agriculture in every circle you're in—social, political, church, and community groups.

"I believe that it is not only necessary but possible to rebuild our local food system. I look forward to the thriving community that results. I'm so glad we're in this together, Bob. Let me give you one more quote that I love, from the agrarian activist Vandana Shiva."

She reached into her handbag and pulled out a small card with some handwritten text that she had copied from somewhere and handed it to me. It read, "The time has come to reclaim the stolen harvest and celebrate the growing and giving of good food as the highest gift and the most revolutionary act."

Like Mumford, wisdom is Lee Warren's key character trait, which is important in a leader. Everywhere she could, Lee was pushing back the shadow of ignorance and fear that hovered over the organic growing fields of the Southeast. Lee, like Mumford, believed that knowledge and education were the most important aspects of a free society.

Wisdom is the ability to contemplate and understand. It can also be defined by the words: knowledge, intelligence, insight, perception, good judgment, and expertise. It is the ability to penetrate a subject, to question deeply, to fully comprehend and understand all its nuances and variables. Wisdom is the innate desire to understand the world around us, and it is a virtue in human beings.

Wisdom and understanding take a prominent chapter and place in our discussion of the environment and sustainability because it takes rigorous, science-based research and understanding to fully know what is going on in our natural environment. It takes open-mindedness and good judgement to make the right decisions and to plot the correct course of action. To Lee Warren and OGS, that course of action means protecting the environment while we build food security, food sovereignty and community resilience.

In describing her years at the head of Organic Growers School, Lee said, "From my first OGS Spring Conference in 2002, to joining the staff in 2013, it has been life changing and enriching beyond imagination."

Lee Warren is one of those people who you meet once in great while and you can sense, right away, a calmness of spirit. She had another thing going for her. She was in charge of an organization with a huge reach. Hundreds of people enrolled in the OGS Spring Conference, a long weekend of educational classes spread out over a college campus. OGS had a database of thousands more people interested in organic and sustainable farming and living. It was a small army. And we needed to build upon that army to create the necessary change in the food system.

Soon after I joined the board at Organic Growers School, I was asked to chair the Advancement Committee, a group tasked with helping to determine the marketing and fundraising efforts for the school. We needed cash, and in my opinion, we needed to greatly expand our reach. I believed that we needed to become a national organization with branches in every region of the country, and I hoped that we could achieve that someday. There were young growers and farmers out there who needed the help and education that we offered, and with the help of organizers and volunteers, we might create regional learning centers that could support larger food hubs across the nation.

The original founders of Organic Growers School were against any kind of activism, but times had changed since it was founded 30 years ago. The world globalized and concentrated, and big brother took over. I was happy to become part of a new board that was willing to radicalize, within reason. We simply weren't going to tolerate the injustices any longer, and we were going to call it like we see it (which in itself is a form of radicalism; anti-establishmentarianism; going against the status quo.) We developed 'A New Theory of Change', and it identified many of the critical problems in the current food system. The list included the environmental crisis, fragmented communities, the loss of regional resilience, increasing poverty, hunger, and systemic injustice. It called out the problems with access to land for beginning farmers, the threats of climate change, and the transfer of knowledge to future generations. It called out many of the other important problems described in this book.

It was a good first step, to call it like we see it, and we could use that kind of messaging to generate awareness about the important things we were doing to fight it all, and hopefully gain some needed financial support for our programs. I wanted to be the guy to spread that message; digitally, in print, and in person, and anywhere I could. I was a radical, a food fighter, after all.

Scaling Up

I knew many of the young growers at the farmer's market. Some of them took classes at the Organic Growers School Spring Conference, and one or two graduated from the year-long Farm Beginnings Class. I knew that these young food fighters could grow enough food to feed customers coming to the market, but most of them grew on an acre or less of land. They didn't grow at a scale large enough to feed an entire community or the larger region.

In the mountains, we didn't have the massive farms that you see in California or the Midwest, but we did have a few mid-size farms that could grow at some scale, like the one owned by Jason Davis, where we spent that afternoon fishing. Those are the farms that seem to be caught in the middle, not large enough to supply the big national grocery stores, but too big for the farmers market, and those are the ones that can really get pinched. At the same time, they are exactly the kind of farms that we would need to support a more diversified and sustainable food system at the larger regional level. And it is the midsize, midscale vegetable farms that we would desperately need in the Midwest as teachers and trailblazers if massive disruption is indeed ahead for the corn belt. I didn't know what was going to happen in the Midwest, but it sure kept looking like the winds of change were blowing.

I hadn't heard anything from anyone else talking about a possible crisis in the corn belt because of electric vehicles. Other writers and academics wrote extensively on the importance of more sustainable growing practices, using cover crops and a more diverse system of crop rotation. Other researchers and writers told us that we need to get cows out of CAFO's and back on pasture in a more regenerative system. But no one said anything about the potential of a coming crisis when corn demand starts to drop. But to me, it all started to seem so obvious and inevitable.

Soon after joining the board at OGS, I started traveling to central Illinois, into the heart of the corn belt, to look at the state of things and to see if it might be possible to transition to other crops, given the existing equipment, people and infrastructure. Western North Carolina had seen this kind of disruption with the sudden demise of burley tobacco, but nothing on this kind of scale. The corn belt is a massive thing.

Illinois is a food desert—there is no other way to describe it, and no way to sugar-coat it. There are literally tens of thousands of large farms, but they grow nothing that you can just pick and eat. So is Iowa and most of the other corn belt states. All the food that they eat in Illinois and Iowa, over 95% of the food consumed there, is imported from outside of the state.[82] They essentially grow nothing but corn and soybeans to feed cows and gas tanks. What's left over goes to making high fructose corn syrup and other corn derivatives.

I didn't want to freak anybody out while I was there, because I didn't really know what was going to happen when electric cars took over. No one did. So, I tried to keep that bit of information to myself in my many visits and interviews with local farmers, officials, and community members.

I knew that until the 1950's, most farms in the corn belt states like Illinois and Iowa grew fruits and vegetables in addition to grains. Farms were much more diversified back then, and most had farm animals running around the barnyard. They had apple trees and strawberries and grew tomatoes and lots of varieties of other vegetables. Most had some cattle that they often rotated onto the fields after harvest. It was a diversified growing system using crop rotation principles that benefited the soil and reduced the need for chemicals. Then Big Ag came in and told them to specialize, and to just grow corn and soybeans. 'Get Big or Get Out' was the battle cry, and the powers that be encouraged farmers to take on more debt and convinced them to start using more and more chemical inputs upon their land in a monocropping system that would devastate their soils. But historically the Midwest did grow a lot of vegetables, and they can do it again. They just don't have the equipment anymore and they lost the technical know-how.

Crops like corn and soybeans are certainly easy to store and ship, and the Midwest has built up the infrastructure over the years to store and distribute these crops in a big way, including the thousands of grain elevators that dot the countryside.

To grow perishable crops like tomatoes or lettuce, you need facilities for washing, sorting, packing and refrigerated storage, and we would need these facilities set up all over the corn belt if we were going to change things. That would certainly take a big investment in infrastructure. We'd need to build the distribution channels and solve serious labor issues to grow these more labor-intensive crops. It will require new, specialized farm equipment and lots of training.

But in the end, it will bring more jobs and revenue to local economies, and it will be worth it because the Midwest will once again be able to feed itself. The refrigerated warehouses and distribution networks to grocery stores and restaurants already exist in cities, so it's really just a matter of getting the produce from the farm to those distribution points in a timely matter. We don't have to completely reinvent the wheel.

Some in government are enlightened enough to understand the importance of conserving our soils and saving our farms, and the Green New Deal proposed in congress is an example. Senators like Bernie Sanders have proposed breaking up the agribusiness oligarchy and making corporations accountable for the pollution and environmental damage that they are responsible for, such as the hazardous run off from large CAFOs. He has also suggested supply management in our corn and soy markets, so farmers don't continue growing way too much of it, by reinstating government procurement and storage for excess harvests to be sold in following years. This system would be designed to keep prices from plummeting after a bumper crop. I believe that these are all good ideas that are worth exploring.

Sanders also proposes paying subsidies to farmers who use regenerative growing practices that sequester carbon on the farm, rather than just paying farmers to grow more unneeded corn. He agrees that public investment is needed for food processing infrastructure for more local, small-scale producers, like lots more regional meat processors, and refrigerated warehouses and regional distribution centers for different crops.

That's if Big Ag doesn't squash it first.

It's much better for agribusiness to keep farmers barely skimping by with taxpayer subsidies and crop insurance while they max out the extraction of resources from the land and the soil. Convincing farmers to grow corn on every inch of marginal land puts that much more in the pockets of the seed and chemical companies, even while the farmer knows how big a risk it is to grow on that marginal land prone to flooding, erosion, or drought. But he also knows the US taxpayer has his back with crop insurance, and Big Ag has the money and power in Washington to make certain there are no changes to the status quo. I knew it was going to be a battle to change anything.

But when somethings not right, your innate sense of justice kicks in, and you just feel it. It's an emotional response. When you know what's going on, when science-based knowledge and understanding tells you something is wrong, are you morally obligated to do something about it? You can vote for justice in the food system with your wallet and your fork. You can also vote in elections, of course. But could we do more than that? The innate desire for justice burned in George Wiley, and as a leader of our ragtag rebel forces, he was going to do something about it.

George Wiley and the Battle of Avery Creek

Our little group of food fighters on Avery Creek Road tried to lay low, and George Wiley tried to keep passions at bay until the right opportunity presented itself.

Wiley came from a family that had been caught in the corporate monocropping system, just like the farmers in the Midwest, only his family was trapped in a system wrapped around burley tobacco, and not corn. His father became dependent on the debt and subsidies that the system created, until he had to sell more and more of his land to cover his crushing debt burden as he got squeezed between rising input costs, lower yields as the soil depleted, and lower prices that the tobacco companies were willing to pay. They had his father over a barrel, and they knew it. Wiley believed it was his destiny to stop this form of corporate bondage and servitude.

To the food fighters like Wiley, the fight was about justice, and a man or woman's God-given right to declare himself or herself free and independent from tyranny in all its hidden forms. Justice is the virtue that inspires this nation towards the ideals of Liberty and Freedom, and to the food fighters, our cause was no less noble.

Justice is the virtue that underlies all healthy nations. Justice includes such ideas as citizenship and social responsibility. The food fighters believed that with enough people standing up for what is right, no matter what the costs or consequences, we might be able to push back the powerful few who controlled the industrialized food system.

Justice is also about giving everyone a fair voice and a chance—it's about fairness. After what Wiley had experienced with his own family farm, he believed that nothing was fair about the current system, certainly not to farmers or consumers. The system was rigged to control what the farmers were paid and what the consumers must pay; whether that was corn, poultry, dairy or burley tobacco, it didn't matter. The entire food industry was rigged. It was designed that way. And the unhealthy processed food that came from it was literally killing people. George Wiley was one of our food-fighter rebels who believed it was possible to create a more just and equitable system.

Wiley was a poet-farmer. He had a full-time job with the county road commission, worked his cattle and small crops in the evenings and on weekends, and wrote poetry late in the evenings or sometimes early in the morning over coffee at his kitchen table.

I met Wiley through another writer and poet that I recruited from Firestorm Books, and I finally recruited him to our rebel cause at the Organic Growers School spring conference. He would quickly become a leader.

Wiley was a serious environmentalist and involved in many environmental and political causes, and he attended the OGS Spring Conference for more than 20 years. He took up our cause early on and became indispensable in our fight for food freedom. He was unafraid to stand up against overwhelming odds.

Wiley could see the big picture and could imagine a better future, but he also was a realist and a terrific moderator. Passions often ran high in our group of food fighters, and many had opposing viewpoints when it came to subjects like organic. Some of our members were headstrong about organic, and others just cared more about helping local farmers, organic or not. Some cared more about sustainability, while others said that's not enough, and regenerative agriculture was the only answer. Some hated GMO's, others were indifferent, and some thought that there might be real benefits from them that could help feed a lot of people in the future.

At one particular meeting in the old schoolhouse, a couple of food fighters got into a heated argument about genetically modified food and Wiley had to break it up.

"Stop fighting," he said. "This is what the powerful ag corporations want. They want to break us apart. And while we're fighting, they take over." He could always see the big picture.

Wiley had an identification with, and an innate sense of obligation to, the common good—the fair and equal treatment of all people. He wanted to fight for what he saw as right and fair for the little guy, the small farmer, and that meant going up against the strong and the powerful.

He was a natural leader because he had the means of getting people to do what they needed to do, and as great leaders do, he kept up good relationships and moral among the group (and he often brought the beer.) But for him, the ideals of democracy were at the root of our food revolution.

Wiley could see a direct connection, a parallel, between the VOC and the mindset of the Dutch East India Company, the British East India Company, and the 400 years of colonial mindset that followed, with what was happening now in the globalized corporate system.

And Wiley believed that now was the time for farmers to determine whether they are to be freemen or slaves to corporate power; whether they are to have any property at all that they can call their own; and whether their homes and farms are to be pillaged and destroyed. The time had come when farmers must choose the course of brave resistance, or the most abject submission.

Farms were indeed being pillaged and destroyed, and farmers were losing their land at an alarming rate. Farms across the nation were being taken over and subjugated by outside parties, including Wall Street investors and Big Ag, and with that, Wiley believed, our independence was being threatened.

The opposite of the human strength and virtue of justice might be described with words like selfishness, egotism, self-centeredness, meanness, prejudice, and cruelty. Not the attributes of a good citizen. At the root of justice and good citizenship is the ability to use moral reasoning to do what is right and fair for all. And let's face it, corporations are not good citizens.

Corporations answer only to shareholders and quarterly earnings reports and don't necessarily have the innate human ability for moral reasoning, empathy, and justice. And yet the supreme court says that corporations are in fact "citizens" and that they have the same rights as people. That really irked Wiley to no end.

The ultimate unselfish and virtuous act of courage is to sacrifice oneself, even his or her very life and liberty, so that others may live and prosper. Many in our rebel group, like Wiley, were ready to do that. They would do a good and righteous act, no matter what the costs to them personally. In the face of what they considered a war of subjugation brought on by the largest and most powerful corporations on earth, the fate of unborn millions now rested in their hands. Healthy food was a basic human right.

But would this young movement have the strength and courage to uphold the values of justice, freedom and liberty in the face of a massive invasion force? The invasion force, this time, was a global food web that included thousands of ships and airplanes.

The rebels had no fighting ships or airplanes of their own, and Wiley, among others, knew that our little island in Appalachia was easy pickings against a force of strong corporate invaders, but he felt it was necessary to at least take a stand. Defenses were in fact already under construction.

Wiley first organized a campaign to protect local dairy and cattle producers in Western North Carolina. There were only two dairy farms left in all of Buncombe County, of the hundreds that had once existed a mere 50 years ago. For decades, a federal law called the Packers and Stockyards Act protected America's farmers and ranchers from abusive monopoly power in the livestock industry. The courts began to water down this law in the 1980's, giving a handful of corporations unprecedented control over meat and poultry production. They had battalions of lawyers and lobbyists pushing the USDA toward relaxing the few laws that worked toward leveling the battlefield and giving small farmers and ranchers a fair chance. Wiley wanted to hold abusive agribusinesses accountable. His fight, our fight, was for transparent, fair, and truly competitive food markets.

Wiley's campaign included organizing a letter writing blitz to the papers and politicians and organizing a large protest in downtown Asheville to save local farms.

The corporate supply ships now just anchored off the coasts carried an invasion force that included thousands of men and millions of pounds of Brazilian beef and Chinese chicken, and it dwarfed the size of our force of less than 100 volunteers, mostly farmers, holding our rebel stronghold on Avery Creek Road. This was the long arm of King Food coming to crush the little rebellious children with one massive blow. The fleet landed at New York and California and began unloading supplies.

How do you fight such an entrenched and overwhelming force as a large multinational in the current food system? George Wiley wasn't blind to the obvious facts. He was far outnumbered by a vastly superior, more experienced and better equipped fighting force than his, and that force was a thousand times the size of the food fighters. Still, he stayed to defend our cause against overwhelming odds. It was almost suicide; it was certainly going to be a rout and he knew it. But he would fight on.

The arrogance of the corporate food executives was in some way justified. If we even popped up on their radar, we were simply a bug to be crushed. To the industrialized, mechanized and hyper-efficient food corporation, our band of guitar players and small farmers probably represented the silliness of human beings in modern America. To the industrial food machine, we would probably exemplify the stupidity of growing food on a small scale with simple hand tools. Really, we were no threat to them, but we would do what we could.

And while the corporate kings of food were using chemical weapons, large equipment and what is essentially slave labor in central America to fill their ranks, we were cutting leaf lettuce with a pair of scissors. Someone came up with the idea of using a hedge trimmer, of sorts, with a basket attached, to speed up the process, which it did, but it was still slow, backbreaking work. Most of our vegetable harvesting was done with a small paring knife. And we were facing down equipment like combine harvesters that were much bigger than an M1-A1 tank.

Instead of blasting a field with chemicals, the easy way, we were buying little bugs, called nematodes by mail order, and sending armies of them out into the fields to kill the other, bad bugs. We bought lots of necessary supplies by mail order and off the internet. We purchased baby chicks by the boxful, shipped Federal Express, packed lightly with paper stuffing so they could bounce around across several states. Our supply chains were miniscule compared to the enemy.

And I was the perfect example, the poster child, of the futility of small-scale farming. As just one example, after failing miserably at growing wheat, the yield being ridiculously low, I tried to process it myself with the simple tools I had on hand. I had the brilliant idea of trying to shuck the shell off the wheat with a blender. When that didn't work out so well, I used the blender to make a couple frozen margaritas, and that worked out fine. But then I had another terrific idea of separating the wheat from the chaff with the help of a leaf blower, which of course blew most of the seed away with the chaff. So, I'm clearly the dumbest farmer of them all. I wasn't going to put up much of a resistance against these corporate food giants.

Our farm sold eggs for $7.00 a dozen. Who in their right mind would pay that? Are we all just crazy? No wonder we were going to get clobbered, and we knew it. But still we tried to set up new growing methods and new distribution channels at markets and restaurants and schools that were outside of the control of Big Ag.

As far as I could tell, this local food thing was never going to scale up enough to compete with Big Food, let alone take them out. And the timing of events wasn't going to help us at all. So it was that George Wiley entered his first battle and suffered his first loss at Avery Creek, and it would be a terrible, humiliating loss.

The Covid-19 pandemic was in full force when Wiley called for a ban on imported beef through his extensive network on social media and a big letter and email campaign to politicians and other influencers. He did this just before reports of beef shortages hit the news, the result of plant closures due to Covid-19. The timing probably scared some people who didn't really understand the issue.

With the disruption and closure of meat processing facilities, local farmers and producers were struggling to find markets for their cattle (and this also played out across America.) Brazil-based JBS, the world's largest meatpacking company, announced that it was about to flood the American market with its imported beef, and to George Wiley, that would be like kicking a US farmer when he's down. It was an invasion that would cripple American farmers and ranchers and that would devastate our own local cattle producers. Prices for cattle plummeted at the stockyard.[83] With meat processors shutting down or cutting back due to the pandemic outbreak and labor shortages, there was nowhere to send cattle. Tens of thousands of chickens had to be simply destroyed and buried on several farms across the country.[84]

On top of all that, the farmers markets and restaurants where our farmers sold their goods were quickly closed down because of the pandemic. The farmers that we were trying to help were left stranded, cut off from the supply lines, and there wasn't much we could do to help them.

The market disruption caused by Covid-19 left farmers hurting across the country. Low prices, processing bottlenecks and drought had put unprecedented pressure on American farmers and ranchers. It should have been a wake-up call.

Wiley made a petition to the US Department of Agriculture, which many supporters signed, for policy changes that would lead to a more decentralized food system. It also demanded a breakup of the "Big Four" meatpacking companies as the first step in creating a more diversified and resilient food system.

No acknowledgement or response ever came. Wiley organized a small rally, with social distancing rules in place, but by the day of the event, the limited number of people that could attend because of Covid rules (less than 10) didn't make for a very impressive protest, and no one from the local news attended.

This was the first of many devastating losses and the beginning of a very trying time for our little Appalachian army. Covid only heightened the awareness of what we were up against, and it greatly limited the food fighter's ability to respond. It was only by courage and perseverance in the face of overwhelming odds that our new food movement would endure. Or perhaps just dumb stubbornness.

Wiley would go on fighting on multiple fronts. He organized an email and social media campaign to build awareness about the devastating loss of farmland in North Carolina, but we kept losing ground in the fight to protect farmland. More than 2,000 acres of farmland were being lost to development every day— including our most productive, versatile, and resilient land.[85]

Our state, North Carolina, was in fact the second most threatened in the nation in terms of the loss of farmland. Our best agricultural land was quickly being lost to poorly planned real estate development, strip malls and apartment complexes. Between 2001 and 2016, 732,000 acres of agricultural land were developed or compromised, 387,000 acres of which were 'Nationally Significant,' or land best suited for growing food and crops, according to the American Farmland Trust.[86]

But stopping developers, and development in general, proved to be a monumental task. Nothing happens quickly enough, meanwhile land keeps disappearing under pavement.

But Wiley pushed county commissioners to triple the funds allocated to land conservation in Buncombe County. With Wiley's encouragement, I wrote articles for local magazines and newspapers asking for more funds for land conservation. And in that, we did achieve a small victory. The Buncombe County Commissioners did vote to triple funding for conservation easements from $250,000 to $750,000. Wiley understood how all things happen in small, incremental steps. Rarely does change happen in one decisive battle. And so, he fought on.

Before 1980, there were no tools to protect farmland like agriculture easements. There were no laws and no land trust organizations. There was only minimal support for better, more sustainable farming practices. The conservation title of the farm bill has, since 1985, provided $115 billion to help farmers build soil health, save water, reduce run off, and sequester carbon. We haven't done nearly enough, but a lot of the groundwork has been done over the past 35 years that we can build upon.

Most of that groundwork has been done in the soil. People talk about different ways for better farming—organic, regenerative, climate smart agriculture, carbon farming. They're not all the same, but they do overlap and use similar practices. And the goal is the same, to maximize environmental benefits while building soil health and sequestering carbon.

Farming contributes over one trillion dollars to our economy.[87] Healthy farmland reduces run-off, controls floods, suppresses fires, protects water resources, encourages wildlife and diversity, and can improve soil health while it sequesters carbon. We need to save the land that sustains us. To Wiley and the food fighters, this was a battle worth fighting.

But long before we run out of agricultural land that we need to feed us, we'll run out of the agricultural land that we need to sequester carbon and restore the planet. In fact, it's likely that we're coming to the tipping point right now as global temperatures continue to rise while farmland disappears.

Our army of revolutionaries was growing. Our email database included hundreds of people willing to volunteer. Attendance at meetings by our core group of misfits increased. But more than just talking about the need for cover crops, more diverse rotational growing practices, and getting cows back on pasture, we were trying to do something about taking back control in the system. With our growing number of sustainable farmers, we were beginning to set up new food distribution systems, and we had some small wins, like increasing the money available for farmland conservation. We had boots on the ground, and I believed that we needed to move some of those boots up to the corn belt where they were going to need reinforcements.

Why do people volunteer to do this kind of thing? Why do people fight these battles when it's much easier to ignore them and go about your business? There weren't any paid positions in our organization, and sure, there was often free food and beer, but that can only take you so far.

Here's what I think: Feelings of self-worth, self-respect, fulfillment, and life satisfaction (let's call that happiness) come from the willful pursuit of morally praiseworthy activities— from doing what you know is right. Doing what you know is the right thing to do, even in the face of hardship or adversity, is what builds self-esteem and feelings of self-worth, which is the key to happiness. It really is that simple.

Living with integrity means doing the right thing, not because of potential reward and recognition, but simply because there must be a consistency between your inner values and your actions—between what you believe and what you do.

I have found a certain consistency among people involved in many important causes; a consistency between what they believe and what they do. This consistency builds a sense of integrity and self-esteem, a feeling of self-worth, a value that you place on yourself. It involves the importance you place on your more spiritual, inner self.

The question becomes, will your values and beliefs be taken lightly, and shrugged off in times when it is more convenient, beneficial and easier to do so? Or will you hold on tight to your inner convictions and values, no matter what the consequences?

The self-knowledge and determination that you will hold strong, regardless of the consequences—this is the greatest source of confidence and strength. We will not flounder, or waffle, or squirm. We will stand and hold against great odds. We will not have to wrestle in anguish with our conscience because the answers, and the required actions, will always be clear, unselfish, and straight forward. George Wiley had that inner strength, and you could sense it. So did Lee Warren.

This is the peculiar happiness of fighting for a just cause. The principles are immovable, unchanging, all-encompassing, and timeless. They are inclusive to all races, gender identities or social backgrounds. They apply to all people equally. And to Wiley and many of our food fighters, these universal principles govern the world just as the principles of the natural world, like gravity, govern in the physical world. Virtue is a guiding force in human beings, and it elevates us.

It would appear then that the true question of life is whether we will live our lives in accordance with these universal principles, or not. Whether we will do what we know is right, or not.

I really don't know if we were radicals or revolutionaries, or how other people might see us. We were just trying to be good citizens and do the right thing. We weren't really trying to bring down society with our little revolution. We were trying to prop it up. Because at the very foundation of government is good citizenship and the sense of duty and responsibility within the people toward the common good.[88]

In truth, this sense of duty and obligation to the common good is the bedrock of society upon which all else is built. Many people in our movement were beginning to fear that corporations and government will grow too big and too strong and start working against the common good and to the detriment of society and the planet.

The food fighters, and I now use that term generally to include all small, organic farmers and gardeners and those who attend a farmers market, come from diverse socio-economic experiences and varied educational and professional backgrounds, but what do they all have in common? They are good citizens. And good citizens make the best radical revolutionaries. This is what it takes to fight the man.

Good citizenship means working for the good of others. Environmentalists, for example, are the ones who usually do much of the fighting for the future generations who don't have a say in current affairs. And I would say that those people who till organic fields and shop farmers markets have a well-defined understanding of good citizenship.

Our CSA members and customers at the farmers market, for instance, as socially diverse as they were, were all socially responsible citizens with deeper connections to the community. They were not innately distrustful, but in truth had a higher level of social trust and a more positive view of human nature than the average person. They believed that if other people understood what was really happening to our food system, our community health, and our natural environment, then they would help to change a few things. This kind of connectedness and trust in fellow man and woman is good and healthy for any individual in a society. Radicals are not bad people. They are the spring of change.

Most people that I have met in the food movement have strong feelings of empathy and compassion for their fellow man, and the feeling of responsibility to help take care of those that needed help. Compassion and empathy are often the emotional responses that motivate people toward great selfless acts. It can often lead people into an inner-city garden, a food kitchen for the hungry, or a great many other courageous and selfless acts.

I honestly believe that Americans have a deep innate sense of fairness. They may not always act fairly, but they know what it is and what it looks like when they see it. Even very young children understand what fairness looks like. Just try giving two kids a bowl of ice cream, one much larger than the other, and watch the reaction. We understand what is right and fair at a very young age.

A sense of fairness and good citizenship involves empathy and the ability to put yourself in someone else's shoes. People who work at food banks or food kitchens can empathize with the people they are serving. They can easily put themselves in those other shoes across the counter when they serve up a hot meal to a hungry person.

We believed our little food revolution had moral authority. We didn't want to completely tear down a political or economic system, just radical change. We did want to break the chains of monopolies and the crazy concentration of power. And we were motivated to do the right thing as good citizens. Resist. Right the wrong. Do something.

CHAPTER FIVE

THE CONCENTRATION OF POWER

We have a small piglet at the farm that we named Albert Einswine, and he's really fast.

He's also very smart. Some research suggests that pigs are just as intelligent as dogs, but I don't know about that. Albert often runs around like a maniac, much like my dog does in the yard and for no apparent reason. I think Albert likes the speed and wants to test his short legs to see how fast he can go. He is incredibly fast, even for a piglet just six weeks old.

Sometimes Albert will screech to a stop and look right at you, daring you to race him, and then he takes off running again in circles around his large pen. The other piglets usually start chasing him like little race cars around a dirt track. I put my money on Albert.

Albert lives a different life than most pigs who grow up, unfortunately, in confined animal feed operations (CAFOs). He eats organic feed and lots of scraps from the garden. He spends his days on pasture at Creekside Farm. He won't ever experience the consolidation and globalization of the industrialized meat business.

One of the food fighters posted a hand-painted sign near Albert's pen at the farm that read, "Whoever controls the food, controls you." It's a bit of a radical, anti-establishment, motivational message that tends to cheer me up when I have some chores to do, like feed the animals or clean the pen.

It motivates me because it hints at a nagging question that has bothered me for years. This valley that Albert and I look out upon was once filled with small farmers, and each one raising at least a few cows, some chickens and hogs, along with their crops. They've all moved on now, and the animals live in a different, almost dystopian world. I think about it as I throw out five-gallon buckets of feed and watch Albert and his siblings jostle for position at the feed bin. And I think about what it all means for the rest of us.

The largest pork producer in the US is Smithfield Foods, which is owned by a Chinese company. This multinational corporation owns over 500 farms in the US and processes far more pork than anyone else. Its 973,000-square-foot meat-processing plant in my home state, in Tar Heel, North Carolina, is the world's largest plant, processing 32,000 pigs a day. That is an incredibly scary number. It equates to 22.2 pigs per minute, 24 hours a day. That's more than one pig every three seconds.

The acquisition of Smithfield Foods included 146,000 acres of land and made WH Group, headquartered in Henan province, China, one of the largest overseas owners of American farmland. One in four pigs living in the United States is owned by this Chinese company.[89]

In March 2020, Smithfield had to close another one of its plants in South Dakota because over 500 workers became infected with the coronavirus. It became the largest coronavirus hotspot in the U.S. at the time. That plant represented 5% of the total meat production in the US. In late April and Early May, meat shelves were empty in many grocery stores as the meat supply was disrupted and hoarding began. Stores began to limit the amount of meat shoppers could purchase. Prices went up.

Other plants were at risk, and others shut down. One facility had to slaughter and bury thousands of chickens in a sickening waste of food because they didn't have the healthy workers to process them, while millions of people were beginning to go hungry. This is the kind of risk that comes from the massive, national processing centers that America depends on.

JBS, the Brazilian owned company and largest meat packer in the world, operates nine cattle processing facilities across the U.S. JBS has admitted that it bribed more than 1,800 Brazilian politicians and officials to secure Brazilian government loans. These loans enabled it to acquire other companies that would allow it to dominate the market. JBS also admitted that this move helped it take over the U.S. beef market as well. Half of its business (51%) now comes from the United States. Many have tied the burning of the Amazon to JBS cattle production in Brazil, as cattle ranchers look for more land to produce more cattle to feed a growing worldwide demand for meat.[90]

Globalization and consolidation continue across the food chain. Three multinational corporations dominate the market for seeds and fertilizer. Four flour milling companies control 67% of the market.[91] Just ten multinational corporations control most of the brands and products that you buy in the center isles of the grocery store (the processed foods). Our food fighters published a flow chart by Oxfam on our web site and through social media that exposed the ten companies and the spider web of connections to hundreds of brands that they own.[92]

And at every opportunity we reminded people of the fact that most of our fruits and vegetables came from foreign soil. We kept hitting the message that one out of every five bites that you take comes from outside our borders, and that the main driver was cheaper labor costs. And all the time people would say, "How can this be?" To anyone who has driven through the vast farm country of the Midwest, through the hundreds of miles of endless fields of green, it makes no sense.

The United States will continue to grow way too much corn and soybeans. These crops are not as labor intensive as other fruits and vegetables, like staking tomatoes or picking fruit. A farmer with a small crew and a combine can harvest thousands of acres of corn and soybeans.

The next obvious question from most people then is what happens with all that corn? As we already know, 40% of the US corn crop is used to make ethanol that goes into our gas tanks, and another 36% is used for animal feed in confined animal feed operations (CAFO's). Much of the rest is exported to feed cows in foreign nations, about 14%. That equates to roughly 90% of total corn production. Most of the remaining corn is used for high fructose corn syrup and other corn derivatives. Only a small fraction, less than one percent, is eaten by humans as corn on the cob or in a can. Meanwhile, half of our soybeans are exported, and most of the rest goes to feed animals here.

With the consolidation of the food supply into fewer and larger food companies, the over-arching message at the School of Postmodern Activities was that we need to break up that power and spread it around a little bit. Saving farmland and our food producing capacity at the local and regional level is critical to strong and resilient communities of the future.

So I say, "Run little pig, Run!"

The Farmer down on Wall Street

The risk to corn farmers that comes from electric cars, and the potential 40% drop in corn demand for our gas tanks, also threatens disruption for financial markets and Wall Street investors. Wall Street owns a lot of farmland these days—millions of acres of it. Here's how that happened.[93]

Many large investors went looking for a safe place to stash some cash after the great recession starting in 2008. Because farmland values have historically increased at a steady pace, some large investment firms and the largest pension funds found a new home down on the farm. Farmland seemed like a safe place in a diversified investment portfolio because it's backed by a tangible asset, real land. And investors might also profit from land leases and agricultural crops while they wait for the land values to rise.

Individual investors can buy into farmland through Real Estate Investment Trusts, or REITs. And while REITs used to focus on housing developments, large apartment complexes, office buildings and shopping malls, they began to package farmland into sellable chunks in the late 1990's. Pension funds soon joined the buying spree, and things went crazy.

Investment groups began buying up all the neighbors and turning those tracts into massive corporate farming operations that are focused on maximizing profit and return while exploiting the land and the labor. It's been a recipe for massive change and disruption in farming communities across the country.

Rising food prices, and the fact that everyone must eat, even in volatile markets, made farmland an attractive asset class. The federal mandate for ethanol promised to keep demand up. And with this built-in law to prop up demand, soon billions of dollars were pouring into farmland across the United States by REITs and the largest pension funds. Police and fire departments, unions, county and corporate pension funds, and other investors are now owners of farmland that by some estimates equates to the land mass of Indiana, or even Great Britain.

Some of the biggest owners of American farmland are

foreign owned companies, including UBS Agrivest, a subsidiary of the largest bank in Switzerland, and the Hancock Agricultural Investment Group, a subsidiary of the largest insurance company in Canada. Here's how one Hancock investment plays out in California.

Hancock is now one of the largest almond producers in California, and most of those almonds (a very thirsty crop) get shipped to Asia as a luxury item. It takes about a gallon of water to produce one almond. In a region that is already experiencing terrible droughts and water shortages and a huge drop in the underground water table, valuable California water is used up to produce a luxury item that is shipped to an Asian country, so that an investment firm in Canada can profit from it. To me, that's just nuts.

Many wealthy individuals are buying up farmland independently. Bill Gates has been quietly buying up farmland and is now reported to be the largest private owner of farmland in the US. But the biggest buyers and farmland owners are investment groups.

The Teacher Annuity Insurance Association-College Retirement Equities Fund (TIAA-CREF), one of the largest pension funds in the world, has invested in vast tracts of farmland. Prior to the crash of 2008, TIAA-CREF didn't own any farmland. It now owns over 500 very large farms, tens of thousands of acres, and has a dedicated staff to manage this investment.

With the average age of a farmer in the US now approaching 60 years old, as much as half of all farmland will change hands in the next 10-12 years as they retire.[94] Large investors with deep pockets are waiting in the wings ready to buy up land, and in the process drive up farmland prices and make it more difficult for the next generation of small farmers to own a piece of land. Rising land prices create a huge barrier to entry for young farmers wanting to get into the business, and the cost of land is directly related to the profitability of the farm. How is a young farmer going to compete for valuable farmland with the deep pockets of a massive pension fund holding billions of dollars?[95]

The USDA estimates that 30% of farmland is now owned by 'non-operators' or 'absentee owners.'[96] Absentee owners generally lease out the land to local farmers. As money has poured into farmland over the past two decades, we've recreated a feudal system of large landowners and tenant farmers.

It would be wise to ask, are these large investment groups creating another bubble that could potentially threaten our food security? What happens when ethanol demand drops, Wall Street panics, the underlying asset value does a tailspin, and millions of acres of farmland go on the selling block with no buyers? Will that land sit fallow because money has dried up, like the millions of homes after the last financial crisis? And what does that mean for food prices?

Maybe US farmland is not supposed to be owned by Wall Street or foreign insurance companies. Maybe it's supposed to be owned by the farmers working the land. Just a thought. Call me crazy.

Farmer owners are certainly going to be better stewards of the land, and we need to ensure that farmers, and not absentee investors, are the future of our food system. Investment firms focus on profit; they are in fact obligated to maximize profits for their shareholders and investors.

Unfortunately, a strict focus on profit can conflict with other important concepts related to the land, like sustainability, soil health, soil erosion, chemical run-off, working conditions and wages, and local community prosperity. The focus is most often on short-term profit versus the long-term health of the environment and the community. There is usually no room for these conflicting concepts on the corporate balance sheet.

When large multinationals purchase vast tracts of land, it leads to the concentration of the land into fewer hands, which can push small operators off the field entirely. Farmer owners are replaced by tenant farmers and workers at the lowest possible wage. Rather than a diverse cross-section of farm owners who live on and love the land, we end up with absentee owners from far-away places that don't really understand or care much about the "microbiome" of the soil.

REITS generally lease the land back to a farmer as a tenant with a short-term lease, usually just 2-3 years for row crops or 5-8 years for orchards. Because he doesn't own the land, this removes any incentive for the tenant farmer to invest in more sustainable, regenerative farming practices that can lead to better soils, better water quality or better conservation measures. There's no incentive for smart farming practices like crop rotation, cover crops, no-till or limited till cultivation, riparian buffers along streams and waterways or preserving pollinator habitats. Building up soil health is a multi-year process. If you've got a 2- or 3-year lease, why do it? And investment managers can't really explain it on a quarterly earnings report. Their intent is to eventually sell the land at a profit anyway.

It's the same kind of short-sightedness that leads to further exploitation of the land, resources, workers and the local community. It's no wonder small town America has been devastated over the past few decades, with shops boarded up and a serious opioid epidemic ravaging the countryside. Many have lost hope.

It comes down to resource and wealth extraction by absentee landlords in an almost feudal system resembling the Middle

Ages. The investment company is the new "Lord" of the land controlling thousands of acres. It represents the concentration of power upon the land, and where there were once many owners, there are now few. Meanwhile, the tenant farmer working the land usually takes on most of the risk of the farming operation, including risks from drought, flood, and pests. The deck is stacked against the farmer; the game is rigged.

This is happening around the world in a global land-rush of astonishing scale. It has been estimated that 500 million acres, which is an area eight times the size of Britain, was bought or leased by foreign or corporate entities across the developing world in roughly a decade, between 2000 and 2011, and it's been increasing since then.[97] This has a major impact on local food security, food sovereignty, and the capacity of people to grow their own food and determine where the food ends up. It also drives up land prices, and not just for the poor in underdeveloped countries, but for the American farmer here. In the US, billions of dollars are raining, pouring, into US farmland by giant pension funds and foreign investors.

As our current farmer population ages out, they might be putting over 400 million acres on the selling block with lots of cash in pension funds sitting in the wings, waiting. And let's face it, large investment firms and absentee owners are not going to be the ones leading the charge for more regenerative or environmentally friendly ways of growing food. Unless of course the individual investors and shareholders start demanding it, which could happen. Investor activists have been vocal and are starting to change the way some corporations do business as it relates to the environment and other issues, like fair labor.

There is, fortunately, a growing group of 'impact investors' who want to know how their investment money is spent, and who invest enough and are vocal enough to influence how and where the money is invested. They may even be willing to accept a lower return on that investment if it does some good in the world, like benefit the environment or the climate. There are important recent examples of how large investment groups have changed their investment strategies, and pulled money out of companies that had a negative influence on climate change. The New York state pension fund, for example, is pulling $226 billion out of fossil fuel stocks, and plans to sell other stocks in companies that might contribute to global warming.[98]

The current system of farming in the US is chemically intensive and harmful to our soils, waterways, and ecosystems. Teachers investing their money in large retirement funds, like TIAFF, could come together to force the change in how farmland is managed within their portfolio. They have a voice. It's their money. A policeman's union in Chicago might be able to do something about the overuse of glyphosate and the super-weeds it has created. Corporations and financial markets don't operate in a vacuum. If large pension funds and investment groups are going to own farmland, then those investors have a say in how the land is managed.

Investors in farmland must focus on increasing living microbes and organic matter in the soil which reduces the need for chemicals and increases the soils water holding capacity—making farmland much more resilient to floods, droughts, and climate change. This protects your long-term investment, which is what you want as an investor. And investor activists can have a say in the matter.

The Elves, Clowns and Kings of Food

Processed food isn't made 'magically delicious' by elves. A food scientist did that with some sugar.

A great disconnect has occurred in our food system, and that has happened by deliberate, corporate design. A hamburger clown or a burger king has nothing to do with the confined animal feed operation. I'm not sure who came up with the clown idea, but food corporations have tried hard to cover the tracks that lead out into the field and pasture. They don't really want you to know where food comes from or how it was processed or what's really in it, or how it got into that box. That disconnect has also led to much poorer diets of processed foods. According to a 2017 report from the National Cancer Institute, "nearly half of all American adults have one or more chronic diseases that are related to poor diets."

And when we lost track of where our food came from, we forgot about the growing process and the people involved. But as Wendell Berry told us, eating remains the final act in a long, slow process called agriculture.

All food, no matter how it's processed or packaged, combo'd or supersized, it all came from a farm and the earth beneath our feet; and someone, some person, took the time to plant, grow and harvest it. We should try to remember the farmer, who for her hard work and labor, makes about eight to fourteen cents on the dollar that you spend for food. The rest goes to food processors and distributors, the retailer and the advertising man, who have cleverly closed the curtain to the factory and the confined animal feed operation.[99]

The daily drama of the farmer and the weather, the heat, heavy rains, drought and pests, all goes sight unseen. Little does the average consumer realize or acknowledge that he or she is a purchaser of products that originate in the soil, that even Cheetos and Cheerios come from black dirt. We've lost this connection to the land as we fell into the trap as consumers of industrialized food production.

We buy what we want at the grocery store, or the restaurant, without questioning or really understanding the relative price charged, the nutritional quality of the product, how far it traveled to get there and how much transportation may have added to the cost (in dollars and CO_2 in the atmosphere.) We don't ask about additives or chemical residue, the cost advertising or packaging may have added to the price of the product, or it's real nutritional value after excessive processing. And where and what country was the cow, pig or chicken raised, and under what conditions? Food today is more of an abstract idea, part of a shrewd marketing strategy, rather than a real thing that sprang from the earth.

But it wasn't always like that. Food used to be more closely associated with the land and a farmer, and in most cases, he had a name. Now it's ground up, broken down, sanitized and chemically distilled, then recomposed with additives into something else quite unrecognizable from its original form. It is difficult for our minds to associate a Twinkie with a farmer in a field, and so we don't.

We have become dependent on industrialized food from far-away places, and the corporations who control it, and so have given up some freedom, because to be dependent is not freedom, as the farmer sage Wendell Barry once told us.

The life and health of your body on this planet is your own responsibility, and so we must try to eat responsibly. And we must understand that the concerns of the industrial food complex are volume and price, and not necessarily your health and longevity. Certainly not the health and fertility of the soil. There is no profit in that.

But there is an escape from the industrial trap. There is great pleasure and freedom that comes from knowing more about the food that you consume, where it came from and how it was grown, and this adds greatly to the taste and the experience of the food. Try growing some of your own food and visit a farmer's market occasionally. Throw back the curtain and see the wonder and mystery. It is the earth that sustains us, not the Frito-Lay factory. It is the farmer who feeds us, and not a clown or a king. And certainly not a cartoon tiger with a coach's whistle around his neck. He's a dead man, by the way.

El Tigre was just a figurehead; he was the fall guy. Butch was right to target the large, multinational cereal companies like General Mills and Kellogg's. But he wasn't just angry about the massive amounts of sugar used in the product and the health effects of that, he was mad at the deceptive way they were doing it, and this furry guy who stood at the front of it all.

He was mad about the environmental damage that comes from conventional farming used in grain production for the product. El Tigre represented the changes in agriculture Butch had seen over his lifetime, and it pissed him off. The US food system is not sustainable from a social, environmental, or economic standpoint, and El Tigre was partly responsible for that.

Reduction in ground water supply. Loss of pollinators and the loss of diversity in insect and in microbial life. Low profitability of farm business in general, with most farmers just barely hanging on. The legal and economic status of farm laborers who do all the work. Diet related illness and disease tied to an unsustainable health care system. Food waste. A fossil fuel-based farm system handcuffed to a limited resource. Pollution of streams and rivers from farm runoff. No wonder he got angry at El Tigre. Anybody who really understood the issues like he did would get angry, and sometimes you need a place, a face, to direct that anger. This face had whiskers.

When it comes to kids and the health of our children, Butch wasn't going to sit quietly anymore. One time when he got particularly riled up, Butch borrowed Mumford's old 1942 Farm All tractor, and said he was thinking about driving it downtown to block traffic for a while. I guess he slowed traffic a bit as he meandered the old tractor along side streets and made his way downtown, and then parked it near Pack Square in the heart of the city. He attached a handwritten sign to the side of the tractor that said, 'Stop Big Ag—Buy Local!'. He sat on the tractor and waved at people as they honked and drove by. The cops never messed with him.

Lots of pedestrians on the street stopped to check out the old tractor, and Butch talked to them about how fucked up the US food system was, and how we needed to reverse some of the problems that we've created over the past 50 years. He told them how we must break the bonds of corporate control in the food system by creating new bonds, new methods of growing and marketing and distributing food products at the regional level.

The man, El Tigre, and the global, industrialized food system don't like that idea. They'd rather you buy everything, and I mean everything, from the few at the top.

Market Concentration

Here's what we we're up against. The monsters of food and agribusiness have locked up the food marketplace through a business model containing the key means of control that – not unlike the tentacles of a giant octopus – strangle the life out of farmers and smaller competitors.[100]

These far-reaching tentacles allow for complete vertical integration, where the company can take control of an entire supply chain, from the farm to the processing centers to the retail store shelves. Meanwhile they build political influence to create regulations that help push the small, family farmer out of business. Large corporate offices have become a revolving door between government and high paying industry jobs, and that creates more influence. These corporate giants take advantage of government subsidies, lending programs, and trade bailouts that only add to their bottom line. The long-reaching tentacles of corporate agri-business are strangling the financial lifeblood out of farmers, ranchers, and rural communities.

In the 1950s, farmers received about 50 cents of the retail food dollar. Today, farmers receive on average less than 14 cents and the rest goes to someone else in the middle, and eventually some corporate CEO will take his share, which is about 300 times what the farmer makes. I can't really say that what the CEO does is more important than what the farmer does.

Why would anyone, really, want to get into farming when the costs and risk involved aren't matched by potential reward? It's no wonder that in a five-year period, from 2007 to 2012, the number of beginning farmers decreased by 20%.[101] That trend has continued. There are other easier ways to make a living without all the risk.

71% of America's chicken growers live below the federal

poverty level.[102] That's because four chicken companies own the birds and the feed, and contract with these growers to warehouse them for a few weeks.[103] They determine the prices a farmer will get paid for his service. And the large corporations save all the risk and cost of taking care of these chickens, including the land ownership and the building and the infrastructure and the labor and the employee health insurance. That risk and debt goes to the farmer. American farmers don't want a handout, they just want a fair shot at a fair market.

The biggest trend in the US economy over the past few decades has been market concentration across all sectors of the economy, which in the extreme, goes against the principles of capitalism. This trend creates less competition and thus more control over supply, information and prices by fewer and bigger companies. With fewer players, assets and capital get concentrated into fewer hands. This is not good for competition, which is the backbone of capitalism. And certainly not good for farmers, food sovereignty, or food security. This is the reason for having anti-trust laws—to ensure there is healthy competition. We just need to enforce them.

While we've become used to market domination in the tech industry with companies like Apple, Microsoft and Google, that same concentration is happening across many other parts of the economy, like manufacturing, banking and finance (where banks have become "too big to fail"), and it now includes food production and distribution.

Antitrust agencies in the United States, including the Department of Justice, the Federal Trade Commission, and the Federal Reserve (The Fed), all use measures of concentration to evaluate company mergers and to ensure competitive markets. A recent Barclays report examining dwindling competition asks whether anti-trust controls are failing, and whether "market power" and concentration are undermining our economic wellbeing by reducing the overall economy's vigor and growth.[104]

How and where we get our news and information has also become more concentrated into fewer hands as concentration in the media has risen steadily over the last decade. Giants such as Twitter, Alphabet, Facebook, and Netflix have completely changed the media landscape.

Winner Take All

Some companies win, and some lose. Some grow, and some shrink and go out of business. That's capitalism and a free market economy, and it's good. It's good at least until market concentration starts to have a negative effect on competition or eliminates it entirely.

A 'radical' in this sense of the word is someone who does not accept the fundamental nature of an unbridled market where monopolies can and do take over, which seems to be the norm or status quo these days across the US economy. This radicalism has no relation to communism or a planned economy but is simply an attempt to control the abusive collection of power in the current status quo. As we've seen, the serious downside of concentration is not just that wealth is concentrated for a few at the top, but the company with market power can manipulate prices of its products and services, the prices it pays suppliers, and the wages it pays to employees (or farmers) since there is no competitor where the worker can take his skills. A monopoly can cut off the invisible hand of the market

Many studies have shown how labor's share of company revenue declines with market concentration, while owners share goes up. Wage earners do not reap the benefits of concentration, and this is part of the problem that we're seeing with the rise of income disparity and the earnings gap in the United States.

More competition can limit those negative effects of concentration because if an employee, a customer, or a supplier feels like he's getting squeezed, he'll take his business or skills somewhere else.

As the Barclay's report shows, market domination is also correlated with less innovation, since companies don't really have to get creative if there isn't another company nipping at their heals for market share. Market dominance also means greater barriers to entry for new companies with new ideas. More power also means more influence in the government that can bend regulations to their favor, giving them, in turn, more power and market dominance.

I'll give another example of concentration in the food industry to stress a point. The state of Wisconsin lost 10% of its dairy farmers in 2019 alone.[105] Wisconsin has been known as the dairy capital of the country, known for cheese-heads, cheese curds, and guys who show up to football games with a hunk of foam cheese on their heads. The consolidation in the dairy industry has squeezed out hundreds of small dairy farmers across the state. Why? Because a few massive dairy companies can take over the entire industry, dictate prices, and push smaller farmers out of business who can't compete with two-thousand head operators.

My neighbor, Lynn Bonham, operates one of the last two dairy farms in our county in North Carolina, which used to have over one hundred dairy farmers just 40 years ago. And it's happening everywhere. To guys like me and Butch and Mumford, that's just not OK. In fact, it's dead wrong. So, call me a radical, but I believed we needed to fight for the little guy, the small farmer and the small independent operator. And I think the cheese-heads are with me on this one. If we can get them as riled up about their neighbor dairy farmers who are losing their farms and livelihoods as they get about a Packers football game, we've got a good chance. They're a passionate people.

The Concentration of Power and Corruption

Now here's what can happen when you mix a little concentration with some corruption.

The New York Times published an article in November of 2019 titled *The Money Farmers: How Oligarchs and Populists Milk the E.U. for Millions.* The article exposes how concentration in food production and farmland ownership have opened the door to corrupt business elites and mafia types across Eastern Europe. You know the guys. Short, stocky guys named Victor or Vlad with a bent nose and a black, button-down leather jacket. These are the guys taking over farming in the former eastern bloc countries.

In the article, the Times reports that the European Union spends $65 billion dollars a year subsidizing agriculture, and it's one of the largest subsidy programs in the world. The $65 billion farm subsidy program is by far the biggest line item in the European Union budget, accounting for over 40% of the total budget, and it represents a massive transfer of public money to a single group—which is supposed to be farmers. But the reality is that a huge chunk of that money goes to gang-land strongmen and corrupt politicians.

As the Times article reveals, the European Union farm

subsidies are being used to prop up oligarchs, underwrite Mafia-style land grabs and create a modern version of a medieval, feudal land system—where land barons take the EU subsidies and pay miniscule wages to tenant farmers who do the work and farm the land.

When the EU brought in former Soviet Union Eastern Bloc countries like Hungary, Bulgaria and the Czech Republic, they knew they'd have to deal with some of the old cronyism and corruption of the communist regime, but they had no idea how bad it could be. And they would soon find out how difficult, and risky, it is to fix.

In Hungary, small farmers now work for a group of land overlords, including oligarchs and political patrons who have annexed the land through shady deals with the Hungarian government. These land barons, as it turns out, are financially supported by the European Union, who pays them huge farm subsidies on that land, and then helps them cover their tracks. The Times reporters said that they had an almost impossible task of getting information from EU officials in charge of tracking the subsidies, where they went, and who got paid. The entire system is shrouded in secrecy.

It would appear that the EU is afraid of shaking things up too much. They're afraid to confront corruption and the political and economic fortunes of the powerful because it might threaten to destabilize an already precarious union, and it could destabilize the food supply at the same time. Better to just make the payments and not concern yourself too much about how the money is spent and who's pocket it ends up in. In some cases, politicians and other influential people may be directly benefitting from the system and so are not motivated to change the system.

The Times article says that the $65 billion in farm subsidies were intended to support farmers around the European Continent and to keep rural communities alive. But in Hungary and much of Central and Eastern Europe, the bulk of the money goes to a connected and powerful few. The prime minister of the Czech Republic, for instance, received at least $42 million in farm subsidies in 2018.

A lot of the money goes into a patronage system, like the one in Hungary run by prime minister Viktor Orban, that enriches friends and family of his political elite, protects his political interests and punishes his rivals. Those who control the land, in turn, qualify for millions in subsidies from the European Union. Meanwhile, a journalist named Jan Kuciak was murdered in 2018 while investigating Italian mobsters who had infiltrated the farm industry and profited from the farm subsidies.

Let's take a quick break for a reality check so that we don't think this kind of thing only happens in Transylvania. The television program 60 Minutes did a segment on May 4, 2020, that exposed how a lot of the federal money designated to help small farmers weather the Covid-19 storm actually went to other groups of wealthy individuals, and a lot of it went to the corporate owners, relatives and friends of the largest farms. Because of loopholes in the policy, lawyers worked quickly to add names to the ownership roster of farms so that friends and relatives could take advantage of the free money, although they didn't actually do any work at the farm and lived hundreds of miles away in Chicago or New York. Add a name, get an extra $250,000 in free money, and it was all perfectly legal. It was shocking and very disturbing to watch the program.

My point is, while we might call it 'shocking' when we see studies repeatedly showing that 80 percent of the EU farm money goes to the biggest 20 percent of recipients, as The

Times report suggests. Or we may say it's 'insane' when we hear assertions that in Bulgaria about 75 percent of agricultural subsidies end up in the hands of about 100 entities—some using that money to amass great political power. But we must simultaneously recognize that in the US, 75% of the farm subsidies go to the top 10% of farm producers, and many of those farms are now owned by large corporations.[106] No matter where you look, farm subsidies are being used to help concentrate power and influence, and it's happening right here in the United States.

Since the Supreme Court said that corporations are 'people' with rights to donate significant amounts of cash to political campaigns, how do you separate the money given by the government to corporations in the form of farm subsidies from the money that flows back to politicians in campaign finance? Money goes from one pocket to the other and back again. How much different is that, really, from what's going on in Eastern Europe? The system is wacky. Our farm subsidies are making the biggest farm interests bigger, and not really helping the small farmer, like it should.

But here's the kicker. According to the Congressional Research Service, foreign corporations and persons own 35 million square miles of agriculture land in the United States, roughly equivalent to the state of Tennessee, and larger than Indiana.[107] These foreign owned entities also take advantage of US taxpayer subsidies. So, your tax dollars are contributing to the profitability of a foreign investment firm, while they buy up more US farmland. Investors from Saudi Arabia own land in Arizona. Chinese companies own vast tracts in North Carolina. And the US farm subsidies don't have to be direct payments. The Chinese hog farms in North Carolina benefit from cheap, subsidized corn feed, paid for by the US taxpayer.

According to the USDA, foreign investors nearly doubled their ownership of U.S. farmland over a ten-year span, increasing from 14.6 million acres in 2004 to 26.7 million acres in 2014.[108] Just in the state of Oklahoma, foreign ownership grew over a recent decade by 475% to over 370,000 acres of agricultural land. Many foreign interests with significant financial resources, including China, Saudi Arabia, and South Korea, are in the market for U.S. farmland due to the lack of enough productive land in their own countries, and in the case of China, because they've polluted a lot of their own land.

In 2014, the Chinese government released a report indicating that nearly one-fifth of its arable land was polluted.[109] Food security is the top priority for the Chinese government, and they're on a farmland buying spree around the world. When China purchased Smithfield Foods and the farms that came with it, a stated goal was to take Smithfield equipment and technology for processing meat on a massive scale back to China.

Vast farms in remote places, including one in Arizona that came with water rights, are now purchased by foreign interests like Saudi Arabia as they attempt to improve their own food security on US soil. As land developers, foreign buyers, and large investment groups buy up more land and continue to push up land prices, more farmers will begin to discover what it is like to be a landless sharecropper. To be landless means there is no place to plant roots. For generations of farmers, land was not just a commodity to be traded on Wall Street—it represented freedom and life itself.

Consolidation has many faces. After recent corporate consolidation in the seed and agrochemical industry, three companies control over 80% of the U.S. seed supply and 70% of the global market for pesticides. And because of consolidation, farmers are seeing their costs go up while their input options (and innovation) go down. At the same time, where and who they can sell their products to is consolidated, meaning the few remaining companies they can sell to will determine the prices that they're going to get for their produce and hard work.

And as one more little tidbit of information that plays into all of this, 60 of the largest companies in the US paid no taxes on pretax income of $79 billion in 2018.[110] Corporations are very adept at tax avoidance. It's why so many companies incorporate in Delaware and other offshore island tax havens in the Caribbean. They don't pay into the system, but still reap the benefits, like the benefits that come from billions of dollars in farm subsidies that reduce their cost for inputs like corn and corn derivatives.

An Army of College Students

With the risks of climate change, desertification, soil erosion and soil depletion, the loss of farmland to development, and water shortages in the West, good farmland will become scarcer and so the land values will increase over time, even without a potential bubble created by Wall Street and foreign investors.

No region in the US has been unaffected by rising farmland prices, but the most dramatic impact has been in Midwestern corn belt states like Iowa and Nebraska, where land prices have doubled since 2009 alone.[111] So, what we're now facing is a massive transfer of land from family farmers to the financial sector. By some estimates, institutional investors and other non-farmer buyers are now involved in 20 percent of all farmland sold across the country every year.[112] When investment bankers and Wall Street are in charge of the farm and our food, what happens next?

The food fighters knew that we would need to enlist college students to join our ranks, and this seemed like a good place to bring them in, since many universities are now investing vast sums of money in farmland through their pension and endowment funds.

I've spent a lot of time on college campuses, and I know how college students and some faculty members can become an army for change. One good example relates to fair labor practices in the manufacturing industry. Student protests have changed the licensed products business, or in other words, the places where college bookstores, sporting goods shops and other retailers can source products with college logos. 'No Sweatshop Labor' was the battle cry for this army of college students, and it worked. Massive companies like Nike and Adidas were forced to pull out of factories in Bangladesh and other locations with unfair labor practices or poor working conditions.

University Presidents and administration buckled under the student pressure and started mandating that product bearing the university marks must come from sweatshop-free factories, or a license to use the school marks would not be granted, and companies had to prove it. In response, companies had to begin inspecting and certifying factories that made those products. The licensed products business is a multi-billion-dollar industry, and it was student action that created radical change.

If more faculty and students were aware of where college endowments and faculty retirement plans are invested, and what farmland investment through REITs is doing to farmland, farmers and the food system in this country, they might have something to say in the matter. Student protests on campus have already changed how many institutions invest endowments and pension funds and forced many to pull investments from fossil fuel companies like Exxon, as one example.

Certain food fighters at the old red schoolhouse on Avery Creek Road, who would prefer to remain nameless because they don't want their names appearing on any lists, started an information campaign that encouraged many students and faculty to look into where endowments and retirement funds were invested. When students start protesting, a campus can (and usually does) react quickly. No university president wants a bunch of student protesters in front of his office—it's bad for business. Just a little subversive message from me, your author, to my young student friends out there who might be interested in creating a little disruption and disquiet between classes— and help a farmer out at the same time. And if you're look- ing for something to chant, I've always liked the slogan used by American Farmland Trust, "No Farmers, No Food!" Short and sweet. Nice ring to it.

If you're not quite ready to radicalize campus, you can at least start by finding out if your university endowment, pension or retirement funds are investing in farmland and potentially adding to the risk of a bubble in our food supply. It should be public information.

I think it's worthwhile to recap some of the consolidation we've seen in the food industry over the last couple of decades. Just three corporations (Archer Daniels Midland, Bunge and Cargill) control 90 percent of the global grain trade, four companies control 60 percent of the poultry industry, and four control 85% percent of the beef industry (Tyson, Cargill, JBS and Smithfield.) Three companies dominate the seed and pesticide market (Bayer-Monsanto, Corteva,

Syngenta) while Monsanto (now Bayer) has a near monopoly on genetic traits (GMO's). Over 95% of corn grown in the US is the same GMO, and most gene patents for crops are owned by two companies.

The four companies who control 60% of the poultry industry are Pilgrim's Pride, Tyson, Perdue, and Sanderson Farms. Contract poultry growers mostly work for them. Got Milk? Two dominant players control most of the dairy products we consume. Dean Foods controls the majority of fluid milk markets (up to 100% in some parts of the country). Meanwhile, farmers in many parts of the country have only one dairy cooperative they can sell their milk to—Dairy Farmers of America (DFA). When you control the market, it's easy to manipulate milk prices so you pay less to farmers while price-gouging consumers. The Department of Justice recently fined DFA twelve million dollars for price manipulation. Go figure.

It all represents a huge change in how food is grown and distributed over the past few decades. The only people who can really deal with the large processors and distributors are the larger, consolidated farms. The little guy doesn't have a chance. How is a small farmer going to negotiate a fair price for his labor when production from his little farm is a drop in the bucket for one massive processor that needs to purchase train loads of raw product to keep their production lines operating. The same is true when they go to purchase their seeds and supplies from the monsters of agribusiness. They have no leverage, no competitor to take their business to, and so will pay what they are told to pay.

While we've seen consolidation in the food industry over the decades, and now in corporate farmland ownership, we have also experienced a systematic dismantling of the old processing and distribution infrastructure across the US. The number of places just to grind wheat or process meat has been concentrated into very few and far-away facilities, adding to the difficulties of the small farmer.

Covid exposed not only weak links at the largest meat processors, but a trickle-down effect at the smaller, regional processors that remain and that many small farmers have counted on for their pasture raised beef operations. As I write this in November of 2021, the few smaller, independent meat processers within 150 miles of my farm cannot schedule to take one of my cows for processing until sometime in mid to late 2022. That's because so many other small farmers and meat buyers wanting to stock their freezers have booked up all of the available production times at the few remaining facilities. Before the pandemic I could call and get a spot at the processor within a couple weeks, now it's six months to a year wait.

It wasn't always that way. It used to be that farmers brought their grain to a local mill to grind and process. Then it went to the local baker. In most regions across the US, there is no local business to bring your wheat, your cow, or your milk for processing. They've all been swallowed up by much larger, regional processors or shut down. The ultimate example of the risk of putting too many eggs in one basket now comes from the food and agriculture sector.

CHAPTER SIX

FIGHTING FOR LOCAL FOOD PRODUCTION

I met with Charlie Jackson at a cozy, warm coffee shop in downtown Asheville. It was a cold December day, but the sun brightly lit the old brick buildings that I could see out the window across the street. A few bundled pedestrians walked briskly down the sidewalk in front of the window.

In the world of food fighters, Charlie Jackson was like George Washington at Valley Forge, and I was like some low-ranking officer in charge of a renegade band of soldiers in some remote outpost on Avery Creek Road.

Charlie and his organization, Appalachian Sustainable Agriculture Project (ASAP), have done more for local food sovereignty than any other organization that I know of. Charlie was highly respected and the executive director of this important organization, and I knew that I couldn't get him involved in some of the anticks that my little group of guerrilla fighters were up to. So, I never really told him about some of the shit we were up to. But I wanted to speak with Charlie, who founded ASAP, about concentration in the food industry and get his take on things. He's been fighting for small farmers and local food production for almost 30 years.

"How do we change the system and spread-out the wealth?"

I asked after giving him about 30 seconds to settle in and take a sip of his coffee.

"We need to rebuild the local and regional food systems. The demand is there—people want more local and sustainable products. We need broad participation to make the big change we need. Policy and infrastructure investments will follow when we take control of the foods we eat. Prioritizing local is a meaningful action for making the personal political."

"What can the average person do?"

"Here's the best way to start—use your wallet. We all eat, and we have tremendous power that comes with where we spend our food dollars. Policy and investment come from getting everyone engaged. Localizing is a deeply grass roots and home-grown approach to building a food system from the ground up that is sustainable and serves everyone. Buy local. It's that simple a first step," said Charlie.

I wasn't sure it was all that simple, and I believed that there were bigger issues at play here, and not just government blindness but government collusion that was making things so much more difficult.

"But what about all the policy hullabaloo that makes buying local not so simple?" I asked. "Some of the crazy shit that's been going on in the food industry lately is absurd. Absolutely crazy," I said. "Everyone knows the Amazon is burning out of control and it's the ranchers who lit the fires."

At the time of this meeting, thousands of acres of rain forest were burning out of control in the Amazon. I continued while Charlie sipped his coffee and let me rant.

"If the president of Brazil is determined to burn and destroy the Amazon rain forest to make room for more livestock production by the mega corps like JBS, under normal circumstances you might think that you could choose not to buy meat from Brazil, or any other farm product from that county. That hurts them where it counts. But without country-of-origin labels on meat products, it's difficult to know where your meat is coming from, even if the label says, 'Product of USA'. That just means the meat passed through a US facility, and maybe got repackaged. Who the heck said that was OK?" I found myself heating up and starting to talk like Butch.

"The first step," Charlie replied, "is to take action. We are not powerless unless we let ourselves become that way. Without broad based involvement we can't make systemic change."

Charlie took another sip of coffee and looked out the window for a second. It was chilly outside, and people were walking at a faster pace than they normally do in Asheville. Usually it's a casual, laid-back stroll, even when late for work, or later than normal. That's just Asheville.

"I'm sure you're aware of the flurry of Wall Street investments in farmland over recent years. Does that scare you?" I asked, and then added quickly, "It does me. It scares the crap out of me."

"It does scare me too, and the recent land grabs could literally change who owns the country in the years ahead. One key component of farmland preservation is to keep farms profitable. That's where local comes in again"

"I just don't think the dangers of this trend toward consolidation in farmland and food distribution can be overstated," I argued. "People need to wake up."

"Local food might be the most promising development in US agriculture that can change the entire system," said Charlie. "It provides an action step for everybody. Unlike many movements, localizing is something we can take direct action on every day. The changes I've seen in the past decade have really surprised me and so I stay optimistic."

"We invest in our future by going local," Charlie added. "That's a better investment than anything Wall Street has to offer. People just need to be made more fully aware of what's going on. It took a long time for us to get to this point in our food system and it will take time to create a new one that better serves us all. The important thing is to act"

It just amazes me that Charlie Jackson has been fighting this battle for three decades. Charlie has an inner strength and calm, and a quiet determination that comes from experience, and that strength has sustained him and carried him through for the long-haul.

I didn't have that kind of patience, and I wanted change to happen right now. Shortly after my meeting with Charlie, I got with a graphic artist dude that I found from a business card tacked to a wall at Firestorm Books and had him create a funky, brightly colored flyer that showed the Amazon burning and the multinational food corporation that would benefit from it. We printed some up and I asked a glassblower who lived in his van to go downtown and see how many places he could hang them. Another accomplice, a poet / unemployed bartender, posted it on some social media sites.

While Charlie and ASAP would have taken a different approach, I felt pretty good about it. We really stuck it to the man on that one, I'll tell you. Some son-of-a-bitch in Brazil probably pissed his pants after we hung up a dozen or so of those flyers. And I think we may have got 30 or 40 hits on the web site from it.

Don't get me wrong. I believe in capitalism, and I believe that a free-market economy is the only system that rewards risk and hard work, which is the driver of growth and economic development. I also believe in smaller government, and I don't like the idea of government officials putting their noses too far into business or dictating who gets to buy from who or how you can invest your money.

The answers to mass consolidation and concentration must come from the customers, and at the grass roots level—the people who vote with their dollars. Spread it around a little more. Root for the little guy once in a while. Everyone likes an underdog, and that underdog can be a local farmer. That is how capitalism and democracy can work together to create a better, more equitable world. I believe this was Charlie's philosophy also.

I don't have all the answers, but I don't know of a better system than capitalism, and I am hopeful that there is some remedy for its own ills—that there is some built-in mechanism to repair itself when it gets out of whack and some companies become too powerful. Perhaps we might make some people aware of the larger issues, and so help to guide the invisible hand.

I concede that it is a stretch to see capitalism as a system that can remedy the very problems that it has designed and created, but this is why anti-trust laws were enacted, to curb monopolies and runaway capitalism. I just have a problem when too much power is controlled by too few, like when medieval kings and lords controlled everything. While it's good to be the king, it sucks when the rest of us have to scratch out a living at the bottom.

"Our economy is strong enough to handle a few prudent and smart conservation measures," said Charlie. "Conservation is really just an investment in our future, and our children and grandchildren's future."

"I agree," I replied. "It's long-term investment in the future versus short-term profit. And I think we can afford to be a little less self-centered and selfish while we look out for the fate of millions of future Americans."

"Conservation and protecting our natural resources are simply the prudent thing to do," he said. Charlie was calm and mild mannered, as always, cool as a cucumber.

"Growth at all costs is not prudent behavior," I said. "I am always surprised that the right isn't more concerned about protecting their long-term investments, supply lines and resources, particularly if there is a possible threat from climate change. It just makes sense to me, as a reformed businessman, to look out for where the axe might fall, and consider implementing some things that might moderate some risk. Putting your head in the sand about climate change is not a wise, 'conservative' business tactic."

"You're right," he replied. "The status quo is not a good, long-term investment. It's a bill that will come due, sooner or later."

Charlie and I both believed in capitalism and a free market economy. We both believed in long-term planning and economic progress over decades, much more than short term profit. That view is short-sighted and dangerous to the overall health of a company and an economy. And we didn't believe that it was right to steal from future generations. The definition of sustainability is to provide for our needs now without compromising a future generations ability to provide for their own needs. A sustainable, conservative business model must look out for the long-term success of the company. You can't do that with your head in the sand or buried in a quarterly earnings report. That's irresponsible.

I think we were both just a little fearful of short-sightedness and capitalism gone haywire, and the concentration of too much power into too few hands. And the truth is, I don't want Amazon to sell me everything that I need. I like to walk through town and spread my money around a little at smaller shops and independent businesses. I like the personal relationships and interaction. I don't want the board of directors at a handful of corporations to determine what I'll be having for dinner tonight. I like variety, choice, and diversity. And I really like knowing who is growing my food.

ASAP Double SNAP

I had asked Charlie to meet for coffee to discuss something else, and finally we came to a point where we could talk about it: the Supplemental Nutrition Assistance Program, or SNAP. SNAP is what many people still refer to as "food stamps."

I didn't come up with the idea, and I'm not sure where that I first heard about it, but some farmers market in Colorado or Bloomington, Indiana or somewhere else found a way to double the value of SNAP benefits as a way to encourage lower income households to attend the farmer's market, thereby boosting access to healthier food choices. Somehow, they found a way that families receiving SNAP could shop at the farmers market and double their spending power. And the beautiful thing about farmers markets is that they not only offer fresh, healthy foods, but a social environment that encourages, educates, and excites people to eat good food.

We've already discussed the serious risks to both human health and the environment that are directly related to our modern processed foods, but how do we make local, healthy, whole foods more accessible and affordable to households with limited resources? I thought the idea was brilliant, so I wanted to talk about it with Charlie because ASAP runs the Asheville City Farmers Market downtown.

"If we can get a grant, or donations to underwrite the thing, it's a fairly simple thing to manage, isn't it?" I asked Charlie. "When people come to your main booth at the market to exchange their SNAP benefits for tokens to use at the individual booths, we simply give them double the number of tokens that they purchased."

I hoped Charlie could try to launch a similar program in early 2019. The program is a beautiful thing, I believed, because it's designed to do two good things with the same dollar; it encourages healthy food choices while also supporting local, sustainable farms and farmers. We would call it 'Double SNAP', and people would know it as ASAP Double SNAP. It turns out, Charlie had run smaller scale SNAP match programs in the past and understood the impact they could have on both families and farmers, and he jumped on the idea right away.

"We don't get as many SNAP users at the market as we would like," said Charlie, "but we've wanted to try to attract more SNAP households, and this will help encourage more to attend. We have a way to accept SNAP cards already set up at the downtown market."

The individual farmers at the market aren't set up to run the SNAP debit cards at their booths, so the SNAP users stop by the ASAP booth on their way in, and ASAP staff run the EBT card through their machine and charge the card for the amount the customer plans to spend at the market, and then gives her wooden tokens for that amount. The customer can then use these tokens to buy stuff at the different booths at the market. At the end of the day, the farmer brings the tokens back to the booth and ASAP redeems the tokens for cash.

"To make this happen, all we really have to do is give them twice the number of tokens when we run their card, and we've doubled their buying power," I said. "That's a pretty good incentive to go to the market, don't you think?"

"It will take us a while to secure ongoing money to support a new program like this," Charlie added.

I knew that funding projects is a never-ending battle for non-profits like ASAP, so I said,

"What if my wife and I guaranteed or underwrote it for now as a test? Then we could start it right away and see if people would come out for it. And then we'd have some idea on how much a program like this would cost. What do you think we would we need to start? $500 in matching funds, or $5000?" I asked.

"I'm not sure," said Charlie. "Probably depends on how many people hear about it. I think people would come out though once they heard about it. Doubling the money that you can spend is a pretty big incentive. And they can buy meats, pasta and breads and other things with their SNAP card at the downtown market, not just fruits and vegetables."

"I could at least guarantee it until we found some donors that would write the checks," I said. "I'd be willing to stick our necks out for, let's say, $10,000 and cap it at that, just in case."

I was afraid my wife would shoot me for volunteering to underwrite something that could cost us $10,000 while we were still in debt from the Agrihood development I was working on. But I felt fairly confident that we could do some fundraising and quickly collect enough money to get it started without bearing all of the financial risk.

Over the next couple of weeks, Charlie worked out the details and I worked on getting some money to support the program from some of our wealthy food-fighters who didn't often attend the meetings.

Charlie started the "Double SNAP" program in early summer, and it worked out great and started to grow rapidly. When people showed up to the market with their SNAP card, we doubled the amount of money they could spend at the market, and most were pleasantly surprised. But once word got out that the value of their shopping dollars doubled at the market, people started showing up who had never been to the market before. It opened their eyes to a whole new world of healthy food and the network of people at the market who are happy to share the joy of locally produced food.

The market is an experience unlike going to a grocery store, with a lot more personal interaction, smiles and lively communication, and it's a great opportunity to learn about healthy food options. And at the Asheville market, it's not just fruits and vegetables. There are several vendors selling meats, handmade pasta, breads and baked goods, deserts, eggs, cheese, prepared goods like sauces, spices, condiments and kimchi, and lots of other goodies. Farmers at the market are always happy and eager to talk about how to cook and prepare their products, so it exposes many people to new types of foods and how to cook them. It's a food adventure.

A secondary benefit was a big increase in sales for local growers at the market and for the local economy. The farmers needed the boost especially when restaurants that they supplied closed down with COVID and left them dangling precariously with financial ruin. It was a win-win for everyone, and the program became even more important during the Covid-19 pandemic. When COVID hit, the program was in place to help people who needed it most.

Renegotiating the Local Food Economy

We need to reevaluate and renegotiate the entire farm and food economy. The problem, as I see it, with many small-scale farms around Asheville is that they produce a lot of food without receiving a fair economic return for all the work. Many are working for wages that put them below the poverty line because they often undervalue their own labor and their family's labor. Or they rely on interns to do some of the work for free or a small stipend just for the opportunity to learn how to farm, which isn't exactly fair in my opinion.

Labor is the most expensive line-item cost for small-scale farms operating with minimal profits, and this is especially true for organic farms that value manual labor over chemical inputs. And let's face it, pulling weeds by hand can be backbreaking work when you do it all day.

When young people, eager to learn about farming, take farm internship positions at no pay or with small stipends just to learn the trade, this props up the small food economy in an unnatural way that doesn't follow the normal market driven rules of capitalism. That's not very sustainable. And it's not all that different from the larger industrialized system that pays people unfairly at minimal wages. We cannot have a food system that relies on the inequities of the system to function.

Under the banner of a 'new moral economy,' small growers often practice a form of self-exploitation because they end up selling their own labor at a reduced cost—often below minimum wages. They want to connect with the earth and grow food to feed people because it is an honorable way to make a living—and it is a noble way to get by in this world. It just doesn't fit into a capitalistic model dominated by the industrialized system. Capitalism cannot rest on the de-valued labor at the bottom. Yet it often does, as it did very early on with the VOC and the Far Distance Company and their dependence on native slave labor in the spice islands.

To confuse matters more fully, we've created an economy

with subsidies to the largest farms that then deflates food prices. And we've allowed massive consolidation that creates huge competitive advantages and economies of scale, further deflating prices and making it nearly impossible for the small grower to compete. The system is breaking down for the small farmer.

And while many of these small growers and workers may have non-capitalistic goals that include some freedom and autonomy and the ability to practice self-provisioning—self-reliance is important to many small, local growers—they are operating in a precarious position that doesn't always align with normal economic and capitalistic principles.

It's true that capitalism has a penchant for profit over people and the planet. And this has naturally led to the consolidation of small family farms and the rise of corporately owned multinational agribusinesses behemoths. Agribusiness has been following the general laws of capital accumulation, so that as large conventional farms grew bigger, they were able to increase productivity and decrease labor costs by the injection of capital into technological advances and through investments in larger machinery, more equipment, and chemicals. Lots of chemicals.

Large farming enterprises have maximized automation in order to minimize labor costs and the need for workers, and this is why corn and soybeans have taken over the Midwest and why we're importing all the more labor-intensive vegetables from countries that might pay the equivalent of $1 per hour for farm labor, or less. Most small growers in Asheville are growing those niche vegetables, and so compete with the world in the eyes of the average consumer.

And for the tasks that cannot be efficiently mechanized on large scale farms, they generally hire migrant workers from other countries, particularly Mexico and Central America. Most of these workers come through the federal H-2A program, which provides seasonal visas for foreign workers to fill temporary agricultural jobs. The reason for this is because it's often difficult to find enough American workers willing to fill these positions out in the fields of American agriculture.

In the face of this tough competition from large, corporate farms and cheap labor in Central America, the United States is witnessing the near complete demise of the family-scale farm. That many small farms have persevered against their corporate competitors this long is often the result of selling their own labor too cheaply. Self-exploitation has allowed them to resist market concentration. They may not even acknowledge or care about the larger market concentration going on around them; they simply hope to provide value added products and compete for a shared customer base, at least enough to survive alongside.

This local economy is also dependent on a small group of shoppers who understand the situation and want to support their farmer neighbors and who choose to pay a little more for healthier local food without all the chemicals or food miles associated with the normal grocery store produce.

I know too many small growers around Asheville and other places that are just barely scratching out a living and some years making less than minimum wage. Some grow food for themselves and to sell at the market but then must resort to SNAP benefits to buy what they can't grow to feed their children. As a self-proclaimed food politics commentator, I must say, that's pretty sad. A country must be able to feed itself and fairly compensate its farmers at the same time.

Developing food sovereignty and food security is perhaps the most important function that a government can do for its citizens—any government, at every level of government, and in every country and community around the planet. There is too much risk otherwise.

A shopper's willingness to pay a little more for produce from a small, local farmer is all part of a renegotiation of the big agrarian question—and that question is—Will the small-scale family farm survive the onslaught of corporate domination? Will the small, local grower even exist in ten or twenty years?

Self-exploitation is not a competitive advantage. But it is happening, and I'm quite certain that many of the farmers that you see at the farmers market are working for less than minimum wage. There are other factors, other values, which are driving them to do this, to be sure. But how long can this go on? Something's got to give.

When I asked Butch about fighting back over ham and eggs at Boone's Corner, a gas station and diner close to the farm, I almost regretted asking him. The floodgates opened.

"The model we have now to compete with multinational food corporations is the small, organic farmer selling at the farmers market," I said. "Is that all we can do? Promote the farmers market and frequent restaurants that buy from local farmers?"

"Yes, you take several pages from that play-book. Then you use some of Big Tobacco's tactics.," he replied. "Espionage, disinformation, propaganda, harassment. Infiltrate their organizations."

I wasn't sure that I was ready for this bullshit. It was early morning, and I hadn't even had a full cup of coffee yet. The coffee probably came from South America by way of a huge multinational, by the way.

"Why not" said Butch over his breakfast, "Fight fire with fire. Look who's behind most of the research in processed foods. Look who's behind the very food pyramid itself. How do you think dairy got on the food pyramid in the first place? Someone paid off someone else for that a long time ago. I mean really, milk on the pyramid. Why not orange juice." He took a sip of his orange juice.

"Listen man," Butch said in a low voice so as not to be heard by the table next to us, "the government in India just bowed down to powerful food companies and postponed a decision to put red warning labels on unhealthy packaged food, food that is clearly killing people in their country, and they know it. When critics spoke up, the government tried to pacify them by creating an 'expert panel' to 'further review' the proposed labeling system." Butch used his fingers to add the necessary quotes.

If it was true, the law would have gone far beyond what other countries have done in the battle to combat soaring obesity rates everywhere. China and India are snacking their way to obesity on the processed food train that originated in the US. And they're heading for a social disaster. From Butch's perspective, someone intentionally cut down the sign that said, "Bridge Out Ahead."

"And guess what, the man chosen to head the three-person committee, this Dr. Boindala Sesikeran, the dude was a former adviser to Nestle. That's just frickin' crazy."

Butch had the uncanny ability to remember names like that. Like his cousin Mumford, he could quote a scientist by name from some obscure research paper written in the 1950's. I don't know how they did that.

"And it gets better. This Dr. Sesikeran is a trustee of the

International Life Sciences Institute, an American nonprofit with an innocent sounding name, right, that has been quietly infiltrating government health and nutrition bodies around the world. It's all espionage, and they don't even try to hide it very well, man. That organization was started by an executive at Coke. Can you believe that shit? Look it up. Talk about placing an inside man into government policy making."

Butch spends a lot of time researching stuff on the internet. How he finds some of this information I don't really know, but he's given me several leads on some of the more shadowy organizations and shady deals going on out there. I looked up the International Life Sciences Institute (ILSI) and quickly discovered that it was created four decades ago by a top Coca-Cola executive. The institute now has branches in 17 countries, and it is almost entirely funded by Goliaths of the agribusiness, food, and pharmaceutical industries.

The 'scientific organization', which once fought for tobacco interests during the 1980s and 1990s in Europe and the United States, has more recently expanded its activities around food in Asia and Latin America, regions that deliver a growing customer base for processed food companies. It has been especially active in China, India and Brazil, the world's first, second and sixth most populous nations, and all with growing appetites for the sweet and salty American diet of processed snack foods and sugary soft drinks.

"That's where you want to place your man!" Butch said, "if you work for Pringles. You want him inside a 'scientific organization' like that so he can advise the government." Again, with the fingers to add quotation marks.

In China, the institute Butch was describing shares both staff and office space with the agency responsible for combating the country's epidemic of obesity-related illness. ILSI and the Chinese government are so interconnected that ILSI's top leaders double as senior officials at China's Centers for Disease Control. In Brazil, ILSI representatives sit on several food and nutrition panels that were once reserved for university researchers and academics.

"What could possibly go wrong?" said Butch. "Let's put a covert food lobby group in charge of deciding public health policy. It's wrong and a blatant conflict of interest. The system is fucked." Butch took a bite of his toast and chewed it angrily as he looked out the window.

It all sounded like espionage in a spy thriller, where the mastermind is a brand manager for Cheetos.

"Here's how it works. I'll spell it out for you," Butch continued. "If you're McDonalds, you don't sponsor a conference on nutrition. No scientist or legitimate nutritionist will come, the ties are too obvious and blatant, even if you offer a nice room in a five-star hotel and all the meals are free, no one will come. So, you hide your sponsorship under the umbrella of some dummy do-good organization. The perks are all there to get people to attend, and you can cultivate allies and influential scientists who might back and support your "research" or your product.

"These things are always held in five-star hotels. How the hell are we going to attract scientists to our cause. We can't afford that. What would we say? 'Come tell the truth and we'll give you a bologna sandwich and a free night at the Holiday Inn?'"

"Why don't we try to infiltrate their dummy organizations?" I said. "Get our own man inside ILSI as a double agent." I wasn't really thinking that we could ever do such a thing. I just wanted to prod Butch a little, like putting some hot sauce on his eggs when he wasn't looking.

He looked off into the distance and I could see the wheels turning. How could we get a man on the inside? Counter-espionage type stuff. A mole, pretending to be a mole for the food industry, inside the fake research organization. After a minute thinking, Butch shook it off and spoke again.

"Most of these insiders are former top government officials that leave government to advise companies like Nestle and General Mills on how to get around the red tape. Then they take a position at one of these B.S. food research institutes funded by the guys they advise, where they fly around all expenses paid to lecture about the benefits of artificial sweeteners and genetically modified crops. When they join government decision making panels, the regulated become the regulators. Total conflict of interest, but it happens every day."

I continued to eat my breakfast but kept my mouth shut otherwise. Butch was on one of his roles.

"So, here's an example of this ILSI outfit in China", Butch continued. "They helped to shape all the anti-obesity education campaigns around physical activity and made sure that no claims or statements about diets of high sugar, high fat, high calorie food has anything to do with the problem or the conversation. Coke uses that strategy a lot. Eat and drink as much sugar as you want. That's not the problem. Just do your 'Ten Happy Minutes' of exercise and you're good. Slimy bastards."

Butch wasn't lying. I looked that up too. China's "fitness-is-best" message, as it happens, has largely been the handiwork of Coca-Cola and other Western food and beverage giants. The program focuses on children and what the Chinese started promoting as 'ten happy minutes' of exercise, and the program says little to nothing about diet.

So that's why Tony the Tiger started looking so buff, I thought, and why he started wearing a coach's whistle. They were just taking a page from the same playbook. Ten happy minutes.

When Michael Bloomberg, as mayor of New York City, tried to fight the "Big Gulp' and limit the size of soft drinks sold in convenience stores, he came up against these giants in the food industry. His was a public health campaign, using the rational that no one really needs to drink a half-gallon of soda pop and add 600 plus calories of sugar to their daily diet. That's just not healthy; but that wasn't enough to stop it. He lost that battle in court, but perhaps he still raised some awareness to the problem. The message was simple enough—We need to cut back on the sugar to save and extend our lives. A few people may have listened.

The 'scientific research organizations' like ILSI are now the ones fighting the World Health Organization as it finally takes a tougher stance on sugar. That's a threat to their business, and so they look for ways to infiltrate and influence behind the scenes.

"It just pisses me off," said Butch.

"Here's the thing," he said, "Developing nations are where the action is. These are places where there's little health infrastructure and a lot of power over information about the health risks of processed foods and junk food. If corporations can get in on the ground floor, they can shape the demand and government policies around their sugar crack. Sugar is so addictive."

"Listen Man," Butch said as he looked me dead in the eye, "I've seen a mother in Mexico fill a baby bottle with Coke. I've actually seen that. She might even think it's safer than the water supply, and maybe it is in some places. Maybe she thinks it's got some 'essential nutrients', like milk? The control of information makes easy pickings for a marketing guy."

"But the corruption of our food supply goes much deeper." Butch's eyes narrowed.

"ILSI received millions of dollars from chemical companies like Monsanto. They infiltrated one committee that issued some ruling that glyphosate [the key chemical in Monsanto's weed killer Roundup] was 'probably not carcinogenic.' The lies and deceit just astound me. It's really no different than the tobacco industry years ago."

Back in India, ILSI's expanding influence has coincided with mounting rates of obesity, cardiovascular disease, and especially diabetes. To India's credit, the government did take some action to combat the rising rates of obesity and disease, including a 40 percent tax on sugar-sweetened soda introduced in 2017. But other efforts, including a ban on junk food sales in and around schools, have stalled out amid strong opposition from food and beverage companies. But still the Indian government was able to do something that Bloomberg and New York City couldn't.

"The power of the food industry is even greater than that of the Big Tobacco industry at it's heyday, if you can believe it," said Butch. "The problem, like smoking in the 50's, is that we don't see the threat. We don't understand the risks. Maybe someday people will look back and see giving a kid a happy meal with a coke was like giving them a cigarette, and they'll say, 'What the heck were they thinking back then? We're people just stupid?'"

Is it possible to change public awareness and perception about unhealthy food? Just as smoking has become socially "uncool", people are starting to realize that unhealthy diets of high sugar junk food is not cool. But what does it take to really create change and improve health and happiness in society? How does change come about? How do we change the values, principles, purpose and meaning of our overall economy? If we're heading in the wrong direction toward some feudal oligarchy that's killing people with junk food, what can we do about that?

"So, how do you start a revolution these days?" I asked Butch as the waitress collected our plates and looked at me funny for saying that.

"Well, you certainly don't go marching around protesting," Butch said. "That'll get your name on some lists. You don't want that."

"What then?" I asked.

"You keep doing what you're doing. Use the media. Write your articles. Write your books. Just leave the heavy lifting, the culture jamming shit to me."

That sounded a little scary. Was he moving up to graffiti on billboards, or maybe something even more sinister? Was he the one capable of hijacking a Frito-Lay truck and burning it in effigy?

Taking Butch's advice, I started writing articles with subversive messages in The Laurel of Asheville magazine in October of 2018. That would attract attention from artists and jazz musicians, the bohemian types, which everyone knows are prone to various forms of radicalism. They could become part of our base, along with the hippies, homesteaders, and tree huggers. There were plenty of those types around Asheville, and I could easily recruit them to the cause. How to place a double agent inside a fake research institute was going to be a challenge beyond me and my pay grade.

I had already published a subversive book and cleverly

disguised it under the seemingly harmless title *"Carrots Don't Grow on Trees"* so that it would fly under the radar of corporate lawyers and their government henchmen. The subtitle hinted at its antiestablishment message; *"Building Sustainable and Resilient Communities"*. The hint of subversion was there: did it mean that our current system isn't sustainable and resilient? I could still fly under the radar.

It was also about this time that we created a web site to disseminate our radical message, and we filled it with information that might threaten to disrupt the industrialized food system. That was just the start of a small wave, a ripple really, that might become a tsunami, and non-profit organizations, local food groups, health providers, and higher education, representing thousands of people, might get behind it. Or so we hoped. But as scary as it sounds, we were about to commit ourselves to some direct action.

Butch asked a question as we got up and walked out of Boones Corner Restaurant, "Your fall harvest festival is at the farm next weekend, right? Do you mind if I set up a stand?"

"For what?" I replied.

"I was thinking about that thing we talked about the other night. What about having a stand and a sign for 'The Organization for the Decency of Naked Animals'" he said. We both smiled.

"No, I'm serious. People would come talk to me with a sign like that," he continued. "I could have people sign a petition and get their email. Dress up a piglet in a Hawaiian shirt or something. Or a sailor suit."

"That's funny, a sailor suit," I replied. "Why is that funnier than a button-down shirt and pants?" We both smiled and thought about it for a second.

"You're right though, that would get people to stop, and

you could talk to them," I said. "You could probably get some outfit like that at a pet store that was made for dogs but would probably fit a piglet like Albert. Just don't get a cop uniform. We don't want to piss-off the cops. We didn't pull any permits for this."

We both laughed and walked away to our cars. It was settled. We would take this fight to the next level.

How Do We Save Farmland?

A farmer friend told me about a real estate developer who boldly knocked on his door and said, "Mister, I can make you a rich man."

And you know what—he wasn't lying.

Rapid development and suburban sprawl are driving up land prices and changing the landscape before our very eyes in Buncombe County, where my farm is located. This is making it difficult, if not impossible, for young farmers to find affordable farmland to grow on. This same scene is playing out almost everywhere across the country as cities sprawl out into the countryside. It's been going on for decades, but in some places, it's now happening at an extreme rate of development.

Farmers are now competing with developers and land speculators for the remaining farmland that's left here around Asheville. Thousands of people have been moving to Asheville from New York City and Chicago and all parts of California because the climate is favorable, and they can get a lot more home for the money than in those places. A lot of wealthy people are building second homes here in the mountains.

Most citizens and long-time residents of Buncombe and neighboring Henderson County value the rich rural heritage of this region. Farming has been an integral part of the local economy for generations, and the vibrant 'farm to table' trend is evidence that we still value farming and local food production. But with rapid growth and development here, as in many places, suburban sprawl now threatens that economy and way of life.

Like many communities across the United States, we need a vision and hope for a future that protects and preserves farming and a rural landscape in the face of the inevitable suburban development pressure. The citizens of towns like Arden, where I live, Fletcher and Mills River have a deliberate and bold choice to make in order to protect what they have left. Namely, a vision for the future that will allow for development in a structured and systematic way and provide for a sustainable economic development strategy that includes farming and agriculture.

When I interviewed with county commissioners for the position on the Buncombe County Land Conservation Advisory Board, I made no mention of some of my more radical associates or my past and pending revolutionary activities, so I got the position. But I took the unpaid position because I believed that one answer to protecting and preserving our farming heritage was to find ways to convince farmers to place their land into land conservation easements, and to try to compensate them in some way for doing that.

And I believed that if citizens of Buncombe County truly value the pastoral beauty and farming heritage of the region, then we could find ways to fairly compensate farmers for placing their land into a conservation or agricultural easement that will lock it down forever.

I believe that the future will belong to those individuals, families, businesses and political leaders who develop a deeper understanding of the transformative and regenerative power of the natural world, and those who balance progress with sustainability and community resilience. That means protecting farmland.

The beauty of the natural environment is what draws most people to the Asheville region. Nature, including mountains, forests, gardens, and farmland, have significant psychological and social benefits for human beings. Studies show that immersing yourself in nature for just 20 minutes reduces blood pressure and improves cardiovascular health. Nature is good for the soul and adds to the quality of life.

But for years we've stood by and watched as farms and nature have morphed into new housing developments, shopping centers and parking lots. Most people living here have seen farmland vanish before their eyes, but until recently there hasn't been a lot of hard facts about the demise of the family farm—mostly just a lot of anecdotal evidence. Research from the American Farmland Trust is giving us a clearer picture about what's been happening around the country.

We should all just say goodbye to Iowa. Over the past two decades, the United States has lost nearly 31 million acres of land to development, which equates roughly to the size of Iowa. That's 175 acres an hour, or 3 acres every single minute.[113]

That same 31 million acres is equivalent to losing all of New York state to development in a 20-year period. And importantly, 11 million of those acres were among the best farmland in the nation; land that is classified as the most productive, most versatile and most resilient land, like the rich farmland in the Midwest. That 11 million acres of our best farmland equates to losing half of Indiana.

In the most comprehensive study ever undertaken about America's loss of agricultural lands, conducted by the American Farmland Trust and using current technologies like high resolution satellite imaging, the researchers show that nearly twice the area of farmland was lost over two decades than was previously thought or known.

As with the rest of the country, the average age of a farmer in Buncombe County is now 60 years old, so as we discussed earlier, a massive land transfer is looming as these farmers retire. We can only hope that land goes to another farmer, but the truth is, with the rising prices of farmland in Asheville now exceeding $30,000 per acre and in some locations much higher, no other farmer can afford to pay that current market value and make a living off that land from farming. The cost of farmland is integral to the profitability of a farming operation. The only person that can afford to pay the current market price for land in this area is a developer, not a farmer. That's a problem.

While we face the risk of losing farming as a viable economic industry, we also risk losing the pastoral beauty of the region that brought many of us here, and at the same time lose our ability to grow some of our own food. As I think we've fairly established, this loss of food sovereignty comes with its own attendant risks, like dependence on food from far-away places. Protecting and preserving our capacity to grow food creates food security, while also benefitting the local economy, creating jobs and adding to regional quality of life. Resilient communities of the future must protect and preserve agriculture and the food producing capacity of their region.

Current programs are available to preserve and protect farmland, like conservation easements that restrict future development, but they don't really compensate farmers for giving up the 'best use' value of the land. By voluntarily giving up future development rights on his land through a permanent conservation easement, a farmer is likely giving up as much as half the value of his land if and when he ever goes to sell it. Without the development rights, you take developers right out of the equation. And since developers won't be bidding on the farm property, prices might remain affordable for the next generation of farmers.

By giving up development rights through a conservation easement on farmland near Asheville, the farmer could be giving up millions of dollars that would otherwise go in his pocket. He or his wife, his children, or grandchildren, may need that money someday. So it takes a farmer with a big heart and a deep love of the land to place a permanent conservation easement on his property. Those that do it are local heroes in my book.

It's all part of a systemic problem when farmland prices rise quickly because of development pressure or Wall Street investors. If the cash value of the land far exceeds the potential farming revenue or income stream, it's at risk for the selling block. Take my neighbor Lynn for example. She operates one of the last dairy farms in the county, milks her 200 cows at five in the morning and five in the evening, every day, including Sundays and holidays. She has to because dairy cattle must be milked every day. And last year, because of lower milk prices, she didn't make any money. Meanwhile she's sitting on 180 acres of high value land that could sell to a developer tomorrow for over $7 million dollars. Why not quit milking cows and just be a rich person? Good question.

Now put a conservation easement on the land that prohibits future development, and the cash value of the land drops in half or more. Lynn would be giving up about $3.5 million dollars in order to protect her land and ensure that it's never developed and always open farmland, forever. That's why it takes a great love of the land to want to protect it forever.

I joined the county land conservation advisory board because I believed that we needed new ideas and funding to financially compensate farmers in some way for conserving farmland, and to encourage more of it. Because if we don't, it'll all be gone before long.

Some other ideas out there include the 'agrihood' model, like what we built at Creekside Farm, where homes are concentrated on a smaller piece of the farmland, and the bulk of the farm is kept intact as a valuable amenity to the new neighborhood.

Other ideas were floating around out there like Transfer Development Rights (TDR's) that allow a farmer to sell his development rights to a developer for cash. The developer can then use those TDR's in another location that has been specifically designated and planned by the county for concentrated development.

Taxes or municipal bonds might be used to help reimburse farmers for conserving land. In Asheville, the convention and tourism board collects millions of dollars from a tax on hotel rooms every year, called an occupancy tax, and a large portion of that money might be used to compensate farmers when they conserve farmland. County and city officials in many regions often find this kind of tax a great source of revenue because people who stay in local hotels aren't from around here and won't be the ones voting you out of office. Nice.

I like this idea because visitors come to this area to enjoy nature and the pastoral beauty of the region and would probably appreciate the fact that a portion of their 'occupancy tax' went to preserving it—since they're going to be paying the tax anyway.

The simplest and best form of revenue for our purposes, it seems to me, is to just levy a tax against any developer or development that intends to cover up farmland with lots of homes, and we would simply levy those taxes as part of the county permitting process for the development. The developer will of course pass along that cost to home buyers. But to me, it's a form of restitution, compensation for the negative impact on our overall community resilience, and it might slow the sprawl. There are often state laws that might restrict a county from doing something like this, so an initiative like this might have to start at the state level.

There are other ideas for sources of revenue that could compensate farmers for placing conservation easements on their land and protecting the future food capacity of a region, probably enough to fill another book.

At the county I was an official, a land conservation board member, and still a rebel food fighter. I spent a lot of time looking at maps and satellite images, like I was planning out the battlefield. Development pressure was increasing on the south side, and we needed to shore up defenses there. Some big shot land speculator was moving bulldozers to the west, try to cut him off. A profitable farm is the best defense, and potatoes and onions, root crops, became our land mines in front of these guys.

I believed that I might have the future on my side if we could hold them off. Because I believed the future is going way beyond green homes and electric cars. It's moving toward sustainability—sustainability to the point of self-reliance, and anyone in land planning or urban design should understand that. The local food movement is booming, and so, for now, we have retained much of the knowledge and capacity to grow some of our own food in Buncombe County. But that is changing quickly as farmland disappears to development.

We're losing capacity before we even fully recognize its value and importance.

The other side of the development equation must be mentioned here. There is a current housing shortage in the Asheville region, particularly for affordable housing. It affects lower-income individuals, including some of the farm workers and food service workers who prop up the tourist industry and help to make Asheville a 'foodtopia.' The only answer I have for that is to try to condense housing and infill as much as we can within city limits and try to limit the sprawl.

The region where I live is blessed with a bounty of natural resources, miles of undisturbed landscape, beautiful rolling hills and green mountains, lush forests, scenic vistas, lots of waterfalls and miles of hiking trails and river frontage. And at the heart of it all are citizens who want to protect and preserve some of that.

In the year 2018, six billion of the world's seven billion inhabitants owned a cell phone (more than a toilet). Yet with all this communication and technology, with a world of information at our fingertips, the world does not see.

The spray-painted message on the wall was this: The revolution will not be televised!

The radicals of the left were supposed to deliver the revolution in the 60s and 70s, and the people would rise up and put down their oppressors.

But that real revolution was a different kind of revolution. And parts of it were televised, between the sitcoms and the game shows. In fact, television made the revolution—the first food revolution. And the people fighting for this food revolution back then were the food scientists in laboratories and Big Ag and the Wall Street traders and the Madmen in the marketing departments. They revolutionized the food industry and changed it forever with a TV dinner. With this the multinationals slowly but surely took over the food processing and distribution centers. Soon, they controlled all of it.

Meanwhile, the radicals on the left became the counter-revolutionaries. They organized farmer's markets and began community supported agriculture programs. They tilled small plots of land and grew food organically and sustainably without all the chemicals. In the latter part of the 20th century, the counterrevolutionaries grew stronger.

So it is that the rebel food fighters are not the revolutionaries, but the counterrevolutionaries. They would not tolerate the systemic changes and tried to put things back the way they were, before all the chemicals and the damage to the environment and the take-over by multinationals. And in that way, they were the conservatives, and rebel food fighters today are still the counterrevolutionaries.

CHAPTER SEVEN

CLIMATE

On the day that the Fall Harvest Festival arrived, there were several radical signs posted around the farm, and they said things like, "To be dependent on food from far-away places is not Freedom."

Another sign read, "Our land is turning to dust while our farmers are going Bust!"

And of course, there was my personal favorite which we often used at other events and sometimes posted at the farmers market, "Whoever controls the food, controls you!"

Other signs said, "Get cows back on pasture!" and "Feed lots only exist because they are subsidized by our tax dollars—$25 Billion Annually!" And closely related to that, "Stop the Confined Animal Feed Operations!"

We had farmer food fighters selling produce and pumpkins at various stands. We had food fighters running the "pet a donkey" booth, and I'm not sure what the whole point of that was, but I think the kids liked it. We had poet food fighters pouring wine and beer at one tent, and some artist food fighters serving salad and fresh baked breads at another. Tents and tables and chairs were scattered around the gardens. Mumford ran his 1942 Farm All tractor and let kids sit on it while parents took pictures. I had a couple of my tractors there on display.

The Creekside Farm Education Center was buzzing with activity in the kitchen and all around the old red schoolhouse.

Butch set up a pop-up market tent near the entrance to the gardens. He was holding Albert Einswine, our little piglet, wearing a colorful, checkered flannel shirt and shorts and sporting a studded leash that wrapped around his belly and front legs. He went with the flannel, I thought. Good choice, very farmer like. Just glad it wasn't the cop uniform.

Butch had purchased the outfit on the internet and the shirt was a little tight on Albert. It must have been made for a smaller dog like a chihuahua, but there was no way to try it on before he made the purchase. Butch didn't bring little Albert into PetSmart to try on outfits, probably because he was afraid that if Albert got loose, he'd be gone. He's really fast, and there is no way in hell anyone would catch him tearing around the aisles and store displays. He's like greased lightning. So, the too-tight flannel shirt would have to do, and Albert didn't seem to mind too much.

Butch made a large banner and draped it across the front of the table that read: "Society for the Decency of Naked Animals." He just stood there holding Albert, who was quite cooperative, and it was a hit. Most people just wanted to check out the cute little piglet, but the sign also intrigued a lot of people and drew them over to his table. Butch got to talk to a lot of people that day. His sign could have said "Free Beer" and he wouldn't have talked to more people.

I stood by and watched for a few moments. He'd start the conversation with something like this:

"We at the Society for the Decency of Naked Animals want to ensure that all animals have the moral decency to wear appropriate clothing. We think it is apprehensible and morally repugnant to allow an animal to prance around naked in this day and age."

He used a lot of the language from the evangelical right and could go on for several minutes in a serious tone without cracking up or even a smile. I don't know how he did it. I think a lot of people at first weren't sure if he was serious or just crazy, until eventually he would start smiling or burst out laughing. Then he'd start talking about other things. How farmers are hurting, about the industrialized food system, about childhood obesity and the globalization and concentration of the food supply. He got over 100 people to sign up for our newsletter and email distribution list.

While most people attending the harvest festival were CSA members or friends of farming and were acutely aware of the very serious nature of the many systemic problems in the food industry, including hunger and terrible injustice, I think they understood that Butch did not mean to make light of these serious issues. It just gave him a platform to talk to people, and they understood that. And it helped him reach a couple people who otherwise might not have stopped by his little booth.

Humor sometimes helps people transcend the moment and look at things a little differently and from an altered state or viewpoint. It can often be a way to break through to someone, and a well-timed bit of humor or satire can sometimes completely change a person's perspective on things. It might at least open someone up to a conversation.

As grumpy as he was sometimes, Butch could be very funny. Wit and humor as a character trait can be linked to creativity and intelligence.[114] This is certainly true of Butch. His humor was often very clever, and he was quite adept at describing the irony of the human condition and the silliness of it all.

Emails from Butch were often full of witty and humorous stories and anecdotes that sometimes could touch a chord and deftly illustrate the incongruity of human nature. Usually, it was related to some dumb or silly act he or someone we both knew may have done, but his humor was never mean spirited or hurtful.

Humor can sometimes be transcendent and connect you to something with a much deeper meaning. And this is the value of humor—it can sometimes replace the hardness, gloom and fear in life with more positive, lighthearted feelings. It was welcome relief given the often-serious nature of our environmental cause. It might even relieve some anger, tension and depression, and may at some point keep a person from saying the hell with it, especially in a fight against what seems an impossible and overwhelming challenge. Butch understood that laughing at the absurd and the irony in the world is sometimes a healthy way to deal with it, both physically and psychologically.

Humor can be a sign of maturity, like wisdom. I think it is related to the insight that the world is an imperfect place, and nothing is permanent or as it seems. This insight leads to a deeper understanding of the human condition and the shortcomings and sometimes the unfairness of life. Nothing in this world is fair or perfect, and sometimes people have to understand that, grow to tolerate it, and ultimately let it go. Humor helps us do that. Butch's cousin Mumford, who could wear a coonskin hat to a scientific convention, understood this imperfection and incongruity, and in his own way mocked it with a fur hat.

Our Fall Harvest Festival was really a local food festival and included tents and booths for other local growers, makers of prepared foods and local crafts, tents for a couple non-profits like ASAP and Organic Growers School, a food truck and a couple of local restaurants that featured local food. The attendees included our CSA member families and friends, food fighters from various backgrounds and occupations, and neighbors from the surrounding community. We had a three-string band playing old time Appalachian music, and more tents with tables spread along the edges of the gardens for people to just sit.

We allowed for one featured speaker, Lewis Mumford, and when the time came, he climbed the steps of porch at the front of the old schoolhouse and began to speak as people started to gather around. After welcoming everyone to the event and thanking them for coming, he said:

"Industrial farming in the US and around the world is ruining the planet and destroying family farms and the web of life in rural communities." A murmur went through the crowd.

"Farmers and growers around the world have shown that it is possible to adopt a sustainable approach to farming that can produce enough nutritious food without destroying the soil that grows it. We cannot stand by and watch, year after year, as many of this country's precious landscapes are slowly diminished in the name of efficiency."

Whispers and grumbles could be heard coming from the crowd, and a small voice was heard "Hear, Hear."

"Huge swaths of this country today are carpeted in large-scale single-crop fields, deploying heavy loads of fertilizer and pesticides, in landscapes that would be unrecognizable a few generations ago. Landscapes that have been dubbed 'green deserts' by some ecologists because they are barren of other life, and food deserts because they grow nothing that we can eat."

Now the crowd was starting to get excited, and the mutter, hum and buzz was growing louder.

"Populations of common birds and insects in North America have plummeted, just as small towns have been broken and withered away. We've allowed industrial agriculture to rip the heart out of the American countryside. And a dark, stupefying shadow has settled over the landscape. And it brought with it despair, meth labs and opioid addiction."

"Stop the Tyranny!" came a loud voice from the back. The crowd began to erupt in a unified strident objection. There were vocal radicals now in attendance.

"The emphasis on producing cheap food threatens the very survival of this nation's farms. Free trade deals have over-whelmed the markets with cheap vegetables, and now meat—food that is produced with cheap labor, almost slave labor, in developing nations!" His tone and volume started to rise to match the excitement coming from the crowd as they grew louder still.

"Nature must be part of the equation, my friends. How we produce food has a direct impact on the Earth's capacity to sustain us, which has a direct impact on human health and economic prosperity.

"With the new federal climate mandates, like transition-ing federal vehicles to electric, should come laws and regula-tions that help to transform the farming economy. Public tax money should go for public good, and not Wall Street investors or corporate monopolies. And that farmland transformation must include protecting bees, butterflies, birds, streams, and wetlands, because a more sustainable agriculture improves the health of the environment that we all depend on."

Cheers and clapping erupted from the crowd.

"Continuing to pay subsidies for agriculture that continues to degenerate the soil and landscape is collective insanity." The crowd roared at this. "No More!" they said.

"By reversing that trend in agriculture, and if we can regen-erate degraded soils around the world, we could capture as much as 70 percent of the world's carbon emissions. Our chil-dren's future depends on this!"

"We must stand together in this fight. We must grow food in more sustainable and regenerative ways. We must cut the food miles associated with our dinner. And so, I ask you, my friends and neighbors, to call your congressmen and women. Send a letter or an email to your senators. Get involved in this food movement and buy local whenever you can!"

Another roar went up from the crowd. Teams of people went up to greet Mumford as he walked down the steps, and they offered to shake his hand with great enthusiasm.

Other than that, we ate some local food, drank local beer, listened to some local music, and tried to be local. We had a grand time.

There is more carbon dioxide in the atmosphere than at any point in the past 3.6 million years.

The last time Earth held this much carbon dioxide in its atmosphere, sea levels were nearly 80 feet higher, and the planet was 7 degrees warmer. Homo sapiens did not yet exist, so we can't know how well our species would have adapted to these conditions. But many paleontologists believe that the extinction of all ancient human species, including homo erectus and Neanderthals, came because of climatic changes. Take a deep time perspective, and you can see that climate change has had some devastating effects on our ancient ancestors and many other species.

Homo erectus, by the way, wasn't all that unintelligent, and I'm not even sure if it's politically correct or not to say that since he is an ancestor to modern homo sapiens. He lived from

1.3 million years ago until about 300,000 years ago, roughly one million years on earth and much longer than the roughly 300,000 years that we've been on this planet. We're still the newbies, the nubes, on this planet.

But homo erectus was, anatomically, very similar to modern humans. The proportions of his arms and legs were basically the same and he walked upright just like us. His brain cavity was smaller, but there is evidence that he kept and used fire. There is also surprising evidence that he was able to build a boat that helped him to leave stone tools and other evidence of his existence on remote islands that were separated by water in his time. That required forethought and probably months of planning.

As a hunter-gatherer he was obviously dialed-in to nature— very much aware of his food source and capable of survival in his environment, which in fact is not true of most modern homo sapiens. Most people can't tell an edible plant from a poisonous one in the wild, let alone identify a particular vege- table growing in a field. And yet there was nothing he could do when the climate started changing but perish. Another species, Neanderthals, would take his place for a while, but they too succumbed to another change in climate. And countless other species of plants and animals have suffered the same fate brought on by climate change over time. Climate—including heat, cold, rain, drought—no matter how well you can cope with it, will inevitably affect your food source.

Evolution has probably made us a little smarter than homo erectus. But maybe we're just a little too smart for our own britches. That's farmer talk, and I'm not exactly sure what it means, but I think it has something to do with over-confidence or arrogance. We as a species have ample evidence of a chang- ing, warming climate, and we have evidence in the historical record how changes in the environment have affected agriculture and led to the collapse of many ancient civilizations. Will the arrogance of man leave us unprepared for the next climatic event?

The Hurricane

Almost all scientists agree that stronger hurricanes and more flooding can be expected with a warming climate.

The full extent of the damage from Hurricane Florence in September of 2018, which dropped 8 trillion gallons of water on my home state of North Carolina, is hard to fathom. While coastal towns like Wilmington and Bern were in the national news when the hurricane made landfall, Florence stalled soon after making landfall and dumped devastating amounts of rain on inland farming communities.

Not far from my home, the rains came down hard and then stopped, and later, the creeks and rivers rose and spilled their banks and flooded the fields and towns long after the rains had stopped. Where was the disconnect? Didn't the river know that the rains had stopped. People were already out and about when the floods came.

When the storm came it was still the height of harvest season – with corn, peanuts, cotton, and sweet potatoes still in the ground. All of it was lost to flood waters as rivers continued to swell and crest banks weeks after the hurricane made landfall.

An estimated 3.4 million chickens were confirmed killed in the floods that followed Hurricane Florence. About 5,500 hogs drowned, according to the Department of Agriculture, and some of the massive lagoons that hold their excrement were damaged, discharging a fecal soup into nearby streams and rivers.

North Carolina has 10.5 million people, 9 million hogs and 830 million chickens. It ranks second among US states in pounds of chicken produced each year, and second in number of hogs. As we've discussed, most of the big farms contract with big agribusinesses, such as Smithfield Foods and JBS. Nevertheless, it was the farmer who took the financial hit from the storm in damages to buildings and infrastructure, and the loss of crops and livestock.

The damage from the hurricane caused other environmental devastation. Of particular note, a dam owned by Duke Energy breached at one of its plants, and coal ash began flowing into the Cape Fear River. Coal ash is known to contain arsenic and other dangerous chemicals. The list of environmental damage from the storm goes on, but the scary thing is that the number and severity of storms like this will continue to increase.

Climate and Agriculture

When most people think about solving climate change, they think about electricity, with wind and solar and electric cars solving all our problems. But as I really began to dig into the subject, I discovered that these are just pieces of the larger and more complicated puzzle.

There are several human activities that produce greenhouse gasses, including building and manufacturing which represents about 31% of greenhouse gasses; producing electricity- about 27%; farming and agriculture- roughly 19%; and transportation- another 16%; and lastly, heating and refrigeration- another 7%. When you add the greenhouse gas emissions from the transportation of food, and the necessary inputs, to the growing of food, it becomes a bigger piece of the climate pie, and could approach 30% of global emissions. Agriculture has a big climate footprint.[115]

What can we do to reduce carbon emissions in food production? While carbon dioxide is the main culprit for climate change, in agriculture it's methane—which causes 28 times more warming per molecule then CO_2—and nitrous oxide, which causes 265 times more warming.

Climate warming methane comes from cow burps and flatulence, and nitrous oxide comes from crop fertilizers. Fertilizing crops for animal feed is a double whammy on climate.

Emissions from agriculture will continue to go up, not just from feeding a growing global population expected to hit 9 billion by 2050, but from a world population that continues to climb out of poverty, and while getting richer, begins to eat more meat. As countries like China become wealthier, they can afford more of the American diet, which means more meat, and meat consumption rates are climbing quickly there.

Producing more meat and dairy will require the world to produce a lot more food because a chicken, for instance, must eat two calories worth of grain to produce one calorie of poultry for human consumption, and a chicken is one of the better converters of calories. A pig eats three times as many calories as it produces, and a cow needs to eat six calories for every calorie of beef.[116]

In other words, as population increases and developing nations begin to eat more of the meat heavy American diet, we'll need to produce a lot more grain, up to six times as much grain. That will significantly increase global emissions from the agriculture sector when the goal is net zero emissions, and really, drawdown—pulling carbon out of the atmosphere and storing it in the soil.

The other big contributor to climate change on the farm comes from fertilizers. Plants need nitrogen to grow, and they'll keep growing as long as they get plenty of it. Plants get nitrogen in nature from ammonia that is produced by microbes in the soil. Making ammonia takes a lot of energy for these little micro-organisms, so they only make it when it's needed. Dump tons of nitrogen on the soil and the microbes don't make any at all— because they don't need to. It disrupts the natural cycle.

But the problem comes from dumping too much fertilizer on the land and it ends up running into creeks and streams causing pollution, and when it escapes into the air in the form of nitrous oxide (again, 265 times the climate warming effect of carbon dioxide.) Several studies have shown that as much as half the nitrogen is wasted from over application at the farm.

If fertilizer makes the corn grow, most farmers might say, let's add a little more just to be sure. And then we'll add a little more for good measure. I do that with tequila when I'm making a margarita, so I understand it. The manufacturing of fertilizer, using fossil fuels, and then transporting it around the world, adds further to the climate effects of fertilizer.

Food waste (in the U.S., as much as 40% of our food is wasted) and deforestation (such as the clearing of the Amazon rain forest for more cow pasture) are other big contributors to climate change from agriculture.

Regenerative agriculture practices, including organic and no till methods of farming, cover crops, and crop rotation are key in the battle for climate. Building microbial life in the soil, including the important bacteria and mycorrhizal fungi, is the key to storing tons of carbon in the soil. Many scientists have come to the conclusion that sustainable farming practices can be our most cost-effective way to pull carbon from the atmosphere. The question is, how do we get farmers to grow more sustainably and regeneratively? How do we get them to reduce soil erosion and use cover crops? New carbon credits might be one solution that can help.

Carbon Credits

Agriculture captures carbon, that's a known fact. It goes back to what you learned in elementary school about photosynthesis. Plants harness the energy from the sun, draw carbon dioxide from the air and water from the soil and then convert it into sugars that they use for growth and energy. Plants also pump more of these carbon-based sugars down into the soil through their roots to feed microbes in the soil, and that's where the real carbon storage benefits come in. Microbes in turn break down minerals and other nutrients that the plant can easily absorb and use. Scientists are just starting to learn more about this amazing reciprocal relationship that developed as plants and microbes co-evolved together over millions of years. This carbon storage mechanism is the key to carbon sequestration and mitigating climate change for the future. I cannot say this enough because it's really, really important.[117]

Forget the sci-fi fantasy that someone will invent a machine that pulls excess carbon out of the atmosphere. Science has already pretty much proven that any such machine will use more energy and generate more CO_2 than it can pull. And the machine already exists anyway. It's called a plant, and the process is called photosynthesis, and it uses the sun's energy to do the trick.

Bare ground releases carbon into the atmosphere. Keeping the ground covered during winter with cover crops also protects the soil from erosion and keeps the plant-based carbon storage cycle going throughout the year. Using cover crops, no till planting methods, better nutrient management, and crop diversity, allows the soil to build its microbiome and the ability to store more carbon. The soil becomes healthier and more resilient to flooding or drought because of its ability to soak up and hold more water. Healthier soils and plants can become a massive carbon sucking machine that covers the earth year-round. Some of these regenerative practices cost money, like seed cost for cover crops. How do we convince farmers to spend the cash? Find ways to give them the cash.

The only really good news for our future is that consumers are beginning to demand more sustainable practices as the effects of climate change are increasingly visible, and sometimes catastrophic. Consumers want to know that the products they're purchasing have been produced sustainably and are not having negative impacts on the environment. They want to buy from companies that are working to reduce their carbon footprint. So, it's good business for companies to go 'carbon neutral', and as more companies pledge to go carbon neutral, interest in creating a market for carbon credits through agriculture is growing.

Corporations can try to reduce their carbon footprint from normal business operations, but they can also pay for carbon credits to offset the remaining carbon that they still emit from their business, and soon they may be able to buy those carbon credits from farmers. This idea may go a long way toward convincing farmers to use cover crops in the winter, simply because we're paying them to do so. Nationally, less than 6% of farmers use cover crops.[118] Here in the Asheville region, about 60% of farmers use cover crops, and that's because they help to prevent soil erosion on our hills and slopes. In the massive corn belt of the Midwest, it's a different story.

While these carbon markets and programs are still new, pilot programs exist that will pay farmers if their soils show a marked increase in carbon storage. And while there's still debate about just how much carbon farmers can intentionally draw from the air and deposit into the soil in the process we call carbon sequestration, these new carbon markets appear to be growing. And from what we know right now, a good goal for any farmer is adding 1 ton of carbon per acre to the soil per year. That seems doable for most farmers using no till or limited till planting and cover crops. A 1000-acre farm could reasonably capture and store 1000 tons of carbon every year. That's not a small number. Let's think about that for a second. That's two million pounds of carbon, or the weight of over 13,000 people standing on that plot of land. It's a lot of carbon.

Under current carbon market prices offered by a few organizations and non-profits, the farmer receives $15 per ton of carbon stored, per acre. That's not enough, because it costs about $25 per acre just for cover crop seed. Prices for carbon credits need to be higher to really combat climate change. A World Bank report suggests prices would need to rise to at least $40 or $80 per ton to drive "transformational change" and get enough farmers on board to realistically bring down atmospheric carbon levels. It's probably going to have to be $35 or $40 per ton just to move the needle.

There also needs to be more regulation and standardization around carbon markets for it to become a real climate fighting tool. Currently there's no USDA farm programs around carbon sequestration or carbon credits, nothing like we have in crop insurance. And there is no consensus on how to best assess soil for carbon gains. Still, by the end of 2021, voluntary carbon market transactions were near $900 million globally for the year, a new record. The trading of greenhouse gas emissions started in the early 1990s, but it has accelerated recently due to a rapid increase of net-zero, carbon neutral and other climate change-related commitments from corporations. That's all good.

For the farmer, there is also a promise of long-term financial savings and increased yields that come with switching to regenerative farming methods. It's just difficult to convince a farmer to change his ways, particularly since his livelihood depends on a good harvest every year. Restructuring existing USDA programs may be helpful, as many farmers point out that those programs, like crop insurance, can actually disincentivize practices like cover cropping. For a carbon credit program to work, the economics must be there.

There is hope that food grown through regenerative agriculture may find its own space on supermarket shelves, possibly through a label like that used for organically grown food. Perhaps a label on packaging might someday say something like "Grown with Regenerative Agriculture" or "Carbon Smart" or "Climate Friendly", or something that has meaning. Again, we need to standardize what all that means. If the farmer uses no till and cover crops on his wheat fields, how do we say that on the packaging for a loaf of bread that will differentiate it from the bread next to it, so a customer can choose?

The world dumps about 50 gigatons of carbon into the atmosphere annually, or 50,000 tons.[119] Regenerative farming practices, some studies suggest, could sequester somewhere between ten and twenty gigatons of carbon dioxide worldwide each year. Twenty gigatons is about the weight of 90 billion people or twelve times the world's current population. It's also nearly two-thirds of all emissions from energy consumption across the globe in 2019, according to the International Energy Agency. Pulling 20 gigatons from the atmosphere, along with limiting emissions with electric cars and renewable energy, goes a long way toward a carbon neutral future. Agriculture cannot do it all, but it can be a quick and affordable part of the solution.

Mike McConnell on Climate Change

If we don't do anything to pull carbon out of the atmosphere, what kind of future are we looking at? I went to see Mike McConnell, former Director of the NSA, to see if he had some answers.

Mike had a second home just across the South Carolina border. He kept a home outside of Washington, DC but was "in the process" of retiring at the time. That didn't mean stop working. I knew that he was involved in the development of a new agricultural community called Riverstead as one of his retirement projects. He was good friends with the developer, who I also happened to know.

We met at a large, beautiful pavilion at this new community in the 'Upstate' of South Carolina. The pavilion was constructed out of trees cut and hewn off the property and overlooking a high green ridge, part of the Appalachian Mountains that ran along the border of North and South Carolina.

After some small talk, and Mike is a very courteous and pleasant person to speak with, I asked him this question.

"I've heard the term agri-terrorism a few times. Can you tell me about that and the NSA's investigations into this threat?"

"Nope," he replied.

Man, that was direct, I thought. Not the answer I expected or wanted but I left it alone.

I changed gears and started asking Mike about the security risks and threats related to climate change. It was the real reason I'd come to see him, and a better question, and he answered by saying:

"The senate oversight committee, who had to vote on my confirmation, said they wanted an assessment from me on the impacts of climate change on national security."

Mike said that he did the work and suggested that I google "DNI (Director National Intelligence) Threat Assessment" and I can read for myself the last several years of reports from the directors, and they all pretty much say the same thing, which is, that the threat from climate change is real.

"So, the fact of climate change is hard to refute. Now we could argue about what causes it or what we might need to do about it, but here's what's going to happen if we don't address it in some pretty dramatic way.

"Warmer climate means two things: floods and drought. Floods in coastal areas like Charleston or Savannah or New Orleans, or San Diego or wherever. That's going to happen. And more incidences of drought mean the areas with modest rainfall will dry up. When that happens, crops fail. And when that starts to happen on a global scale mass migration becomes a strategic problem."

Not to mention a humanitarian nightmare, I thought to myself.

"There will be food shortages. There will be border wars. There will be water scarcity and countries will fight over water. Countries will fight over the fact that migrants are going from one country to another."

This was scary stuff, and my mind wandered, and I started to wonder if there was anything that we could or would do about it. Was it really just related to the difficulty of identifying cause and effect in our modern world? We may see the train barreling down the track, but we do nothing, frozen. Maybe we just fail to recognize that a little pain now saves a lot of pain later. And perhaps it's all related to our selfish inclination. It's easier to just ignore the warning signs and keep it rolling, full speed ahead.

Maybe it wasn't related to our inability to identify cause and effect, like ice caps slowly melting, but maybe sometimes it is just so annihilating to face the truth. What is the motivation for inaction? Is the potential devastation too scary to talk about, to deal with it, to even anticipate it?

It couldn't just be greed, I thought, that causes us to ignore a possible outcome, could it? We're certainly smart enough to understand the risks and potential outcomes of our actions but are those outcomes just so overwhelming that we simply bury our heads in the sand. Why is it so hard to get people to understand the science and to see the truth?

"So, what happens next, Mike?" I asked.

"What this will lead to is a rise in simple solutions, known as populism."

We were already seeing the trend toward populism in relation to migration on a large scale. Brexit was a direct result of British fear about an influx of migrants from the Middle East and Africa into the United Kingdom. President Trump was elected largely for the same reason and his promise to build a wall. People are migrating from Central America for various reasons, and the wave of populism that swept through this country, as it has the world, is related to this movement of people.

Later Mike told me that he spent a lot of his time flying around to meet with top banks, businesses and universities trying to warn them about the need to improve cyber-security. He said, "Ya' know, almost all of the banking transactions end up going through four large banks, and mostly just one in New York."

My stomach tightened, though I was not surprised. Of course. Food is consolidated and we can see how it benefits a few at the top. It follows that banking is of the same design. Mike said he was a little put off by some of the arrogance and neglect he encountered among some of the CEOs at the largest banks. Fortunately, he was in a position to make them listen, and he probably ended up saving them billions from hackers.

Mike still mows his own lawn. His wife tells him that he can certainly afford to pay someone to mow the lawn, but he thinks men should mow their own lawn, and so he does. And it's a big yard that takes him four hours to mow, he told me. I asked if he ever considered planting an edible yard of perennials, and that went over like a fart in a space suit. So I asked if he had a big Z-turn mower for the job, which he does. A Z-turn mower is the kind that has two handles in front, not a steering wheel, and professional mowers use them because they're fast and they turn on a dime. I told Mike that I have one at the farm also, which I love almost as much as my tractors. This led to another brief story.

"Ya' know, as director of the NSA I got to drive an M1-A1 Abrams Tank once. And that tank drives with handles just like a Z-turn mower."

"Really? Did you get to blow anything up?" I asked.

"Yea, I got three shots with it. The first was bad, I was a little jittery and didn't aim properly. But the second shot, I blew the hell out of a tree." I felt a slight carbon burn from that, but I have to admit it sounded exciting and I wished I was there to see it.

"Dude, that is so cool." I just called the man 'Dude', and

I thought, 'I have got to get one of those!' Excessive and unnecessary, yes, but we could park it down on Avery Creek Road when the zombie apocalypse starts, so it would be a justifiable purchase.

By this time, I'm thinking Mike's a pretty cool guy with a very interesting life. In addition to many of the nation's highest military awards for meritorious service, Mike holds the nation's highest award for service in the Intelligence Community. He was highly regarded and highly sought after by the private sector because he knows what he's talking about.

I asked him, "What are the risks we face related to climate here in this country?"

"If we don't address these issues involving climate change and social order, like mass migration, then we're in trouble. The immigrants who are fleeing El Salvador and Guatemala and Honduras are leaving there because the living conditions are already unbearable. So how do we really address migration? Helping to change the living conditions in those countries is a good start."

Then he rattled off the risks in quick succession, and it sounded like the unfolding plot of a disaster movie.

"Global climate change, crop failures, water shortage, drought, mass migration, global coastal flooding, border conflicts that could result in chaos across the region. These are some of the threats. Mass migration has to be addressed in a variety of forms from climate change, but there are also endemic issues and problems in various governments."

It was a scary list that came from him without having to think about it for a second. I had to wonder how the problems in those countries might be connected to America's corporate-dominated politics, trade, and foreign policy. Somehow it was all connected, I thought.

"What can or should the United States do about these global threats?" I asked.

"It is wise to do our homework and try to be prepared," Mike replied.

"That is the value of foresight and planning," he said. "To see something coming and do something about it. That is what makes a community resilient."

Foresight requires a person to understand cause and effect, and a theme kept emerging for me that explained a lot of our problems. It was man's inability to see and recognize cause and effect in the modern world—our inability to put the two things together. That or our blind refusal to acknowledge it.

People have difficulty seeing connections in the modern world. Our world view is often complicated, distorted and confusing, and it is often difficult to determine and distinguish cause and effect when we cannot even accept and agree upon obvious facts, like the polar ice caps are melting because the world is getting warmer. There is often a long delay in the timing of cause and effect, and then another delay in the mind's recognition and understanding.

The axe in the Amazon flashed in the sunlight as it raged toward the tree. Across the river and at some distance, a rancher saw the sparkle of the silvery axe as it came down on the tree, but he heard nothing. A few moments later, the sound came with a crack that echoed across the river.

There was another delay in recognition, while his mind put together the two things, the flash of the ax and the sound that came later.

Climate Migration in Buncombe County

After my conversation with Mike, I decided to do a little more research on this climate migration thing. You can plan for a more resilient community and region, one that can feed and support itself with locally produced goods, but rapid migration can screw up the best of plans, like having a bunch of uninvited guests show up for a dinner party.

Unless everyone is preparing for a future that could include climate disruption, then we're all at risk. The entire southwest faces a serious water shortage problem. Large parts of Florida and the eastern seaboard face flooding and sea level rise. Huge cities like Miami and Houston, with large populations, could overwhelm other regions if people needed to migrate en masse. I did some reading, and then decided to talk to some people who might have something to say about climate migration closer to home.

My original concern was related to the loss of valuable farmland around Asheville. Lots of people were already moving here and farmland was getting developed at a worrying pace. If we did nothing, it would all be lost to development, and then we wouldn't have the capacity, the land, to feed ourselves. On top of that, we'd lose our farming heritage, which is a terrible thing to lose.

I had to ask the question: Are the threats of more frequent and severe weather patterns, including risks of drought, wildfires, hurricanes, and flooding, already causing some early signs of 'climate migration' into Buncombe County? Are we already seeing now the early signs of a more ominous, long-term migration in this country?

And who did I ask? Your friendly, neighborhood real estate professional, of course. I wanted to find out what they've been hearing from their clients as reasons for moving here. I hunkered down for a few days and spoke to about 50 of them. I emailed hundreds more from an email database that I received from a friend in real estate.

I asked this simple question; "Regardless of whether or not you believe in climate change, have you had a client say that they are moving here from Florida, Houston or New Orleans because of concern over hurricanes or flooding?"

As a sidenote to all of this, I had to preface the question with "Regardless of whether or not you believe in climate change" because after a test email blast to about 50 agents, I received an abrupt response from one guy that said, "There is no such thing as climate change! Take me off your email list!"

I didn't care what the old fart thought about climate change, I wanted to know what his clients might be saying about climate change and did this influence their decision to move here.

The answer was, almost unanimously, yes. Of over 100 surveys and emailed answers, almost all said yes, and most respondents had a personal story that they wanted to tell me about a client. One poor guy lost two homes to wildfires in California before he finally gave up and moved here. In almost every case, it was the client's belief or perception of risk that was driving the move to Asheville.

"It's not crack-pots, preppers or survivalists," said John Haynes from Retreat Realty in Asheville. "It's normal people looking for some kind of safe haven in a time of uncertainty."

And they were coming from all over, from coastal Florida to Houston to California, to avoid some perceived climate related threat. One agent said many of his clients are worried about rising sea levels, and "want to get out now while they can still sell at a decent price." Another said that the rising cost of insurance will make many homes on the coast uninsurable soon.

"Mother Nature didn't intend for millions of people to live in the desert, but people still move to Phoenix and Las Vegas, even though huge battles are now raging out west over water rights," said Josh Smith with Walnut Cove Realty. It didn't make any sense in the context of climate change. Phoenix is not a very resilient place to live with the heat and lack of water, and it's almost impossible to grow food in the desert.

John Haynes owns a firm that specializes in security, and he says many of his clients are concerned about the power grid, food and fuel shortages, a banking collapse, or other threats that could result from a serious natural disaster, and many want to relocate away from large population centers. About half of his clients are wealthy business owners and CEO's looking for "a strategic safe haven" for their families. "Many are very well educated with PHD's," said John. "I've sold to several Hedge Fund Managers and the very rich. I've sold to many who paid over a million dollars for their land—in cash."

Some of John's clients are ex-military or law enforcement. About half of his clients are not really wealthy and would be considered 'homesteaders' looking to live closer to the land with a smaller footprint on climate and the environment. "But all have the same needs—land for crops, some livestock, and access to good water." John was describing people who were trying to bring food security and food sovereignty down to the level of the family homestead.

"It's not all about some big conspiracy theory," he said. "I see it more like the Boy Scout motto—'Be Prepared.' Our great grandparents were all 'preppers' around here, by the way, who grew, canned and stored food for winter. We need to relearn some skills that we've all forgotten."

"A lot of our risk is not necessarily from natural disasters," said John. "A lot of it is man-made. Remember that blackout several years ago that darkened the entire Northeast? A downed tree did that. Our grid is vulnerable. Many of my clients can afford to install solar and do. It's more sustainable, but also more resilient."

"We're so arrogant," John continued. "We live on a razors edge. All it takes is for someone to pull the power cord. You've read Bill Forstchen's book, One Second After, right?" Indeed, I had. I knew the guy.

"When the book came out, I sent out 700 letters to people in Charlotte offering a free copy of the book." That's an interesting marketing approach, I thought. John obviously sells a lot of property, and I wondered what Bill would think of his book being used as a real estate marketing piece.

The Asheville region is somewhat resilient compared to other cities and regions in the country. We're growing more of our own food locally and so retain some of the knowledge and capacity to grow food, which makes us less dependent on food from far-away places. And the mountains protect us and give us the first drink of water. There's plenty of rain for crops, as of now, and scientists say that we'll likely become wetter in the future with climate change. It's a good place to hunker down.

The Dust Bowl of the 1930's is our clearest example of cause and effect when it comes to poor agricultural practices, climate, and mass migration. It's also a warning about the deepening hardship and hunger that comes from not managing our farms wisely and with some foresight.

The severe dust storms that greatly damaged the ecology and agriculture of the American prairies was for the most part a man-made problem created by intensive tilling of the soil, breaking up grassland cover that had been in place for thousands of years, and then failing to plant cover crops for the winter to protect the soil from erosion. Severe drought and wind caused the inevitable devastation, which no one could see coming, because no one was looking. Periods of severe drought are common in the region.

With a complete lack of understanding of the ecology of the plains in the 1930's, farmers went about deep plowing the virgin topsoil. The native knowledge that would have helped, and the native, deep-rooted grasses that normally trapped soil and moisture even during periods of drought and high winds were tilled under, and the soil was quickly blown away.

During the drought that came in the 1930s, the unanchored soil turned to dust, which the prevailing winds blew in huge clouds that blackened the sky. These choking billows of dust – named "black blizzards" or "black rollers" – traveled cross country, reaching as far as the East Coast and darkening cities as far away as New York City and Washington, D.C. Smoke from fires in California, coincidently, is doing the same thing today, darkening skies on the other side of the continent.

On the plains, the dust storms often reduced visibility to 3 feet or less. Several people died in the storms, lost in a cloud of dust, but found later not far from their homes, sometimes just a few yards away from the front door. Many more died later from lung disease or pneumonia complicated by the dust. Thousands of farm animals also died as the farm lost its valuable topsoil, until there was nothing left to grow on. The farmers packed up old jalopies and hit the road for California, and they weren't always welcomed there. Now some of their descendants may be forced to migrate again out of California because of drought, water shortages and wildfires.

We're still blindly doing this same thing today, with only about 6% of US farmers using cover crops, and the loss of topsoil in the Midwest has been devastating. Many regions, once fertile, are now completely devoid of any topsoil at all.

Take ignorance and a lack of concern about the natural environment, tie it to man's arrogance, and then combine it with technology (like the tractor) that can magnify our impact, and what do you get? The perfect recipe for man-made devastation in the environment and the food supply. Because of the rapidity of events, the dust bowl just happens to be one of the most obvious, clearly defined examples of man's pride and ignorance related to the destruction of the environment that we can use. When things happen slowly over a longer period, it's harder to spot the problems and even harder to motivate a response from people. The ocean rises in centimeters.

A Giant Sucking Sound

As a farmer and regular food politics commentator, I have a fair understanding of food production in the United States. One of the biggest problems that we face in agriculture today, as I see it now, is an over-dependance on drought-stricken California for the bulk of our vegetables.

While we're all too familiar with the terrible wildfires in California that captured news headlines for months over the past several years, all of it related to ongoing droughts in the region, those same droughts are now disrupting food production in this country.

California is known as the vegetable basket of the country, and for good reason. Former North Carolina farmer and author of the book *Perilous Bounty*, Tom Philpott says, "Just a few clusters of water-stressed counties in one state (California) provide 81% of US grown carrots, 95% of broccoli, 78% of cauliflower, 74% of raspberries, 91% of strawberries, 66% of lettuce, 63% of tomatoes," and includes a significant amount of U.S. meat and dairy. And here in Western North Carolina, we're just as dependent on California's Central Valley as the rest of the country.[120]

After several years of drought in the Sierra Nevada mountains, the annual snowpack that feeds rivers and irrigation canals in California has been slowly receding, and as the climate changes, the situation is predicted to get much worse. A severe drought in California from 2011 to 2019 was the worst in recorded history and it followed one that was only slightly less severe from 2007 to 2009. In early 2022, scientists reported California's drought was the worst in over 1200 years.[121] Reduced snow melt forced farmers to pump more water from underground aquifers—to the point that they're reaching a critical state. If you could hear it, it would be a giant sucking sound.

Farmers in the Central Valley of California have relied on pumping more and more underground water to make up the difference for reduced rain and snowfall, until those aquifers have become dangerously depleted, and in many cases, they're already tapped out. Because of the rapid depletion, access to those underground aquifers is becoming much more regulated under the California Sustainable Groundwater Management Act of 2014 that began enforcing water pumping restrictions beginning in 2020, in the hope that the aquafers have a chance to rejuvenate to some sort of balance.

But it's a pay to play system, and large almond growers (a

high dollar specialty crop) with huge investments in infrastructure and Wall Street money behind them, are more willing to pay for water under these restrictions then vegetable growers. Millions of acres are now planted in almonds, a very thirsty crop, mostly for export to countries like Japan and China. We cannot continue draining the aquifers to produce a luxury item for export.

With the looming water crisis and water wars that are already underway, California needs to scale back agriculture to bring it in line with water realities there. US lawmakers, says farmer Philpott, "should consider putting public policy and resources behind a strategic ramp-up of produce" in other farming regions outside of California. As water resources dwindle, we can no longer depend on California for most of our fruits and vegetables. We need to diversify food production regionally.

Philpott says that California should just focus on feeding the fast-growing cities in the southwest, like Phoenix and Las Vegas, and stop trying to grow vast monocultures of almonds for China and lettuce for New York. And he's right, all farming regions of this country, and around the world, need to reorient their farm business models to feed local and regional consumers.

The Ground is Sinking

Because of the drawdown on underground water tables over recent years, the ground has been sinking by more than two feet annually in some regions of the Central Valley. With research from NASA's Jet Propulsion Laboratory, Philpott points out some of the obvious damage that has resulted from this sinking ground, which includes damage and breaks in irrigation canals, dams and pipes in the above ground system that brings snowmelt from the Sierra Nevada mountains to the Central Valley. The new dips in elevations have led to major leaks and jams in canals, reducing flow by 20 to 60% and thus creating more reliance on underground water reserves. The sinking ground has also damaged bridges, roads, houses, and other infrastructure. It all makes for a fairly obvious sign that something unusual is going on.

Farmers are having to drill deeper and deeper to hit shrinking underground water supplies. And as the water levels drop, salinization happens when minerals become more concentrated, requiring new and expensive filtration systems to reduce salts that would otherwise kill most plants and makes the water undrinkable. This puts pressure on rural communities and residents in California's Central Valley for drinking water that comes from those same aquifers. Many rural communities are forced to drink bottled water now as the minerals like salt get concentrated in the remaining underground water table.

As we become less dependent on California, which is inevitable given depleted aquifers and more drought from climate change, how does a nation learn to feed itself regionally? We can start by transitioning some of the corn belt into other crops, like vegetables and pasture raised beef to feed nearby cities like Chicago, St. Louis, and Minneapolis. The reduced demand for corn and ethanol that will come from electric vehicles should free up enough land for these other crops and grass-fed cattle operations.

But as noted already, it will take time to develop the infrastructure, resolve labor issues and distribution systems, and it would be wise to get started now. Wells drilled into the underground aquifers in California are starting to make that sucking sound you hear when a kid hits the bottom of a milk shake with a straw. Not a happy sound.

Crop yields in many breadbasket regions of the world that are at risk from climate change include places that produce massive quantities of grains, like the high plains in the United States and rice producers in Southeast Asia. Extreme weather events have undoubtedly increased in size, intensity and frequency and are playing a role in more recent food price spikes, says Cynthia Rosenzweig, a climatologist at NASA.

We're already seeing the effects of a warming planet on food production. Greater spring flooding in the Midwest has led to much later planting of corn and soy crops and reduced yields. Drought wilted rice fields in Thailand and Indonesia, and scorched sugar plantations across the tropics. Severe drought in California is causing price spikes in vegetable, meat, and milk products. Recent record-breaking heat waves in Europe have affected many of their crops, including a 13 percent decline in French wine production.[122]

That's right, French wine production is being affected by all this, and I know what you're thinking. Not the wine! Say it isn't so! But it's true. The French better start taking this whole thing seriously or they're done for. Because it's not just the wine. It's the bread and cheese that go with it. Crop yields in French breadbasket regions are at risk. The droughts also affect animal growth rates, so there goes the cheese. They'll be devastated.

It wouldn't be the first time.

The French Revolution

Food has always been a flashpoint for revolution. If history has anything to teach us, it's that when people start to go hungry, they get scared and angry and quickly turn to the streets.

The French Revolution created upheaval in France that lasted for over a decade, from 1789 until 1799, and it had far-reaching social and political implications across much of Europe. The Revolution overthrew the monarchy, established a republic, experienced violent periods of political turmoil, and finally culminated in a dictatorship under Napoleon and war throughout Europe.

The causes of the French Revolution are complex and are still debated among historians, but most agree that bread played a major role in the beginning. Bread was a main component of the French working man's diet, and it was closely tied to the French national identity, even more so than today. Food historian Linda Civitello writes that bread was so important to the French diet and sustenance, bakers were even considered public servants. The police would oversee all aspects of bread production, from supply lines to quality of ingredients and how it was produced. According to researcher Sylvia Neely, the average French worker spent about half of his income on bread, and it was the main component of his diet.[123]

When grain crops failed two years in a row in 1788 and 1789, says Neely, the price of bread shot up to 88 percent of the worker's wages. The resulting famine and economic upheaval were blamed on the ruling class, and the coming revolution may have really started with a Women's March to protest the price of bread.

The march began among women in the marketplaces of Paris who, on the morning of October 5, 1789, were near rioting over the high price and scarcity of bread. Other radicals with their own political agenda joined the marchers, and the bread demonstrations quickly became intertwined with others who were seeking liberal political reforms.

The market women and their various allies grew into a mob of thousands. They ransacked the city armory for weapons and marched to the Palace of Versailles. The crowd besieged the palace, and in a dramatic and violent confrontation they pressed their demands upon King Louis XVI.

Most patrimonial governments like the one that existed in France at the time are based on political systems in which members of an elite group of rulers regard the state as a type of private institution from which they can directly profit. As we'll discuss in a little more detail shortly, this is one of the main causes of poverty among lower classes. It's also the cause of great indignation that can lead to unrest, particularly if the government fails to provide some of the most basic necessities of life: food and water.[124]

Violence has often been necessary to overcome deeply entrenched actors and institutions within a political system that try to block any possibilities for change. Sometimes these actors are so powerfully connected that the only way to get rid of them is through violent revolution. This was true of the aristocracy and office holders of the *Ancien Régime* in France who had to be physically dispossessed of land and title during the French Revolution.[125]

I'm not sure if multinational food corporations wield this kind of power, but history shows us that poverty is not always determined by geography or the environment but is very often the result of corruption and the way power has been controlled and monopolized by a narrow elite, much like the aristocracy in France prior to the revolution.

Many countries in the world today are controlled by a few

privileged insiders and the politically connected who have organized political and economic institutions for the systematic accumulation of wealth, and always at the expense of the masses and the nations environmental resources.[126]

We've seen this same scenario play out time and again in poor countries around the world where dictators use the country and its people as a personal banking system to accumulate vast wealth, and the institutions that they set up are usually geared to that sole purpose. Often devastating civil war arises when different groups attempt to take control of those corrupt institutions to line their own pockets.

I have to ask myself, are we seeing this same kind of organized wealth accumulation by elites happening at a different scale in an inner-city grocery store, or in a rural farming community? Do multinational corporations now wield that kind of power over our lives in their systematic accumulation of power, control, land and wealth?

If we allow monopolies to control vast amounts of power and resources, and that begins to affect prices and supply, will some people finally rise up? The French were fighting an entrenched aristocracy. Are we now fighting and entrenched corporatocracy? I never anticipated our little revolution escalating to the point of violence or anything like the storming of the Bastille. But maybe this is because I felt relatively safe. I wasn't on the edge. I wasn't living in poverty, not knowing where my next meal would come from. I couldn't really know what might happen.

A zombie apocalypse, however, that was always a distinct possibility in my mind.

"True happiness," said George Wiley "is found where family and friends come together around a table to share and celebrate food and a few drinks together. Everything else related to food is just the stuff of marketers and brand managers."

We were sitting on my front porch at the farm and drinking iced tea, socially distanced, on a bright summer day during Covid.

Wiley continued, "I think people are discovering this more now with the coronavirus and the lockdown and social distancing. What people really miss isn't all the 'stuff.' They really miss the connections with others. This is a good lesson to learn, I think."

"Because of all of the disruption and shortages we've seen," I asked, "do you think the virus will lead to less dominance by corporations over our lives? I mean, do you think we'll find a new economy, and a stronger local and regional economy?"

"I'm not sure, but I do think we'll see change," said Wiley. "People are understanding the downside of globalization. For one thing, I've been waiting for a part for my truck for six months. Must come from China." He looked at me and smiled.

"How do we find the ways of social and political organization to combat global power?" I asked. "I mean, we're just a puny bug to be squashed. Our struggle is really one of David versus Goliath, don't you think?" I didn't give him a chance to answer.

I started on a rant now and Wiley let me run with it. And I knew just enough on this subject to be dangerous. I felt like Karl Marx on a soapbox. But I'm also a pig-dog capitalist, so I felt conflicted.

"That's why we have bank bailouts, excessive pay for CEOs, exploitation of national resources, exploitation of the people and the treasury, globalization and free trade agreements that cripple entire regions and destroy self-reliance, all the while creating more dependence and income inequality."

I was rambling off the list of injustices in my head, and each one getting me just a little warmer.

"I remain adamant that it's not the result of free market capitalism. I'm a capitalist Wiley, you know that. I'm no socialist or communist. But our problems are the result of the rise of corporatization. Global corporatization is the antithesis of free market capitalism. It's the monopolistic organizations and banks acting in ways that block the natural workings of a free economy. It concentrates power and kills the entrepreneurial spirit and vitality of an economy!"

Wiley calmly replied.

"The growth and concentration of corporations has certainly increased their influence over government," said Wiley. "It's not just their size, their enormous wealth and assets that make multinational corporations dangerous to democracy. It's their capacity to influence, and often infiltrate, governments around the world to expand their commercial interests."

"Doesn't that make you angry? Come on Wiley, get a little agitated, would you?" I wanted to see some kind of reaction from him.

"To be truthful with you Robert, I'm more scared of banks and financial institutions than I am Kellogg's or Coke. They can ruin us all quickly with their schemes and make a lot of people go hungry."

In December 2014, after the financial meltdown just six years earlier, a spending bill required to fund the government was modified late in the game to weaken banking regulations. The modification made it easier to allow taxpayer-funded bailouts of banking "swaps entities", which the Dodd-Frank banking regulations prohibited. Citigroup, one of the largest banks, had a role in modifying the legislation. That is power. And I understood why Wiley was so concerned about banks. They must be the true capitalist pigdogs! Let's get 'em!

No, wait a minute—this book isn't about them…

As I've said before, I'm a capitalist, and I know of no better economic system. I believe that within capitalism we can strengthen and enforce our banking regulations and our anti-trust laws. And we need to be diligent about enforcing the anti-trust laws, especially when it comes to food security.

But back then, when I was talking with Wiley, I was thinking that maybe it's about time to storm the Bastille or something. We'll get those bourgeoisie bastards! According to the general laws of capitalist accumulation, the longer the capitalist controls all means of production, the more power and capital they will accumulate, leading to both higher profits for the capital owners (the bourgeoisie) and to worsening living conditions for the poor people who live by their labor—the proletariat chumps! Let's get 'em! Viva la révolution !

CHAPTER EIGHT

GLOBALIZATION

A Call from Jerry

"This is Jerry," he said. "I'm standing in the frozen food section of Whole Foods."

The call came from one of our low-level insurgents who didn't have much security clearance, but he had my cell number.

He was a member of the underground resistance, and a vegetarian. For years he went to the farmers market, but on this day, he became a covert operator and my spy on an important reconnaissance mission to Whole Foods.

I received a frantic call from Jerry Barnhouse on a bright and warm Saturday morning. Jerry owns a small print shop in Asheville, a one-man operation, and he owns a couple of large format printers and mostly prints larger signs and posters for the Asheville community. I've used Jerry for years for road signs and posters, some now with subversive messages. He's a good guy, normally very composed, mild-mannered, and low-key, but he sounded very upset when he called this day.

"Yea Jerry. What's up?" I replied.

"You're not going to believe this. I just found a bag of sliced, frozen zucchini, and guess where it comes from. Turkey! Can you believe that? Turkey! Since when is Turkey known for growing zucchini, and how the heck can they grow it, cut it, package it, freeze it, and ship it halfway around the world cheaper than we can grow it right here."

"I don't know Jerry. That sounds pretty crazy, but a lot of crazy stuff like that is going on."

"It says 'organic' on the package, and it's here in Whole Foods, but how the heck can you trust that it really is organic anyway. I mean Turkey. Isn't that an arid country in the first place?"

"Yea, I think so. A little unstable too, right? Been in the news a lot lately," I answered. I've never been to Turkey, but it probably has some climate variety and a diversity of growing regions, like most countries. Tension at the border between Turkey and Syria had been in the headlines lately.

"I guess I'm just really upset because zucchini is so easy to grow here. Why would we need to import it from Turkey of all places? I mean it's so far away. I have some growing in my backyard right now, more than I can eat. It's so easy to grow. It'll take over if you let it."

He had a good point. "Don't get too upset about it, Jerry," I said. "It's messed up, I know, but I'm glad to see that you, at least, are paying attention. Most people are pretty clueless how food comes to us. It just sort of magically shows up at the grocery store, and they have no idea where it comes from or how it got there. At least you're reading labels, and that's good."

When you start a radical, local food movement, your network can build rapidly, and you begin to learn about the secret lives of others that you had no idea existed, even though you may have known a person for years. I didn't know that he had a garden and grew his own vegetables.

I felt bad for Jerry. I knew he was pretty upset about the whole thing, especially since it happened in a store that he believed in, that he trusted, a place that was part of his own personal value system. I think he felt a little betrayed by Whole Foods.

"Thanks for reporting in, Jerry." Since he was now an operative, although he may not have known it yet, I wanted to say, just for fun, "Did anyone follow you?"

Jerry shopped at Whole Foods and Earth Fare, and for a guy in his 60's he seemed like a very healthy man. We had a conversation in his small print shop one day about how so much food travels around the world, and the importance of local food. But I suppose finding zucchini from Turkey was a big letdown for him and put him over the edge. It brought home the fact that 'organic' says nothing about food miles or where a product could come from. Neither does shopping at Whole Foods. And my phone call with Jerry happened before one of the wealthiest people in the world acquired Whole Foods, whose businesses are certainly part and parcel of the monopolization trends in Corporate America.

From that day forward Jerry would become a full-fledged member of our resistance organization, and I knew that I could count on him to put our rush jobs in front of other work. But I must say that I was intrigued by the phone call, and later that day I stopped into Whole Foods to find this mysterious international package of zucchini.

It wasn't hard to find, but what surprised me even more was a package laying right next to it. Frozen soybeans from China! Even I, a hardcore local food fighter, was set aback. Almost stunned by it. Here I was holding in my hand organic soybeans from China. I said to myself, out loud, "You have got to be frickin' kidding me."

A lady shopper nearby obviously heard me talking to this very naughty bag of frozen vegetables, and she did one of those wide turns with her cart to steer clear away from this 'weird-o' as she passed. I'm sure that kind of thing happens to you. It happens to me all the time.

I knew of course that we as a country grow way too many soybeans. Take a road trip through the Midwest and all you see are endless fields of corn and soybeans for thousands of square miles. Like Jerry, I thought, how the heck can China grow, package, freeze, and ship (on freezer containers) soybeans cheaper than we can produce them in the US. I am dumbfounded by the whole thing.

I called Jerry back from the store to report back to him about what I had found. We commiserated for a moment in disbelief, then I purchased a package of each, the soybeans and the zucchini, to store in my freezer as proof and evidence of the absurdity of all things laid bare in this very book. They're still there, taking up room in my freezer, and I'm not throwing them out and I'm not eating them.

According to statistics from the USDA, we import 64.7% of our zucchini from foreign nations. More surprising is the fact that we import 95.6% of our asparagus, so that if you're eating asparagus, the odds are almost certain that it comes from a foreign country, most likely Central or South America, and probably Peru. But that's not nearly the end of it. For avocados, it's 86%; cucumbers 74%; bell peppers 60%; and tomatoes 57%, all imported from foreign nations.[127]

The list goes on, and it holds true even when tomatoes are in season somewhere here in the US. Food travels the world on boats, planes, trucks, and trains in an endless worldwide web of food. The food miles associated with one meal can easily equate to the circumference of the planet, or 25,000 miles, without you ever knowing it. Many studies of food miles for a simple lunch, or even breakfast, have born this fact out.

There is no question that having access to fruits and vegetables is a good thing, if it means people eat more of them, particularly in the wintertime. But the problem arises when imported produce supplants or replaces our own production, because that leads to the loss of farm capacity and infrastructure right here at home- the land, equipment, people, and knowledge to grow our own food slips away. It's risky business importing so much food and becoming dependent on it.

We're outsourcing more of our produce to foreign countries and the trend continues to grow. I know I said this before, but it's worth restating. Research from the USDA suggests that in less than a decade over 75% of our fruits and half of our vegetables will come from a foreign country. 20% of the total food Americans eat, including grains and meats, comes from a foreign country. That's one out of every five bites that you take.[128]

A lot of food circles the globe just for processing. Salmon caught in Alaska is frozen and shipped to China for processing into fillets, and then shipped back to us. The reason is cheaper labor. The same is true for fish caught in Norway—it's also sent to China for processing. Chicken grown in the US is often sent to China to process, then shipped back as chicken nuggets. And here's a fun fact, there are ten times more cows in Mongolia than people but walk into a store in Mongolia and all the milk comes from England. Go figure.

We can talk about many of the problems in the US food system over breakfast. Coffee is going to add a couple thousand miles to this conversation, just so you know. Norway conducted a survey to determine the food miles associated with an average breakfast in that country and discovered that the food miles equated to the circumference of the earth, or again, over 25,000 miles. The coffee and orange juice really piled on the miles, but so did the wheat for the bread and the dairy, the jam, and the cheese. Yes, like most Europeans, they eat a lot of cheese for breakfast. And a lot of cold cuts too, like salami. I know that's weird. It's lunch meat. Have it for lunch for goodness sakes. The whole thing just pisses me off.

An American breakfast has a lot of those same miles and CO_2 emissions from all that transportation. Ninety-five percent (95%) of the food that people eat in Iowa, in the center of farm nation, comes from out of the state. If a farming state like Iowa can't feed itself, what does that say about the rest of us?[129]

Some researchers have calculated that in most nations around the world over two-thirds of their food supply comes from a foreign country.[130] That's true for many rich nations as well as poor ones. War and civil unrest can spread across borders and disrupt the food supply over a vast region. And now, with a few clicks of a mouse, a cyber-terrorist can do serious damage to the food supply in a matter of seconds and even bring a rich nation like Great Britain to its knees in nine meals.

"If shit really hits the fan, God help us," Butch said over beers at the clandestine drinking club we called a school, strategically located at the edge of the forest.

"People will come up here in hoards from Raleigh and Charlotte. They'll say to themselves, 'Oh, mountain people are nice. They know how to survive. They'll help us. Maybe we'll catch a deer.' Millions of them coming up I-40 thinking we can feed them. And we can't."

No matter what he said, I knew that if it came down to it,

Butch would help them any way he could. I knew also that he had just finished reading Bill Forstchen's book *One Second After*, and it scared the crap out of him. I read it first and then gave it to him. It scared me too.

On this particular evening, there were five of us sitting around a table at the School of Postmodern Activities, drinking beer and having a discussion about postmodern activities, and in this particular case, we were talking about 'way postmodern', a time far off in the future where we revert back to the stone age. Core members of the group, who probably drank more than others, included Butch, his cousin Mumford, a poet, an artist and a real estate guy.

"All it takes is an EMP, or a CME, and we're all dead," Butch said as he took another swig and wiped his mouth with his sleeve.

An EMP is an Electromagnetic Pulse that can come from a nuclear warhead detonated in the upper atmosphere. Military scientists understand that you don't have to target cities with lots of nuclear warheads in a large-scale attack; one well-placed bomb in the upper atmosphere can put an entire nation back into the stone age instantly. Bill Forstchen described this terrifying scenario brilliantly in his book, and the setting for the book happened to be right here in our neck of the woods, in Black Mountain, just 10 miles down the road from Asheville. Recognizing the towns and places that he describes in the book made it all seem more real and even scarier for the people living in this area. It was a hit locally and a bestseller nationally.

One nuclear explosion in the upper atmosphere will likely knock out the entire power grid for months, or even years, and take out communications satellites and systems, and with it the entire banking and financial system, the health system, and just about everything else that runs on an electrical current including computers, cell phones, cars and trucks.

Butch was wearing a t-shirt that says 'Awful Arthurs Oyster Shack' that he got at a restaurant on the North Carolina coast, and he claims to have won it for eating the most buckets of shrimp in some competition there. His cousin denies that, and says he was just given a coupon for a discount at the t-shirt shop next door. Butch often wears camo pants and likes to bow hunt. He eats venison throughout the winter. He's still angry at the developers of The Cliffs community, after 15 years, for putting in a golf course on land he used to hunt. For a guy who seems tough, a guy that grows some of his own food and knows how to hunt and fish and how to survive in the woods, Forstchen's book upset him, and he wanted to talk about it, so we spent most of the evening discussing the subject matter.

The book tells an apocalyptic story about a town, Black Mountain, North Carolina, just after a rogue nation like North Korea or China, we never know who, sets off a nuclear bomb high in the atmosphere that knocks out the power grid, even the satellite driven cell phones and the electronic ignitions in cars. The small town instantly loses all connection to the outside world. No one knows what just happened. In just one second, the event sets them back to the Middle Ages. No communication, no vehicles for transportation, no refrigeration, no pumps for running water. Cars suddenly stall out on interstate 40 that runs through Black Mountain. People get out of their stranded cars, clueless.

The living standards become immediately worse off than the Middle Ages because at least back then we had horses and wagons, wells for water, and people had the skills and knowledge of the time to grow and process food. They knew how to live in the Middle Ages. We don't.

"Starvation and mayhem, man," Butch said. "When those hordes of people from Charlotte and Raleigh start the death march up here to the mountains looking for food, what are we going to do? It'll be like the 'Walking Dead'. What happens when they find out we can't help them? We can't feed the tens of thousands of migrants that will flood up here. We won't be able to feed our own people."

"Shouldn't we be telling people about this? Shouldn't they all understand the risks?" Butch asked. "Maybe we should rework some of our posters to show a giant mushroom cloud in the background."

It was all too apocalyptic. And I wasn't sure if anything like that could ever happen, but I must admit that the books prologue, written by Newt Gingrich, past speaker of the house, was a bit concerning. Apparently, they had a lot of discussion about this kind of thing in the house and senate, and the idea wasn't all that far-fetched. It could happen, and Gingrich knew it, and said so in his prologue. And now you can see the marketing brilliance of John Haynes, the real estate guy, who sent copies of the book to potential clients in Charlotte. I wonder if he included a little note, like, "Better to get out now" with a smiley face.

A large solar flare, or coronal mass ejection (CME), can do the same kind of damage as a nuclear warhead in the upper atmosphere. One just missed us, in fact. It was known by scientists as the Solar Event of 2012. It would have devastated our communications, banking, transportation, and food systems, had the timing been different and the earth took a direct hit. Billions would have starved, particularly in the developed nations. The CME crossed the path of the Earth's orbit just before the Earth got there. Lucky galactic timing on a near miss.

A similar event did happen in 1860 that took out the telegraph system for months while lines had to be replaced and repaired. The only thing that really saved us was our lack of dependance on electronics at the time. The northern lights, or aurora borealis, was visible across most of the country as energized particles from the sun slammed into Earth's upper atmosphere. That event, interestingly, also started several new religious movements. Our power grid and digitally dependent world make us so much more vulnerable than they were back then. It's scary stuff.

Butch wasn't a prepper or survivalist or anything like that. More like an ultra-realist. And when he saw a problem, he wanted to smash it.

"We need to be able to fend for ourselves," Butch said. "Grow more of our own food. Relearn the old ways. Learn to be a little more self-reliant, or at least not so dependent on other places. If it's not a CME or an EMP, it could be a Russian hacker on the grid, but one thing is for sure, the trucks, trains, boats and planes will all stop running. Everything's digital now, and we're like little babies in the woods, we're sitting ducks, and most people today are totally clueless how to survive."

It may have been the beer talking, but there was always a hint of truth when he said stuff like that. We should try to mitigate some of the risks out there that we've created in our industrialized, tech savvy, digitally dependent world. A simple packet of seeds stored in your freezer is like a backup hard copy of your supper.

Globalization, Colonialism and Corporatization

One of my personal heroes is barrel chested and mustachioed Teddy Roosevelt, who wasn't afraid to break up Standard Oil and other monopolies controlling commerce in his era. Pro-business does not mean pro-monopoly, and the United States has a long history of business 'Robber Barons' crossing the line. The modern meat industry is the perfect place to start the modern breakup.

History repeats itself, again and again. Corporatocracies that started with the Far-Distance Company and the Dutch East India Company on the Indian subcontinent quickly expanded into the Caribbean with the Dutch, Danish, British and French "West India Companies". The Hudson's Bay Company operated not only a monopoly right here in North America, but was the de facto government in the late 1600's. What's happening now is not unusual.

Then there was the British South Africa Company, and later, the United Fruit Company (which became Chiquita Brands International) operating as a banana republic in Central America. The Standard Fruit Company quickly followed in Honduras and other countries. The same theme plays out again and again; monopolistic, colonizing power that comes with the control of food production, labor, and prices. What we're seeing today in the food industry is nothing new. The forceful takeover of land, people, resources, and knowledge has been going on for centuries. Back then it was called colonialism, which is the intentional domination of land, people, and resources. For colonialism to work, it required the erasing of smaller, self-sovereign nations of people and erasing regional self-reliance. It required dependence.

Colonialism began as soon as ships could sail at a distance, and it won't be easy to defeat that kind of long-standing mentality—that 400-year-old thinking. But when companies get too big and powerful, bad things happen. More competition from lots of smaller companies is better for everyone. Regional and community self-reliance, and regional food sovereignty, helps resist corporate colonialism in the food system.

I was thinking about getting some sheep. I had another hair-brained idea that might make some money on the farm and stick it to the man at the same time.

A Mexican friend of mine named Cerillo had a nice little side business cooking sheep in his backyard and selling it to families in his Mexican community down in Hendersonville, about 15 miles south of my farm. He would buy live sheep from a farmer, bring them home and process and cook them in a pit that he dug in his backyard. He had a large network of Mexican families around Hendersonville that would buy the cooked lamb for special occasions like birthdays and graduations.

On some weekends over the summer, he cooks six or seven sheep at one time, and I thought that was pretty cool. Food to the people, man. It was a small-scale community food network that fed people directly. Cerillo gave people what they wanted, and something you can't get anywhere else in town—lamb meat slow cooked the traditional way, in the ground. He was giving his neighbors a food product that was a big part of their own cultural heritage.

Cerillo had a full-time job in construction but would sometimes help me out at the farm after work or on some weekends, and I had known him for about ten years. So, one day I talked to him about going into business together. We could buy young lambs and raise them at the farm, I told him, and perhaps cut his cost on the sheep.

Who cares that it was all illegal? It was about feeding people, man, and he was cutting out all kinds of powerful, monopolistic organizations like the confined animal feed operator, the chemical companies like Monsanto, the meat processors like JBS, the USDA, the large grocery store chains and the truckers and distribution warehouses. He was selling direct to the consumer in a tight food chain like the old days in Mexico and the US. And knowing someone close by who can simply process and butcher an animal is good news if shit ever hits the fan. It makes the community a little more resilient.

Cerillo's meat was cooked in a hole in the ground, the traditional way, and certainly not something you could purchase in retail stores. The whole idea of killing a sheep and cooking it in a hole would definitely, absolutely freak out a food inspector. There was something a little exciting about it, I thought, flying under the radar of the commercialized food system and feeding people directly in a communal way. We were rebels. Lawless.

But you know what, Mexican families have been cooking and sharing meat this way within their communities for hundreds of years, and they're going to keep doing it. And I don't know how many times I caught a fish or shot a goose, cleaned it, and cooked it in camp that day. Who am I to say it's wrong to kill and cook a sheep like that for your neighbors, if it's what they want? It felt like some indigenous thing or ancestral way, so I didn't judge.

Many of Cerillo's customers worked in the food chain growing and picking vegetables at farms in the region. The irony of the food system must not have escaped them when they went to a grocery store, where they paid about 25 times more for a vegetable than they were paid for growing, picking and packing it.

When Cerillo cooks, it's an eight-to-ten-hour event, and he'll always cook several at a time. He starts a wood fire in the brick-lined pit that he dug in his backyard, lets it burn down for a couple hours to get some good, hot coals, spreads the coals around with a little dirt and some aluminum foil on top and lays in the butchered lamb meat right on the coals. Then he lays more aluminum foil over the top and buries the whole thing with dirt again, letting it all slow cook for about eight hours. And when it's ready eight hours later, he digs it all up.

The meat comes out tender, smokey flavored and delicious. Once word of mouth started spreading through the large Mexican community in Hendersonville, people came knocking. He usually cooks on Saturdays, and people start showing up at his house at 5 o'clock in the morning the next day to purchase the cooked meat. He usually sells out by 7 or 8 o'clock that morning, within 2 or 3 hours. To me, that's a terrific little local food business that celebrates a long-standing food tradition and cultural heritage—and at the same time, it really sticks it to the man. Naturally, I wanted to be part of this clandestine, subversive food operation that was actually much easier and more efficient than my beef operation.

Our farm has a meat handlers license so that we can store and sell meat, but when I need to process a cow, I must drive it one and a half hours away to the nearest small scale, USDA inspected facility to drop it off. Then I have to go back a couple days later to pick it up. It's a pain. In 1968 there were about 10,000 total slaughter facilities in the United States. Today there are just 835 USDA inspected facilities and another 1938 "other" facilities, less than a third the number of butchering facilities.[131] Meanwhile, the population has increased by more than 50%.

As the number of facilities decreased, many of the remaining ones got much bigger, so that today just 50 facilities slaughter and process about 98% of all US cows.[132] That's an average of one large facility per state, or one facility per 6.6 million people. With all the consolidation, it's no wonder I have to drive so far to butcher a cow at a licensed and inspected facility.

One of the more radical food fighters once said to me, "License? We don't need no stinking license!"

To learn about the sheep business, and perhaps purchase some, I went to see Raphael Bravo in Columbus, North Carolina, who owned a sheep farm about 45 minutes south of me. I did learn something about raising sheep and rotational grazing, but in one of those 'small world' chance happenings, I also met a man who once worked *for* the man.

It turns out, Raphael spent a career working as a big shot on the executive team for Campbells Soup in New Jersey. That was before he retired to the mountains and started sheep farming. Raphael was a head buyer for Campbells and spent most of his long career buying mushrooms. He got paid well for that, and loved his job, he told me.

"Until one day," Raphael said, "they came to me and said that I was making too much money. Can you believe they said that? And these were guys that I worked with and knew for years. So I told them to keep their money and keep their job, and I left the company after 25 years with them."

Raphael speaks with a Spanish accent. It was very different from the Mexican Spanish accent that I was more used to hearing, and it sounded like it had a little Italian mixed in. He was raised in South America, in Venezuela, and he received his master's degree in agricultural economics from a university in England, where he met his wife.

"All of my life I wanted to be a farmer, so when I left, I had made enough money to start this little farm, so it all worked out. I'm happy," Raphael said. He had a beautiful farm of about 30 acres and spends his days tending to about 40 sheep. He milks a cow and makes his own cheese from it to fill in his day. It's a peaceful, pastoral life that he has going now.

Campbells is one of the largest buyers of mushrooms in the world, and Campbells Cream of Mushroom soup is the number three seller for the company, says Raphael, which surprised me. I would have figured it was the #1 seller since my mom put it in everything. To her, Campbell's Cream of Mushroom soup was like a rich sauce that could go on top of meat like chicken, in tuna noodle casserole (which we ate a lot with seven kids) or on top some side dish like green beans. We ate so many meals with a creamy white mushroom sauce that, growing up, I thought we were French.

"In the early days," Raphael said, "Campbells bought mushrooms from farmers. Then they started their own mush-room farms, and we had eight of them strategically placed near our soup plants located in the United States, Canada and Mexico."

"Then for some reason, my boss wanted to close those farms, which are really like mushroom factories, huge buildings where mushrooms are grown indoors under very controlled environments, and everything is automated like a factory. So, we closed those farms and I started buying mushrooms again from other large mushroom farm factories all over the world."

Since Raphael left, he says that most of the mushrooms now come from factory warehouses in China, and they're frozen, and not fresh. I didn't say anything, but I thought to myself, the global food chain strikes again. They're saving what, a few pennies? My mom would be turning over in her grave.

I imagine that the supply chain was much easier to manage when the ingredients are frozen and come on massive container ships and so aren't perishable, but I'm not sure what that means for taste. Would my rich French pallet be able to taste the difference between fresh mushrooms and frozen from China? Probably, which is why Campbells won't be winning any Michelin stars from me anytime soon. My tuna fish noodle casserole will never taste the same. I realize that I'm nit-picking about fresh mushrooms in a can of highly processed, high sodium industrial food, but gosh darn it, can't we just leave some things alone.

Raphael told me about his career with Campbells while we sat in his barn and had a beer (which he insisted) and my little farm tour turned into a four-hour long visit. But it was interesting to learn how a large food corporation can pay an executive so much money just to purchase mushrooms. It was a beautiful Friday afternoon, and we had a chance to become friends, and I tried some of his homemade cheese which was quite good.

We drank cans of Sierra Nevada, which started as a microbrewery and then got big, and eventually opened a large brewery in Asheville to service the East Coast, and as I sipped from the can I wondered if they were big enough now to pay an executive a large salary just to buy hops. God help us if they come frozen from China, I thought. There would be riots in the streets of Asheville if that ever got out. It's a local institution, and you don't go messing with a local institution.

And you shouldn't be messing with my mom's secret, white mushroom sauce either. We're French, you know.

Banana Republic

There are about seven thousand different edible crops on this planet, which makes the Earth a very accommodating place for omnivores like us. But today, over 95 percent of what we eat comes from just thirty plant species, and the bulk of our calories come mostly from just four: wheat, corn, rice and soybeans. It's like we're walking into a restaurant and ordering the same damn thing every time, when so much more is available.

Mass production of a limited number of products is a key to efficiency and profits, so the industrial food complex likes it this way. Grind up these four core grains, add some sugar and brightly colored packaging, and you can create about 7000 different snack foods.[133]

While there are literally hundreds, even thousands, of varieties of corn out there, about 95% of the corn grown in the US is the exact same genetically modified organism.[134] By exact same I mean an identical, carbon copy. The same thing goes for some other fruits and vegetables. Bananas, the most popular fruit in the world, are a good example. While there are hundreds of varieties of bananas, the Cavendish banana from Chiquita dominates the world, and every Cavendish is an exact clone of each other; copies that came from creating a seedless banana, and so identical in size, shape, and color.

In political science, the term banana republic usually describes a politically unstable country with an economy dependent upon the exportation of a limited-resource product, such as bananas or minerals, and usually comes with the exploitation of its citizens and labor.

Typically, a banana republic is a society of extremely stratified social classes with a large, poor working class and a ruling-class, mostly composed of the business, political and military elites. The term banana republic today usually refers to a dictatorship that accumulates power and wealth through kickbacks from the exploitation of citizens in large-scale plantation-style agriculture.

In 1901, the American author O. Henry coined the term to describe Honduras and neighboring countries that were being exploited by U.S. corporations, such as the United Fruit Company. Companies back then would often finance guerrilla wars and presidential campaigns, and sometimes finance entire governments to keep the business running smoothly. Bribes are still commonplace and just part of the business model in many parts of Central and South America, and really, all over the world.

But the environmental effects of deforestation and monocropping bananas has taken its toll on the Caribbean countries. Entire tropical ecosystems have been destroyed, which has devastated biodiversity. With a loss in biodiversity, other natural processes necessary for native plant and animal survival have been upended. What we're seeing now in the Amazon, the clearing of rain forest to make room for industrial beef production, is nothing new. It's happened in other regions for palm oil, for coffee, and for bananas. In Brazil, it's just happening for hamburger. And without country of origin labeling laws for meat, we unwittingly contribute to the demise of the rainforest, one bite at a time.

Like the early spice traders who, flying a flag of corporate immunity, sailed the sea in search of valuable spices, and ended up decimating native groups and environments, we see the same thing happening again over bananas and palm oil—400 years later. When will we learn?

Lewis Mumford on Global Trade

Our society seems caught in the epic battle between the spiritual and material world, between human virtue and our more selfish inclination. We can do some pretty dumb things in the name of self-interest and profit, and we can easily lose our connection to nature and the environment.

The subject of insane trade came up often at the farm and at meetings in the old red schoolhouse. It was affecting our business at the farm to be sure, and it became a favorite subject of discussion for some of our rebel food fighters.

Lewis Mumford never actually said much during our meetings in the old schoolhouse. He preferred to listen and learn. When COVID-19 hit hard in the spring of 2020, we stopped meeting in person and started emailing each other more frequently.

I sent Mumford an email on a cold December morning during COVID. It read:

"The Congressional Research Service said in a report that the US imports over $100 million worth of tomatoes per month, even during peak US tomato growing season. We currently import over 72% of the tomatoes we consume in the U.S. from foreign countries. That's crazy, don't you think?"[135]

"Yes, it certainly seems that way," Mumford replied from the socially distanced comfort of his study at home. "But I find it really disturbing how food products are shipped around the world just for processing. African-grown coffee is being packed 3,500 miles away in India, then shipped to consumers around the world. Canadian prawns are processed in Iceland, and Bolivian nuts are being packed in Italy. Global food trade is a perplexing subject."

Mumford knew a lot about global trade, and this started a back-and-forth email chain that turned into a fun little exercise for me. I'd search the internet and then reply. It was like researching the ridiculousness of human beings.

"California imports exactly as many cherries as it exports," I wrote. "Doesn't make any sense at all. Why not just keep the cherries you grow?"[136]

He replied the next day: "Mexican cows that are fed and raised on cheap, subsidized, imported American corn are shipped to the United States, where they are butchered for meat, which is then sent back and sold in Mexico. How about these companies just build a nice meat packing plant down there and save all that transportation fuel?"

That's absurd, I thought. And how about this, let's quit dumping cheap subsidized US corn on Mexico in the first place, and let them grow their own corn to feed their cows. But I had another comeback ready for Mumford.

"In 2007, Britain and Australia exchanged 20,000 tons of bottled water with each other. They're both drinking more bottled water, so that number has gone way up since then. Why don't they just ship the fancy labels—it would be much cheaper and better for the environment."

This was getting interesting, I thought, and Mumford was right there with me. He replied the next morning.

"Butter from New Zealand costs less in the UK than butter produced right down the road, even though it's shipped half-way around the world. Must be the result of subsidies paid to dairy farmers in New Zealand, and of course fossil fuel subsidies. The equipment they use is the same, and the cows aren't much different."

But what does that mean for the farmer down the road, I thought? Don't people give a hoot about that guy? They probably see him in the pub all the time. They'll share a pint with the guy, and then go buy butter from his competitor on the other side of the planet. People often talk about efficiencies of scale, but the truth is we couldn't have produced a more wasteful system. My turn.

"There are apples grown in the UK that are flown to South Africa just for a wax coating, and then flown back to the UK." The whole process involves incredible amounts of waste and CO2 emissions. There was no way he could beat that one, I thought.

He replied that evening. "More than half of the seafood caught in Alaska is processed in China, and then much of it is sent right back to America's supermarkets. How stupid is that?"

"Why don't we just try to convince the fish to swim to China," I quipped, "so they can be processed and sent back to us. It would save at least one long boat ride." Dumb joke, I know, but Mumford sent me a smiley face emoji anyway.

Mumford was already aware of this, so I'll just tell you instead. U.S. beef from cows raised in CAFO's is usually too fatty to be sold as hamburger meat. So, some of that beef gets shipped abroad, and leaner grass-fed beef gets imported from far-away New Zealand and Australia to mix in with our fatty meat. You're often eating an international hamburger, and you don't even know that it's a blend from different cows raised on opposite sides of the planet. I think it would be much wiser, and certainly much better for the environment, if we just moved some of our own cattle out of the CAFO's and back to pasture.

"How is it cheaper to ship food across the world for processing than to process it where it was grown or caught?" I finally asked.

"Globalization," he said, "is this unseen force that supposedly eliminates inefficiencies through the magic of trade, but it's actually very inefficient and has radically disconnected us from our food supply. It's mostly about saving some labor cost, and not efficiency. It takes much longer for products to get to market and burns a hell of a lot of fossil fuel in the process."

Mumford continued. "Companies often relocate labor-intensive work overseas to minimize costs. Scotland's minimum wage, for instance, is about four times that of China, which explains why Scottish fish is often processed in China. As in many countries, like the U.S., taxpayers subsidize fossil fuel costs, so we prop up this craziness."

With global fossil fuel subsidies, both direct and indirect, on the order of $5 trillion per year, this energy-intensive way of doing business is often less expensive for large food exporters and distributors, though it carries great costs to the environment and to jobs and livelihoods in the food's country of origin.

"All the costs, including taxpayer subsidies and future costs of climate change, are not considered in the cost of production," said Mumford.

"But there are other reasons that a country might want to 're-import' their own products," he said. "Like tax policy loopholes. In many cases, companies export and re-import goods to benefit from these tax policy loopholes. For example, China's value-added tax allows businesses to claim tax rebates by exporting their products, while other businesses can then re-import those same products to claim rebates of their own. It's a complicated shell game, but some people are making a lot of money at it."

Flunk me. Really?

The email went on. "Fossil fuel subsidies, which greatly reduce transport costs, help make this a viable strategy. The results are absurd, I know. But in most years since 2005, China has imported more from itself than from the United States – despite being the US's third-largest export market. It's a racket. They just 'export' to some offshore location and someone else 'imports' right back. Really stupid."

Importing stuff from yourself. That was a new one to me, and he had me with that. It's impossible to beat that. So, I asked another question.

"Farming is seasonal in most parts of the world. You can't grow food in the upper Midwest in the wintertime. Because the availability of crops varies seasonally, is this really the main justification for global food trade?"

"Not really," he replied. "Even in the height of apple season in the northern US, apples from New Zealand and Chile flood supermarket shelves – and regardless of origin, many supermarket apples stay in cold storage for up to a year, so the season doesn't really matter. Distributors source from wherever product is least expensive. Supermarkets will choose apples from 10,000 miles away if they're cheaper than apples grown just 10 miles away. There's no loyalty to local."

I know a guy who was paid well to buy mushrooms like that, I thought. He wasn't a bad guy. That's what they paid him to do.

"So, Mumford," I asked, "would you say the main contributing factors to this crazy food trade system are subsidized fossil fuels for transportation, free trade agreements, import-export tax rebates, and differences in labor costs, and perhaps lax environmental and safety regulations? As opposed to the seasonal availability of fresh produce?"

"Yes, and it happens all over the world, even in the remotest places. Cod caught off Norway goes on a 10,000-mile round trip to China to be fileted and returned for sale on the local market. It's crazy, for sure. Even used batteries crisscross the planet. All of this while CO2 levels are threatening our very survival."

"How badly does global trade affect the climate?" I asked.

"I just looked this up," Mumford wrote. "Back in 2012, commercial ships produced over a million tons of CO_2 per day — more than the total emissions of the UK, or Canada, or Brazil, and more than the US coal industry. That's roughly 4% of the world's CO_2 emissions — and it's set to grow to 17% by 2050 if current trade rules continue. The growing aviation industry will produce an additional 20% of global emissions by 2050. And that doesn't account for the infrastructure need-ed to support long-distance trade — like cement production for docks and warehouses, which already contributes 8% of the world's emissions per year. We might get close to 50% of glob-al CO_2 emissions by 2050 just from transporting all this stuff back and forth."[137]

The food miles were piling up quickly. And I understood how climate agreements like the Paris Accord do not account for the emissions from international trade, and that was not by accident or an oversight. People keep praising global trade without fully accounting for the affects it has on the planet. The CO2 emitted by the thousands of oil tankers, container ships and cargo-carrying aircraft that crisscross the globe do not appear in any nation's accounting for emissions. Why? Because policymakers believe that trade, the growth of glob-al GDP, and the profit margins of their corporate political donors, is more important than the climate.

Mumford summed it up this way, "It's really quite troubling."

I summed it up this way, "Somebody totally screwed this whole thing up, and made it all a lot more complicated than it had to be—all to turn a buck—which is fine, except when it uses up valuable resources, impacts the environment and compromises our children's ability to feed themselves in the future. Then it's just stupid."

Trade agreements were established to increase economic activity and prosperity, but what has resulted are countries importing and exporting almost identical quantities of produce. I looked up some numbers on important items where imports and exports were nearly identical in the U.S. and U.K.[138]

US Imports and Exports per year:

	Imports	Exports
Potatoes	365,350 tons	324,544 tons
Sugar	70,820 tons	83,083 tons
Beef	953,143 tons	899,834 tons

UK Imports and Exports per year:

Milk	114,000 tons	119,000 tons
Bread	174,570 tons	148,710 tons
Eggs	21,979 tons	30,604 tons
Pork	158,294 tons	258,558 tons

A day or two went by, and I had a chance to search the internet before my next question, which was related but went in a little different direction.

"In terms of volume, world trade is nearly 32 times greater now than it was in 1950. Were we less happy then without all of this stuff circling the globe, do you think?"

It was a loaded question. I'd seen studies by several research groups that suggested 'Happiness' in the US actually peaked in 1957 and has steadily gone down from there. Maybe we've come to expect too much, and so we often feel disappointed. Maybe after the war people were more grateful for what they had. A great deal of research says that gratitude is a key to happiness.

"I don't think we were less happy back then without all the imported stuff," Mumford replied. "But I do think that by purchasing locally grown foods, you help maintain farmland and green, open space in your community, and you feel more connected to it, and I do think that adds something to happiness. I certainly like to drive by farms and green space. I think most people do. We don't want that to go away."

I replied with more of my recent research, "A study in northeastern Iowa showed that greater income and employment was generated by farms with local sales than by regional grain farms. Higher income levels do add to happiness, at least to a point, right?"

"Yes, I believe that is true. But food grown in the local community is less likely to be disrupted by transportation issues, largescale food-borne illness outbreaks, weather, and higher fuel costs. That can give us some peace of mind and can limit the 'unhappiness' that might come from disruption. So, I suppose local food could add to happiness in that way also."

Food and happiness and food security and food sovereignty can and should be linked together. More research in this area—happiness and food sovereignty—should be done, I thought. I know most people who attend the farmers market seem to enjoy the experience and the connection to the farmers growing their food. Plus, I remembered what Lee Warren had told me about the positive mental health impacts of gardening and working with the soil.

"To reduce CO2 emissions, create more jobs, and build stronger communities," I wrote back, "we have to say 'No' to some of this crazy food trade. People need to speak up, don't you think? – to share facts about what is going on. We need to call for an end to corporate subsidies and tax breaks and fuel subsidies that support it. We all need to critically question the free trade dogma, don't you agree?"

Mumford replied, "Yes, we do absolutely need to account for the real costs of fossil fuels for the products sold. Only with a full-accounting system that accounts for the subsidized fossil fuels will we realize that a chicken from 10,000 miles away is actually much more expensive than a local chicken, particularly when you factor in the affects and costs of climate change.

"And we need to support local economies because that helps your friends and neighbors," he added. "I try to buy local food and other local products, because it helps build local food systems and local business alliances, and that's good for community resilience. In the end, I think it also benefits our general happiness."

Long-standing surveys have asked Americans, "Are you happy?" Why did happiness in America seem to peak in 1957? We're much richer now, and we have three times as much stuff. What happened?

Globalization happened. Globalization is the deregulation of trade and finance to enable businesses and banks to operate globally. It is the emergence of a single world market dominated by massive transnational companies that are hurting small business and that end up putting a lot of mom and pops out of business. We all work for the man now, and he dictates prices and wages.

Yes, globalization allows some people to buy cheap stuff at Walmart. But globalization is also the powerful force that changed small towns and jobs and it has also changed how and what and where we buy things today. It's not really unlike the early spice traders who conquered and dismantled local, self-reliant economies and enslaved their populations. Where there was once autonomy and self-reliance, there is now dependence.

We're all now much more dependent on China and Walmart now. In many places now, they're the only game in town now, and they dominate the local economy and the products bought and sold there.

In the mid-20th century, colonialism gave way to a more subtle and sinister form of enslavement—debt. Crippled with debt, nations fell deeper into poverty, which allowed multinational corporations to extract cheap resources and cheap labor. Today those transnational corporations have become so large and powerful that they can influence and even control governments and economic policy. All the while they keep demanding more deregulation to further globalization. It's an agenda that has major implications for people and ecosystems around the world.

Globalization is not just affecting manufacturing and food industries. Everything from IT administrators to accounting and tax analysts, to X-ray or CT technicians and other white-collar jobs, they all have moved to India and other nations with lower pay scales. We're outsourcing our service industry now on a massive scale so global companies can save some labor cost.

The promise of globalization was to outsource all the hard work, like factory and farming jobs, so that Americans could all have nice, cushy white collar desk jobs in an information economy. I guess our largest corporations didn't get that memo because those jobs are now leaving fast. And who said there's something wrong with farming and factory jobs in the first place?

Where concentration and the consolidation of power has led us to too little competition, and large companies can dictate prices, perhaps globalization has led us to too much competition in a global economy where we can't necessarily compete with cheaper labor, and so we lose jobs.

As I began to put all these pieces together, I opened myself to deeper, more ominous questions. In this global race to the bottom, where prices and then wages continue to fall, will we eventually come to a place where no one can afford even the cheap stuff?

Are We Really Feeding the World?

In 2018 we exported over 16 billion pounds of meat to other countries.[139] With slow population growth over the past two decades in this country, our meat consumption has remained relatively flat at about 220 pounds of meat per person, per year, which comes to over one-half pound of meat per day.

Large meat companies like Tyson see their future growth in developing nations, "where a growing middle-class population for the first time can afford to eat meat and visit drive-through windows", said former Tyson CEO Don Tyson.

But many might respond to that statement with the question, "why should the US become the meat factory for the world?" The whole business, from monocropping corn to confined animal feed operations is an environmental catastrophe. Eating more meat is also not helping to create better eating habits in countries that already eat a healthier, grain and vegetable-based diet.

The reason companies like Tyson want to turn the US into a meat factory is cheap, taxpayer subsidized corn and soybean feed. Never mind that it's a dirty, smelly business that pollutes our waterways as it diminishes our soils, China is taking advantage of lax environmental laws and cheap inputs and raw materials to feed its growing appetite for meat. If Tyson has its way, we'll become the industrial scale pig farm for China and other countries growing meat consumption. And the environmental wreckage certainly doesn't deliver lots of high paying jobs and prosperity to the Midwest. As corn and soybean farms have scaled up and mechanized, pushing thousands of smaller farmers out of business, those that remain are still just hanging on because of the subsidies.

The jobs created in the meat processing plants are not necessarily jobs that many Americans want. It's hard, monotonous, and very dangerous work. Over half the workers in the slaughterhouses are foreign born, many from Mexico and Central America, some illegal.[140] Many are refugees running from political turmoil and violence in their home countries, and so are more willing to take any kind of work that they can get, and over recent years they have been filling the ranks in the meat processing factory lines that can slaughter over 977 hogs per hour, or 16 per minute.[141]

I'd hate to burst anyone's bubble, but we're not really feeding the world's hungry or providing some huge humanitarian service like Big Ag wants to claim. According to a 2016 report by the Environmental Working Group, half the soybeans and 15% of the corn grown in the U.S. is exported, but almost all of it (86%) goes to feed animals in industrial confined animal feed operations in twenty highly developed countries with very low rates of hunger.[142]

About twenty nations that do have food shortages and hunger import a meager 0.5 percent of total U.S. ag exports. Even with food aid, the massive U.S. ag industry contributes just over 2% of the food supply for the poorest nations.[143] That equates to roughly seven days' worth of food in the year. These hungry nations must fend for themselves or get help elsewhere for the rest of the year. Let's not kid ourselves and feel good about it. We're not really feeding the world's poor and hungry like agribusiness wants you to believe.

Localization

Localization is a viable answer to both concentration and globalization. Localization is certainly an alternative to global corporate control of capitalism. And the truth is, we simply cannot continue to destroy our soil and water in this global-ized, industrialized system. As I've mentioned previously, it doesn't mean eliminating trade, nor does it mean absolute self-reliance. It's simply about creating a more sustainable econo-my by producing and consuming goods closer to home. And this localization must happen in all regions and in all countries around the world. If the U.S. is going to help other nations, we need to help them become more self-reliant and self-sustaining in regenerative food production.

Localization, or as some call it, regionalism, or bioregion-alism, simply means shortening the distance between the producer and the consumer. It's also an important leveling of the economic playing field that currently benefits the biggest corporations and banks.

We can bring transnational corporations under democratic control—you know, by the people, for the people—because we vote with our dollars, but it's difficult because of their market dominance. We can try to regulate product imports and exports with taxes and tariffs, and we can try to subsidize the things we think are important with taxpayer money. If a fraction of the subsidies that go toward subsidizing fossil fuels went to renew-able energy, or if a fraction of the subsidies that go to corn production went toward sustainable farming practices, there is no telling what we might achieve in terms of food sovereignty. And regionalism is a way to step back from the edge of cata-strophic destabilization of the biosphere. It also comes down to self-reliance, which is at odds with globalization.

We can begin to favor local and regional production, and we can take more pride in what we produce locally and regionally. When economies operate at the more human, local scale, we can see the impact of our purchasing choices. We can know if the environment has been positively or negatively impacted, or if the local economy and jobs are improving. It's much more accountable, and we will know if workers are being exploited or chemicals are being dumped, because it would happen under the watchful eyes of people nearby and within the community.

Money tends to stick around and circulate a few more times in a local economy. One study showed that $100 dollars spent at a locally owned store (versus a chain) kept $45 dollars in the local economy. $100 spent at the chain left $13 in the local economy. Three times the money stayed in the local economy from shopping at a local store. That's three times the jobs it supports and three times the tax proceeds for the local government.[144]

When it comes to local food, you're not only supporting a local farmer and the local agricultural supply line including seeds and soil amendments (as long as the farmer is buying inputs locally), but you shorten the distance between producers and consumers, cutting out food miles, cutting out CO_2 emissions and oil dependency, while you're putting money straight back into the local economy. You're gaining some control in your own communal life.

I began to realize that inside of my ominous questions about the modern food system there lay a redeeming hope. Break your carbon chains; gain freedom and add to the quality of life in your community. At the deepest level, localization is about connection. It's about re-establishing our connections with others and the natural world, and this connection is a fundamental human need. We can change many of our social and environmental health problems by changing the local food economy.

Mumford on Fixing Stuff

"Corporations have a meticulous attention to costs, profit and most importantly, standardization. This would include the standardization of people," said Mumford.

On this warm summer day Mumford was tinkering with his old, 1942 FarmAll tractor manufactured by International Harvester, and it was a telling part of his character. He fixed everything. A lot of the things he owned were old but still in good running order, including the old oil-burner furnace that he used to heat his home. He didn't run out and buy a new piece of equipment if he could fix the thing he had first. This led us to a conversation about technology.

"Many people do not understand that there are limits on the possibilities for technology and progress, limits that are set by nature," he said. "And a shiny new toaster may create happiness for a few fleeting moments, but that's about it. The damage to the environment by mining the metals for that toaster are more lasting."

Mumford has probably fixed more than one toaster in his life, which would be inconceivable to most younger people today.

"The drive for riches, for mass production and consumption at all costs, these are dangerous things. Can you hand me that screwdriver?"

I reached over and handed it to him.

"What's that, Mumford?" I said as I pointed to a strange looking part attached to the old tractor.

"That's a magneto. Works like a distributor cap. Sends the spark to the plugs."

He stood up for a second and said, "I enjoy working on old tractors like this. It's kind of like a puzzle to be solved. Sometimes it takes a lot of patience, and I try to remember that I'm in charge here, not the machine. I'm the boss, not the technology. It will succumb to my will, not the other way around." He smiled at me and then bent over the engine again.

In the context of what we were talking about, that was pretty deep. I let that sink in for a minute and didn't say anything.

"Technology is running rampant and controls so many lives now," said Mumford. "Who really cares if we reach a technical proficiency without happiness and fulfillment? Where does art, or human relationships, or nature come in? What about human desires and goals?"

Mumford disapproved of the modern trend of technology which emphasizes constant, unrestricted expansion, mass production with little regard for quality, and a 'replacement' mindset. Most things are made cheaply to break down so you can replace it. He grew up in a time when people fixed toasters.

"Modern technology and industry fail to produce lasting, quality products because companies employ business concepts such as 'planned obsolescence', low-cost design and materials, and frequent superficial 'fashion changes.'"

Fixing stuff was his way of standing up to our throw-away society. But at a deeper level, Mumford hated the idea of the standardization of people around the globe. A new Domino's Pizza store opens every 6 hours somewhere on the planet, and over half their sales come from outside the US now. We've been exporting our wasteful lifestyle as we've exported fast food restaurants around the world. Localization can mean keeping some of your local food and culture safe from this kind of corporate onslaught. Who wants to go to Italy and eat at a McDonalds anyway?

CHAPTER NINE

RISK AND RESILIENCE

Cause and Effect

The great advertisements went out from the advertising men in New York and Chicago, and the billboards and TV commercials and radio and print ads went out, all promising the abundance of cheap food. Cheap and ready to eat food just for the taking, anytime you want it. Just reach out and grab it, ready in less than a minute, and you don't even have to get out of your car. But the American farmer, who used to make 50 cents on the retail dollar, was now making less than 14 cents.

And the global web that supported all this was good for the investors and Wall Street men. Material costs went down but the prices and profits went up. The Peruvian farmer sold his cucumbers for mere pennies to the hamburger corporation who would turn them into pickles, sold worldwide.

Because of their concern about all the chemicals, some people started growing their own food and sharing it, and they sold some at a farmers market they set up in a park. The fat cats saw a drop in sales coming and so endorsed the organic label and said there ought to be some rules about it, and they made the rules so that the small farmers could no longer use the word organic, even though they started the whole thing.

The food corporation executives, always nervous as dogs in a thunderstorm, sensing the change but not knowing the nature of the change, only fearing the immediate thing, the quarterly earnings report and the results, and not knowing the causes—did not realize that they themselves were the causes of their own demise.

There was no love for the land, it was just an asset class, where crops are bought and sold before they were even planted. A hunger for food was replaced by a hunger for profits. And if a crop failed there was no gut-wrenching fear of hunger, only anger. It was just money, precious money.

The old-time farmers who knew the old ways of the earth and used manure to fertilize their land were not very good businessmen. And their love of the land did not account for much when the bankers and finance men took the land, and all the small family farms got consolidated and became one big farm enterprise. And if the Wall Street men wanted to buy up all the land, they could do it, and then they could feed us all.

The corporate farms kept growing bigger and the owners fewer, and they had become farmers of paper. It wasn't a diversified crop but a diversified portfolio that mattered. And the changing economy was ignored.

But some hard men and women still tilled the tiny patches of earth wherever they could find it. And more patches popped up and those patches became networked. The food corporations could not see the cause and effect of it, this rebellious uprising, because the effect came much later, so that they could not see that they were the cause of their own demise.

The loss of topsoil happens in millimeters, and so it was hard for them to see. A new superbug develops resistance over time, and it is an effect of the devastation, not the cause, that the corporation created over years of spraying, but they could not see it or recognize it

The black soot on the walls of the church came over hundreds of years of burning coal and then gas and oil, and they could not see it because it was happening so slowly over several lifetimes in shades of grey and black as it crept up the stone walls of the church. But tiny molecules of CO_2 also floated up into the atmosphere, so small as to be imperceptible, and they kept floating upward, until they blanketed and warmed the earth.

A young man gets shot in Chicago. The bullet killed him before he heard the blast from the gun, because bullets travel faster than the speed of sound, and the sound came later but he did not hear it. And the corporations got bigger and richer, as the jobs left the city and wages were cut and the neighborhood got much harder.

A kid in LA drinks a soda pop and tosses the bottle at a garbage can but misses. Diabetes comes much later as an effect. Years later, a plastic bottle washes up on the shore of a remote Polynesian island and a fisherman has no idea where it came from or what the cause.

Another kid gets sick from a poisoned river and does not know the cause that is a factory miles upstream. The river is like a timeline, and it was only a matter of time.

An opioid addiction was caused by a doctor trying to do some good, wanting to help others by relieving pain. The cause might have been a sales contest for representatives at a drug company. Another sales contest at Monsanto added a few million tons of chemicals to the soil and in turn the waterways, and had its affects felt years later on.

The coal came up a deep, long tunnel that runs for miles underground, and then boarded a train for a long ride to a city hundreds of miles away, where it was burned and then took another trip up the tall smokestack. Particles floated in the air for weeks, and then triggered an asthma attack in a kid in another town. And the particles partially block the sun's rays from reflecting off the surface of the earth and escaping. The rays and the heat became trapped. And all that traveling and distance becomes a timeline that makes it difficult for anyone to agree on the cause for certain, but the earth is warming.

A dam in China stops the water from flowing to a farmer in India, and the farmer's family goes hungry.

In Southeast Asia, organic palm oil comes from a mono-cropping plantation that replaced a native forest and a diversified ecosystem. A woman thousands of miles away in Seattle reads the words "vegetable oil" on the side of a package and doesn't know what that means, but she thinks it's good.

A farmer in South America with a wife and kids wishes he had another acre of land, and dreams about what he could do with that acre, and how that acre would make his life better. A rancher nearby, also trying to better his life, just needing another piece of land for more cattle, and the forest is so big, who would ever notice or care, and so the sound of a chainsaw is heard by monkeys in a nearby tree who do not know the cause and they run for their lives.

A farmer in Iowa keeps planting the same crop of corn on the same land for 30 years with diminishing returns while killing his soil. He requires more and more chemicals to improve the yield, just to stay afloat, so that he gets further and further into debt, and can't understand why. "I'll just have to work harder," he tells his wife.

Road Trip in a MANNA Truck

My small farm in Arden, like many other regional farms, often donates surplus produce to MANNA FoodBank, and we have for years. You can never plan out just right how much seed to put in the ground. Some things will do well, and some things will do poorly, so you plant extra, just in case. If something grows really well, we'd have more than enough for the CSA or what we could sell at the farmers market, and so we would donate the rest. We also had a few generous CSA members who purchased an extra CSA share just to donate to MANNA every week. It's just another example of how local food systems can help to build food security and community resilience.

To get an idea where some of this food goes, I jumped on a MANNA food truck and took a pre-Covid ride deep into the countryside. Way deep. Far into the hills and hollows of the more rural and remote mountain regions of Western North Carolina, where hunger hides among the green hills.

My drivers for the day were Bill Bass, a retired builder, and Bob Pace, a retired IT guy, both MANNA volunteers who make these runs regularly. Our plan was to set up a "pop-up food market" for the afternoon, with tables just, like a farmers market but, with food free for the taking. Volunteer drivers like Bill and Bob made nearly 800 trips since the inception of the program and traveled 60,000 miles around the 16 counties that MANNA serves.

Bill averages two road trips like this every week and has made more than 125 trips since he started driving for the MANNA Volunteer Driving Program, which began in 2016. Although he's retired now, he's still as strong as an ox. As I found out, it's a lot of work unloading and setting up all of that food.

MANNA distributed well over 19 million pounds of food

over that year, with more than 1.1 million pounds distributed by 50 volunteer drivers like Bill and Bob. If you average it out, they distribute more than 1,200 pounds of food to hungry households on every pop-up market trip. That's a lot of boxes to move around.

Bill says of the work, "It keeps me active." That's an understatement.

But there are two sides to this story. This food not only helps feed hungry households in Western North Carolina, where one in four children face food insecurity, but the program also reclaims tons of food that would otherwise be wasted and end up in a landfill. The fact is that the amount of food we waste in the US would feed another country—a very large country. About 40 percent of our food is going to waste, and that represents about 20 pounds of food per person per week. It comes to about $165 billion per year in wasted food. And it comes from points all along the food chain.[145]

Potential waste comes from grocery stores and distributors as food approaches the "sell-by" date, or because it has a slight blemish or is misshapen in some way. At home, we throw out about 25 percent of the food that we buy. The greenhouse gases that we emit just to grow all that wasted food, using our fossil fuel-intensive system, is enough to rank third in the world for emissions.[146] The vast amounts of water we use to irrigate that wasted food is more water than is used by any other country.[147]

Food waste makes up a big, gooey chunk of the municipal solid waste in landfills and it's the number two item that goes in there, behind paper.[148] Food waste emits serious greenhouse gases in the form of methane as it decomposes. Simply reducing food waste will go a long way to reducing the effects of climate change.

Thankfully, in partnership with more than 60 grocery

stores, retail businesses and produce packing houses, MANNA rescues much of this perfectly good food that would otherwise end up in a landfill. From surplus milk and cheese to fresh fruits and vegetables to pasta, canned beans and corn, nothing gets wasted and people get fed.

More than 80 percent of the food MANNA distributes is donated. In addition to food received from the grocery partners, MANNA receives food from more than 60 local farmers, food drives and individuals. The perishable produce that can't be distributed goes back to a farm to feed livestock and will end up on a plate as bacon someday. MANNA is a local leader in green waste initiatives.

When we finally reached our destination where we would set up shop for the day in the parking lot of a small church, people who came for the food began helping to unload the truck. They grabbed boxes and brought them over to the eight tables we had set up, opening the boxes and arranging the food nicely. It turned into a colorful display, a little island of brightly colored cans and fruits and vegetables, an oasis of colorful food in the middle of a food desert.

I was standing on the back of the truck with Bill when a little kid came up to me and asked, "Can I have one of those watermelons?"

Bill said with a big smile, "Sure you can," and he leaned way down and handed the boy one off the truck. As he stood back up, he looked at me and said, "That's why I do this."

Mumford on Soil Health

Mumford was out working in his garden again when I stopped by the day after my MANNA road trip.

Mumford always focused on the health of the soil in his vegetable garden because he believed that ecosystems and soil health are directly related to human health, and he believed that the time he spent improving the soil in his garden was actually time spent improving his own gut health. Plants depend on bacteria and microorganisms in the soil to break down minerals and nutrients that their roots can absorb. In the same way, the human body needs bacteria and microbes in our own gut to break down the nutrients that we need into a form that our bodies can absorb and use. Without them, we're dead.

Our bodies are an ecosystem, and we need a diversity of high-quality foods to feed a diverse, high-quality ecosystem living in our gut. The microbes in our gut include over 500 species of bacteria that weigh about 3 pounds, as much as the human brain. You couldn't survive without a brain, and you can't survive without the micro-organisms living in your gut. It's that simple.

I said before that there are more microbes in a tablespoon of healthy soil then there are people on the earth, over 6 billion of them. Some soil scientists say that there are more microbes in a small handful of good dirt than all the people who have ever lived on this planet. It's hard to get an exact count on that many little creatures in the soil to be sure, but there's a lot of them. Billions and billions. When we add fertilizers, pesticides, herbicides, or even plow, we can damage or destroy that underground environment.

As I approached him in his garden, I recalled his statement from several weeks earlier that stuck with me somehow, it lodged in my brain, and kept popping up: "We don't belong here anymore." It was a sad statement about the human condition, and I hoped it wasn't true, and I didn't want to believe it. Could we ever redeem ourselves and reunite with this world?

"How long do you think it takes to improve soil health that has been damaged by chemicals, or dead soil?" I asked him as we stood looking at his garden. I wanted to know if we still had a chance.

"From my experience, you can radically improve soil health very quickly, in just two years," he answered. "I've seen it done and I've done it myself. No till farming, adding multi-species cover crops, and I mean like 10 to 12 species including deep root tapping plants and various grasses and legumes, all grown in wintertime when you're not growing crops, so it doesn't even stop you from farming.

"A lot of it dies when it starts getting hot out because they're winter crops, but it still covers and protects the soil from sun and rain erosion. Worms, bacteria, spiders and other insects, and fungi all move in right away. Roots create spaces and channels for water and break up the soils. Next spring the farmer just rolls it all with a crimper, flattens it to a carpet—not a plow, and then uses a drill seeder to plant the next crop. Pretty simple stuff, and it doesn't cost a lot. Just some cover crop seeds."

Mumford went into how he adds minerals and nutrients to his garden, including worms and worm casting tea from his worm farm in the garage. A farmer on a larger scale can't do that, but he can easily add compost or manure.

"It's cost effective to let nature do its thing, because by the second year, the farmer won't need pesticides or herbicides anymore, and the crops are just about as productive at a lower cost because less fuel was used to spray and no cost for the chemicals."

Agrochemical companies obviously see no advantage to changing the system to more sustainable and organic growing practices. And right now, they're in the driver's seat, leading the farmer to believe that he's locked into the chemical system.

Most farmers are afraid to get off the chemical train because they fear weeds and pests will take over, or their yield will drop significantly and cause them financial ruin. In truth, there isn't a lot of margin for error for these guys, so you can't really blame them for being hesitant to change.

Mumford continued.

"Modern agriculture operates like a machine with a minimal number of steps that require no real understanding of nature, biology, ecosystems, history, or long-term consequences."

Mumford looked down at the black dirt and got quiet for a moment. I stood there and didn't say anything. I was trying to picture a chemical rep in my head, like so many salesmen I'd met before. In the 50's, when it all started, they probably wore a white, short sleeve shirt and a skinny tie, I thought. Now they probably wear khaki pants and a polo shirt with a logo embroidered on the left chest. That was the uniform, a soldier's uniform, and there was now an army of these guys stationed in just about every county across the country.

I imagined the chemical rep saying things like this:

"Just listen to me, Mister. I'll tell you what you need. The new Bug-Buster 2000. That's the ticket for you, friend. Kills 'em all deader than a doorknob!"

And if he says it enough times, and says it loud enough, you start to believe him.

"Plants have natural defenses," said Mumford, bringing me back to the present and to the garden. "They can produce toxins, which is what we often sense as flavors, which discourage a pest when attacked. Stress and survival in the natural environment are what often creates the flavors and smells for us, the quality and nuance of vegetables. If a plant is grown in a stress-free environment, we get a generic food without all the flavor or potential benefits."

What he was saying made sense to me. Many of our leafy greens and tomatoes come from greenhouses now, and that's why they taste so bland. They've had a sheltered life, with no chances to stretch their legs or build their ecological muscles. They're weaklings in the vegetable world, bland and lifeless.

"You want to eat strong, healthy vegetables that have been around the block," said Mumford, "something with some environmental bite to it. Some flavor."

Here's the kicker. In 1944, before all the chemicals, about one-third of our crops were lost from field to market because of pests, shipping, and storage. Since then, we've done massive damage to our soils and ecosystem with chemicals and killed off entire species of insects and animals. Meanwhile, the average crop loss today is still the same, about one-third.[149]

"But now," said Mumford, "we're addicted to chemicals because we've killed off all the good, beneficial predator pests—the bugs that eat the bugs that eat our crops. We went down the wrong path and it's time to change course."

The global agrochemical industry has annual sales of about $40 billion and it keeps rising fast.

"But do you think they're just going to lie down now and let someone disrupt their business?" I said. "The agrochemical business was zero in the 40's, with virtually the same rate of crop loss, but now they're monsters. It's going to be tough to fight that kind of infrastructure in order to convince farmers to do things another way. Maybe some farmers will listen, but it's going to be an uphill battle."

About $23 billion worth of those chemicals are sprayed on U.S. soil annually, which means we're using more than half the ag chemicals here in this country.[150] The U.S. only represents about five percent of the global population, so that means, somehow, lots of people around the world are still able to eat and use less chemicals, or none at all. How could that be? Maybe it's all bullshit? Maybe we're not all going to starve and die a horrible death if we stopped or slowed down the use of all those chemicals?

Mumford continued while he worked the soil with a rake. "We just can't keep spending massive amounts of money on chemicals that create more problems and haven't really solved any. It's also fossil fuel dependent so it's just not sustainable. We're going to run out of fossil fuels eventually. Then where are we going to be?

"The real problem with pesticides is that they kill everything, and not just a targeted pest, like helpful spiders and lady bugs and other beneficial predators. Cotton is a good example. Cotton is now a very, very chemical intensive crop and we've got a lot more serious pest problems than we've ever had since we started blasting them with dangerous chemicals."

"And we're exporting most of this cotton, almost 80% of it. So were trashing our soils and waterways here again for an export commodity," I said. "That sucks."[151]

In the late 1940's there were three primary cotton pests; the boll-weevil, boll worm and leaf worm, and they were devastating crops in the south in large part because that's all they were growing, and they didn't rotate in other crops. They kept feeding these pests the particular plants that they liked to eat, and the population kept growing.

When DDT was introduced, farmers thought that it was a game-changer. It killed those pests, but only for about five years. Then the pests gained resistance, as they are known to do, and came back fighting. And then the problem was, when they came back, they brought five other pests with them. Now it wasn't just three pests, but eight pests attacking the cotton crops. Today there are about 33 different pests attacking cotton.

The reason? By applying DDT, we killed off all the preda-tors in the fields—the spiders, lady bugs, praying mantes, lace wings, grasshoppers, and anything else that was going to eat those other bugs. So many of those pests that would have been suppressed by the predators had free reign. A smorgas-bord of green, leafy food. The only bugs left were the ones that eat cotton, and none of the bugs that eat those bugs were around anymore. As I started to learn all this, I started thinking how narrow minded we were. Why didn't anyone anticipate this happening? Why did we think we could just outsmart mother nature?

"The greatest damage from chemical pesticides," said Mumford, "aside from risks to human health—is that they kill everything in their wake, including predators, and it opens the door for more leaf eating pests, so we have to keep applying more chemicals for more pests. It becomes a vicious circle. And we eventually lose that chemical as the pests gain resis-tance to it. The same happens with herbicides, and there's now a superweed in the south that is resistant to Round-Up. We're just pouring gasoline on the fire, I think."

The other side of the equation is how we've started to mono-crop a single variety of plant and how that makes us much more vulnerable to pests and disease because it limits genetic variation that might help us in the battle. As noted previously, over 95% of all corn grown in the US comes from one single variety—dent corn, so called because there's a little dent in the kernel when it's dried. It's also called field corn. Thousands of miles of corn are planted with virtually no genetic diversity.

Large multi-nationals invest in creating corn and soybean GMO's because there's money in it, billions of dollars. They don't waste their time with brussels sprouts because the huge return isn't there.

"We don't have the gene pool now that we once did, and that's part of it too, isn't it?" I asked.

"I'll tell you what," said Mumford, "If nature or some crazy bioterrorist wanted to design and spread a disease that attacks a certain genotype, then we could risk losing every plant—and experience massive worldwide devastation on an industrial scale. Mother nature can be a bioterrorist. Look at the potato famine in Ireland in the late 1800's."

"I have ancestors that came over from Ireland after that tragedy," Mumford continued. "They were all growing the same variety of potato, which was a mistake, and when a particular fungus carried by the wind wiped out virtually every potato crop across Ireland within a couple years, it led to mass starvation and mass migration. But I learned later that the starvation wasn't all caused by the potato fungus, or course." My ears perked up. Of course it was. What did he mean by that?

"There was still food in Ireland," Mumford said, "but not everyone could afford it. In the year just after the potato famine, Ireland exported vast quantities of pork and wheat to England. I guess some wealthy landowners could get better prices in England."

I had never heard this before, and I couldn't help but think about how that statement tied into other discussions in this book related to systemic power and control of the food supply.

"I think a lot of people died not from a lack of food," he said, "but from a lack of money to buy it, which was related to unfair labor practices that kept small sharecroppers at the bottom."

What kind of an asshole, I thought, or group of assholes, would export food when people at home are starving? Were prices and profit so important to them?

"Still, the Irish were vulnerable to disease because of a lack of genetic diversity. Perhaps another variety may have been able to resist the fungus, I don't know. But when you have absolutely no genetic variation in corn, with every plant being an exact copy, that creates a tremendous amount of risk for a fungus or disease to spread rapidly and wipe out everything.

"The essence of nature, the essence of survival for a species is genetic variation because that will help it adapt and survive in an ever-changing environment. We've put all our eggs in one basket. Really dumb. We're just asking for it. And we do it with bananas and lots of other fruits and vegetables."

"There are efficiency benefits to this GMO, that's why they're using it, right?" I said. "Most of the corn is Round-up Ready," meaning that it was genetically designed to survive being sprayed with the herbicide in Round-up. "The farmer can go through the field and kill all the weeds but not kill the corn. It makes things a lot simpler for him, right?"

"Yes, and the corn is all nicely laid out in a uniform height, and a uniform size and shape, and it all grows and ripens at the same time, which makes it much easier for the farmer to harvest. But it's a very fragile system, and just begging to be disrupted by nature."

Herbicides like Round-Up are just part of the problem with industrial ag. The increasing use of neonicotinoid pesticides closely corresponds to sharp declines in bees, butterflies, and other pollinators, as well as birds who eat the bugs. But honeybees are like the canary in a coal mine. They're the first to go.

These newer pesticides are more lethal than DDT and are not only incredibly toxic to honeybees, but they can remain toxic for more than 1,000 days (over two and a half years) in the environment. They are also systemic insecticides, which means plants absorb them and incorporate the toxin into their tissues— stems, leaves and all. I hope you're cool with that because you may eat from that plant in the future.[152]

Other studies have suggested that only 5 percent of the toxin ends up on the plant when it's sprayed; the rest ends up in the soil and the environment. Most pesticides readily dissolve in water, and that means what's used on the farm won't necessarily stay on the farm. With irrigation and rainwater, they wash into streams, ponds, lakes, and wetlands—contaminating those bodies of water.[153]

As I continued my underground research, I discovered a 2014 international study of 452 species of insects, and it estimated that insect populations had declined 45 percent over 40 years.[154] Another study reported that 81 species of butterflies declined by an average of 33 percent in the last 20 years.[155] A major 2019 study warned that 40 percent of all insect species face extinction due to pesticides.[156] Climate change and habitat destruction were also exacerbating the problem. The evidence was mounting, and it didn't bode well for bugs or human beings.

In 2018, the European Union banned neonicotinoids for field use based on their harm to pollinators. In 2019, Canada also passed restrictions on the use of the most widely used neonicotinoids. But here in the U.S., it's still full steam ahead. I was starting to understand why so few bugs were hitting my windshield in that earlier experiment.

Forget for a moment the damage to the environment, the devastation to pollinators and the risk to our own food supply, the massive use of these pesticides doesn't make economic sense for the farmer. Studies have shown that farms using neonics had 10 times the insect pressure and half the profits compared to those farms who use regenerative farming methods that work with nature, and not against it.[157]

Regenerative agricultural uses cover crops, no-till and other methods to increase on-farm biodiversity and soil health.

Keeping predator bugs, and giving the plant a fighting chance with healthy soils, are mother nature's way of supporting the biosphere in which we all live and depend on.

"It is the arrogance of man to think he can outsmart mother nature in the long run. He can't," said Mumford.

Let's add the 400 years of colonial cultural training to that arrogance, I thought. This isn't anything new, culturally, for the European colonial mindset. The indigenous peoples they would encounter had a completely different understanding of nature. They believed that we are all part of nature, and if you didn't respect that, well, then you're on your own.

Farmers who are dependent on chemicals are going out of business. It's painful to see that when we have tested, scientifically sound solutions that don't require the massive and expensive inputs. Working with nature, instead of against it, is just good business.

At Creekside Farm, we haven't used chemical pesticides or herbicides on our vegetable crops in six years, and two farmers feed about 200 people (80 households) the bulk of their produce needs for a good part of the year. That's roughly one farmer feeding 100 people. The average farmer in this country, growing conventionally, feeds about 120 people when you add in all the support personnel from distributors, truckers, and chemical suppliers in the conventional ag business to prop up that business.[158]

I'll describe food production on our farm in a little more detail later, but the fact is the whole food system won't come crashing down just because farmers stop spraying massive amounts of chemicals. I believe food production might actually increase.

The Definition of Resilience

Resilience is a word we hear a lot these days. But what is resilience, and why is resilience important? To answer that question, ask yourself this one.

What happens if you flip the switch, and the lights don't come on?

What happens if you turn the faucet, and no water comes out? Do we have a backup plan?

The real question related to resilience is this: Can we take a hit and get back up? Can we take a hit and not shatter into a million pieces?

Resilience is the ability to withstand and recover from some type of serious disturbance or disruption, and the truth is we must plan for it. It doesn't just happen. We must build resilience into our systems. Why? Because there are certain threats and risks out there that can cause serious disruption to society.

What risks? Take your pick—from rogue nuclear states like North Korea, to Russian hackers trying to shut down our power grid and gas supply or hack and disrupt our electoral process, to terrorist groups bent on our destruction, to rising sea levels, to climate change and more frequent and severe storms, draught and more frequent and severe forest fires, solar flares or an EMP burst in the upper atmosphere that would knock out all power, communications, banking and financial systems for months, if not years. There's a lot of risk out there. If you don't want to take my word for it, I've got some backup from security experts on the subject.

A Meeting of Security Personnel

As I continued my journey into fear and confusion about the inherent risks of a global food system, I participated in a meeting with a group of men that kept me up for weeks thinking about it. It was a different group that gathered at the old schoolhouse this time, different than the usual beer drinkers and radicals, I mean. These men were serious, intelligent, and respectable, and they drank black coffee and some smoked cigarettes.

A wealthy and well-connected developer friend of mine pulled together this group of security experts, ex-government men and resilience thinkers, for a meeting at the old, red schoolhouse just before the first COVID lockdown happened. We had all just heard some news about a mysterious viral outbreak in China, but not much else. We all showed up for an open discussion about the greatest risks threatening the US and the world, and how these things might impact us closer to home here in the Southeast. We had no idea what was about to happen.

The six men came from varied backgrounds, and included Mike McConnel, former director of National Intelligence and the NSA, who talked about cyber-security and the threats from Russia and China. "I fear social disorder, chaos and border wars," said Mike.

Michael Pritchard, former Special Agent in Charge for the US Secret Service, discussed the risks of coastal flooding around the world and the security risks of mass migration that will come from that. "Populated coastlines around the world," said Pritchard, "are three times more exposed to sea level rise than previously thought. The potential security implications of the loss of these major coastal urban areas are enormous and could lead to massive migration and disruption of social order around the world."

When it was Jim Anthony's turn, and as a large developer of real estate, his comments came from that perspective—how climate change affects where we live. "The risks of climate change, such as sea level rise or extreme heat and wildfires," said Jim, "are risks to assets and investment portfolios, and show how vulnerable our financial markets are. Entire metropolitan areas are at risk, and that represents a serious, global economic threat when these assets become worthless."

Many investors are uncertain how long insurance coverage will be available for assets in highly vulnerable locations. As Jim noted, "A plus-4-degree world is not insurable. Who would underwrite that? You'd have to be crazy." We had already seen the trickledown effect in 2008 when global financial markets went into a tailspin, and how it affected the most vulnerable in society. This wasn't just about the impact on the portfolio of the wealthy, because it would bring everyone down with them. "It could devastate the entire worldwide economy," said Jim, "and push millions more people below the poverty line."

Bill Forstchen has written several apocalyptic best-selling novels, including the one that scared Butch earlier called One Second After. Bill has probably spent more time writing and thinking about the end of the world than just about anyone I know. I don't know how he ever sleeps at night. His novels are well-researched and as a history professor he adds an element of historical human experience to his apocalyptic work.

"Some of the things that concern me the most?" said Bill. "We've dodged the bug since 1918 with the flu pandemic that wiped out millions of people. With air travel, a serious virus can now spread around the world in just 72 hours. That could break down the distribution of food quickly as fear and panic take-over. There's less than 20 days of food on hand in the current US food system. Grocery stores will be cleaned out much quicker than that."

That statement was almost psychic—he described the global pandemic just before it unfolded. And while food shortages did occur, the results were not as devastating as they might have been if the disease had been even more life threatening. The timing and foresight of his comments were unnerving as they began to unfold a few weeks later.

When it was time for me to chime in on this conversation, as the president and farm CEO, I spoke from a food and farming standpoint, and I said, "I think the argument that we need to make is that it's good business to grow smart. At the same time, it will make the food supply much stronger and more resilient just in case some of these things that we're talking about come true."

"I've spent a lot of my time recently thinking and reading about global food supply channels. I think it's basic economics. It's long-term investment and return versus a quick buck. It's irrational behavior to act solely out of short-term benefit. There are ways to make supply channels and business so much more resilient to disruption, and that effort doesn't really cost that much."

We went around the table several times in this open discussion and talked about a lot of different threats that might impact our region and the world. I couldn't help but think later on, for days after the meeting, how much of what we talked about related to threats to the existing system, a system that was precariously built like stick buildings on the edge of the sea, waiting for a storm. There was no redundancy, no back up plan. It was a system built on risk, the kind of risk that Wall Street bankers were willing to take, but the risk threatened everyone now. It wasn't just about wealth and security, markets and asset values, it was about people and communities—the human cost of all this risk. I realized that my own comments were simply related to how a cereal company might protect its interests and profits—a profit centered mindset—coming from Mr. Bigshot farm president.

The Covid pandemic would strike a few weeks later, and that meeting probably influenced how I reacted to it. And at the deepest level, I was more worried about hunger and starvation than asset values in Miami Beach.

Resilience Thinking

The U.S. food system is facing the triple threat of peak oil, climate change, and serious public health problems. The food system should be *THE* key public health and national security concern in this country, and all countries around the world, but it's not. We can't fix this nation's public health, energy independence, or climate change challenges without understanding their close connections with the industrial food system.

A more resilient, regional food system must include farms growing a diversity of food locally and sustainably, and just as importantly, the regional processing and distribution centers for that food. It also means changing our food culture away from processed and fast foods and teaching children about the importance of healthy food and what that looks like.

Resilience is the ability to prepare and plan for, absorb, recover from, and more successfully adapt to adverse events. Laura Lengnick, a friend and resilience expert, and author of *Resilient Agriculture: Cultivating Food Systems for a Changing Climate*, was the first to teach me about the subject of resilience. When something bad happens, communities must be able to "bounce forward" from these events, she told me, not bounce back. A bounce forward means solving problems and preventing or limiting hardship in the future, says Laura.[159]

Laura's book presents a story of transformation. The kind of resilience thinking that she advocates promotes a "bounce forward" and not the "bounce back" philosophy for a very good reason. The reasoning— industrial culture is not resilient, that has been proven, so it makes no sense to "bounce back" to 20th century structures, processes and standards. Resilience thinking invites us to "rethink" the way we design and manage communities so that when there is a damaging event, we can invest in recovery efforts that transform our food system, says Lengnick. For example, instead of rebuilding pork production facilities damaged by hurricanes in North Carolina, we can instead restore the floodplain that the pork farm was located on. In this way, we can enhance community resilience by promoting the ecosystem services that reduce the risk of flooding. Another example, instead of rebuilding massive, concentrated pork production facilities we can invest in re-diversifying and re-regionalizing pork production into smaller, regionally based facilities to feed major southeast population centers. "Bouncing back" is not the appropriate response for food system transformation and it, ironically, actually supports "business as usual" and the problems that got us here in the first place.

The rise in monster hurricanes and devastating heat, drought and wildfires in the West, as well as the persistence of terrorist threats and internet hackers, have awakened us to an understanding that what is happening to others can also happen to us. No one is perfectly safe. We must recognize our vulnerabilities and try to come up with a plan.

The global climate is changing, there is no longer any question about this, and the impacts of that are already being felt around the world. Global sea level has risen by eight inches since 1880 and according to NASA is anticipated to rise another one to eight feet by 2100, perhaps much sooner.[160] Along the coasts, some communities are already experiencing tidal flooding with significant frequency, even daily.

We are all living at risk. The challenge before us is to determine how we, together, respond to the specific risks, including extreme weather events, rising rivers and seas, economic stresses, Wall Street turmoil, failing infrastructure, internet hackers, terrorism, political division, fractures in social cohesion, aging populations, refugees and mass migration. There is a long list of potential threats and disrupters that we need to keep an eye on. And any one of them, or a combination of them, can affect food production and distribution.

A regionally based food system is key to helping us mitigate some of the risk in this world by securing our local food supply, or at least part of it. Local and regional food systems are the path to food sovereignty and food security. It's harder to solve other problems when you're hungry.

CHAPTER TEN

HUNKERING DOWN

When the Covid-19 pandemic hit hard in the spring of 2020, I began to get really concerned.

It was as if I knew too much. The former Director of National Intelligence told me personally—to my face—about the vulnerabilities in our food system. People I knew started losing their jobs left and right, and all I kept thinking about was this, what if people in the food system just stopped going to work?

We didn't know how bad it would be at first, but I wasn't the only one asking the question, "Will people risk the life and health of their families by going to work for minimum wage, out in the field, or at the meat processor, or at the food distribution warehouses, or at the retail stores?"

I had spent the better part of ten years studying the food system, and I knew something about the consolidation and centralization that has happened in the food supply, and how the shut-down of just a couple of key facilities could drastically reduce the supply of important food categories. I knew how far food traveled to get to our tables. And I knew intimately about our own food producing capabilities in my region and in my community, and it wasn't nearly enough to feed us all.

Mumford hunkered down at his home and didn't go

anywhere. I stopped by his house in late March 2020, and we sat outside on his porch, both wearing masks and socially distancing.

"From what I've read, this could get much worse, Robert, if this thing mutates," said Mumford. He continued,

"If this thing mutated and turned into anything like the black plague that ravaged Europe and Asia in the 1300's, the food system would shut down, and we'd really be in trouble. That pandemic wiped out one-third to one half the people in the known world. Whole towns and villages disappeared from the map. And it was a gruesome way to die, with boils and pustules and a sickening, terrifying thing to witness, I'm sure. If the symptoms of this pandemic, or the next one, ever manifested themselves in any way like that one, we'd really be screwed."

"For now, it's killing mostly older folks," said Mumford. "But if it mutates and starts killing younger people, like the Spanish Flu of 1918 did, I think people will start acting a lot differently. If this pandemic were as deadly to younger people as it is to older people, I'm sure the general response, and people's attitude, would be a whole lot different right now. It's sad to say that, but I think it's true."

"And if it becomes more deadly," he continued, "who would go to work if they might bring something home that could kill their children? Who would drive a truck across country? Would you go to work at a grocery store for minimum wage? The whole food system would collapse, almost overnight. And it could still happen. Viruses mutate, that's what they do. Nature designed them that way." It scared me to know that he was thinking the same way I was. Even a short term shut down in food distribution would create massive panic.

The scientist in Mumford had been researching this thing

since early January, and I trusted his opinion. I stood confounded on the spot. All I knew was that we were woefully unprepared, and a worrying lack of sense came over me.

People started buying more guns, and I started to get more worried. The news reports showed that gun and ammo sales were skyrocketing, and I tried to think about what all of that meant. Obviously, I wasn't the only one worrying about what was going on, and clearly many people were already going into some defensive, 'hunker down' mode. This is the Appalachian Mountains, and people here own a lot of guns and know how to shoot them. I pulled my shotgun out of the gun safe in the basement and stuck it in a closet closer to the back door. Don't ask me why.

In early April, I began to feel extremely uneasy, and I started to really regret the time I spent binge-watching episodes of The Walking Dead. People had to start realizing by this point, surely, that something had gone wrong with our globalized system. We were dependent on important drugs, like insulin and penicillin, from companies in India, who were themselves dependent on the chemicals to make those drugs from China. We didn't even have the capacity to make our own masks and gowns and other PPE supplies. We're like a baby in the woods, just like Butch said, and the system didn't let us down—the system was designed this way.

Because of outbreaks at the massive meat processing facilities in Kansas and Nebraska, many grocery stores began to run out of meat in May, and other stores limited the amount of meat you could buy, which was unnerving. Many of my friends in the restaurant industry, cooks and waiters and bartenders, suddenly lost their jobs. Other farmer friends, who supplied all those restaurants with meat and produce, stopped getting orders, and they were starting to panic. It happened overnight.

If this thing got worse, I thought, and the global food system actually collapsed, people would begin to starve, and people would die. It was as simple as that. Food riots would start quickly, within days. Countries would start hoarding food and other supplies, restricting shipments at the ports and borders. And I knew that no one could save you. No helicopter would come down from out of the skies and drop you needed supplies. No rescue teams would find you and feed you, because the same problem would be happening all over the country and around the world. None, I suspected, would even try.

Maybe I shouldn't have read Bill Forstchen's books. He spelled it all out in graphic detail. Bears and coyotes would come down from the hills and feast on the poor, starving and dead souls who were unfortunate enough to outlive the funeral directors and grave diggers. It was an absurd notion, I thought, but I couldn't help myself. All the fearful possibilities made my head spin, and I was getting paranoid.

People started hoarding, and things like toilet paper were suddenly in short supply. I thought about how long perishable food actually lasts, and it's not very long. I was acutely aware of the fact that toilet paper was the least of our worries in the bigger scheme of things.

This whole thing was becoming worryingly inexplicable. How did we become so vulnerable? It just didn't make sense— It was happening so quickly that all I could do was sit there bewildered by our lack of foresight, our imprudence, and our blind arrogance as a nation. Why did we outsource so much of our food production to far-away places and foreign nations? Are we just blind? Here was my ultimate fear manifest. Years of asking what the effects of outsourcing so much of our food might be was potentially about to answered before my eyes.

Would the local government take control of the food supply

in order to put down food riots? Would they lock the doors and station cops in front of the grocery stores so that food rationing could begin, like in Bill's book? I'll admit I was getting a little crazy in my thought process. But the irony was that we were reportedly the most powerful country in the world, and yet so quickly brought to our knees. The economy came to a screeching halt. Millions were suddenly out of work. People would start to go hungry.

I knew that we as a community did not have nearly enough food production capacity to feed our citizens, and what we could grow wouldn't be harvested for several months. We were alone on the edge of wilderness in the heart of the Appalachian Mountains. There was no map for this, no clear idea of what might lay ahead; just a worrying lack of sense in it all. Are we all just plain stupid? Someone should have seen this coming and done something about it, right? People in many rural, "under-developed" regions around the world, I thought, would fare much better through this thing simply because they were closer to their own food production.

In early June, I began to feel extremely uneasy. There was, after all, nothing that I could do by then. It was too late. If we plowed under hay pasture and started planting corn or potatoes right then, we wouldn't be harvesting anything for months, at best, except for perhaps some salad greens if we planted them also, but they don't go very far in the calorie department.

Even more people started losing their jobs, and more by the millions. With the chicken coop so close to the road, I became worried that someone might try to steal some chickens, or the whole coop, if things got really bad for them.

"Who knows what some people are capable of when they've got hungry children at home," Butch told me over the phone. "You probably better move it."

The 'egg-mobile' was a movable chicken shack that housed about 100 chickens. It was on wheels so we could move it to different fields and gardens and let the chickens scratch up bugs and fertilize different sections of the farm with the best fertilizer known to man. I hooked it up to the truck and pulled it from a garden down by the road up a hill and closer to the house, where I could more closely watch over them.

Then I started to worry about the cows, and would they be next? I couldn't know how far people might go when they get hungry, when their families get hungry. I just remembered what Mike McConnell said, and how the U.K. was 9 meals away from riots in the streets. It wouldn't take long, I thought.

There was a certain incidental disquiet that I was on my own here on this farm in the middle of nowhere—a disquiet deeply and vividly heightened by the fact that my closest neighbors were not really that close, and the closest one, a quarter of a mile away, was 94 years old. No telling how good he was with a shotgun. What if we needed to block off Avery Creek Road to keep the hordes of hungry from coming up to the mountains to ravage our fields and livestock like some zombie apocalypse?

I had to stop thinking like this. Damn Bill Forstchen and his books! I was getting myself too worked up. With any luck, we might get through this with just a warning from nature. I pressed on with a queasy uncertainty. The first thing to go is always toilet paper, I told myself. Just the rumor of a shortage caused the thing itself. It was all so predictable. Maybe that would be the extent of it, I hoped.

Then it was masks and PPE gear, then ventilators, then antibiotics and other drugs. Then it was chicken and hamburger and other protein. The global supply lines were showing stress. Shut down a few massive factories and the shortages come quickly. Big lesson in that one. But was anyone paying attention?

The bottle neck at meat processing factories caused the long supply line of animals waiting their turn for slaughter to back up. With factories closing because of outbreaks, farmers had nowhere to sell or slaughter their cows and pigs and chickens. It was the domino effect as businesses tumbled backwards toward the farm.

People st ocked up on dry goods and non-perishable goods and Cheetos and frozen pizza. They stopped going to the grocery store every week for milk, eggs and fresh foods like vegetables, and so demand for some of those items dropped quickly and food started rotting in the fields and warehouses, and milk was poured on the ground. It was all so predictable.

Some of the people that were laid off and lost their income started getting hungry. Small children started getting hungry because they had to compete with older siblings for food. And soon one out of five children in the United States didn't have enough to eat. And with school out, there were no free school lunches to make certain they got something to eat.

In the middle of May 2020, the news was getting scary to watch.

"People will be getting out of the city soon. I wouldn't be sitting around New York either, not when the food riots start," said Butch. "How are they going to feed 9 million people, when half of them don't have any money or savings. Most people live paycheck to paycheck, and now a heck of a lot of them have lost their jobs and don't have a source of income. Two weeks and things will start getting out of hand."

Butch continued speaking, at a distance and wearing a mask, while we stood in front of the old schoolhouse. "You're going to need to do something to protect your cattle when things get crazy. People will do anything when they get desperate and hungry. You need to get them up on top of that hill and away from the road. It's more strategic and defensible."

What Butch was talking about started to seem unreal. "You got a rifle?" he asked.

I did have an old rifle but wasn't even sure if it still fired. I went down into the basement and pulled my uncles old WWII M1 carbine rifle out of the gun safe. The standard issue rifle was used by infantrymen in WWII and up through the Korean and into the Vietnam wars.

My uncle Bill, long gone now, used this gun while serving in WWII, so it was now pushing 80 years old. I kept it clean and stored it well, so maybe it would still fire. I had a couple boxes of ammo that were more than 20 years old, probably from the last time I fired it. I had no idea how long ammunition lasted, so just in case I decided to drive by my local gun and ammo shop to pick up a couple new boxes.

A line of 15 people stretched out the door. Because of new regulations allowing only 10 people in a store at one time, including workers, I wasn't sure I wanted to kill an hour or maybe much longer standing in line to buy ammo. I went back the following Monday morning and only a couple people were standing outside. When I got in, I asked the dealer how his business had been in recent weeks.

"Crazy busy," he said. "We've run out of a lot of gun styles and ammo. Most of them, in fact."

"What type of guns are you out of?" I asked.

"AR-15's were the first to go," he said.

It was a little unsettling to hear the dealer say that his biggest sales came from assault weapons. Some people were really hunkering down around here, I thought. The fear and uncertainty of what was happening was causing a lot of people to think about protecting their homes and families with semi-automatic weapons. I purchased a box of carbine ammo for my WWII rifle and went home a little more unnerved. That little excursion to the gun shop didn't make me feel any safer at all.

What was I going to do anyway? Shoot at some guy for trying to steal a chicken? The whole thing was absurd. I put the gun and ammo back in the gun case in the basement, locked it and hid the key. I knew the whole food system balanced precariously on supply chains with weak links that could be broken, but this wasn't me. I needed to stop listening to guys like Butch and hope the weakest links in the chain would hold till this thing ran its course.

For months, all that dominated the news and the minds of the people was the Coronavirus. Everything else would take a back seat, even while our local farmers were facing bankruptcy.

Almost all our small farmers in the region sold to restaurants and at the farmers markets. Both outlets were shut down quickly, and so farmers had produce coming up with nowhere to sell it. They needed another way to sell their produce, or it wouldn't be long before they were out of business and the local farm economy collapsed.

The Corner of Market and Walnut Streets

The downtown Asheville City Market, run by ASAP, finally opened back up with social distancing rules in place. I was still worried and nervous about what was going on but needed to get out of the house, so I went to the market early, before it opened, to help our farm manager set up. We weren't even sure if people would come. I could see the concern in other farmers eyes, which was all I could see of them. Would anyone come now with Covid everywhere?

Then people started arriving. Cars were lining up in the parking lot and along the street as social distancing rules limited the number of people in the outdoor market at one time. A great sense of relief came over the farmers and growers as people started walking between the market tents lining both sides of the street, still trying to keep socially distanced from each other. And then something amazing happened.

The Creekside Farm tent was located near the end of the row of market tents, and I could see the crossroad and the bus stop at the corner of Market and Walnut streets. A large city bus pulled up and stopped, and a whole lot of people got off the bus and started walking towards us. About one-third of them were people of color, which at first surprised me because normally the market didn't attract that many people of color, not in that ratio anyway, not one-third the people getting off the bus.

The sky behind them was a bright white from the early morning sun, and it appeared that some of them didn't exactly know where to go, but the growers at the first tents warmly greeted them and welcomed them home. And they told the first timers how they could purchase vegetables and meats and pasta and rice and prepared foods like sauces and baked goods like breads and even cookies. They told some of the new arrivals where they could go to redeem their SNAP cards if they had them, and how the market worked and how they could use the new Double SNAP benefits to double their spending dollars.

As the day wore on, the cars and busses kept coming and unloading passengers, and more busses and more people came. The farmers and growers were very busy, and everyone was talking and laughing and coming and going, and it was a community built around food again, but this time it was the whole community, not just the well-to-do who could afford to pay a little more for healthy food. It was a beautiful, wonderful thing to see and participate in.

Our little market had suddenly become much more diverse, and because of that, it was much busier and livelier than it would have been, and it continued to grow over the next several weeks and months.

It turns out, the Double SNAP program was working better than we expected. The county health and human services office had posted information and given out bus route maps to the market. MANNA FoodBank and other non-profit organizations had helped to spread the word through social media and other channels, and then word of mouth started to spread the news even further and deeper into the community.

What started with a small $10,000 commitment to underwrite and test the idea, and then the financial backing of some of our wealthier food fighters (who still didn't attend the meetings), the ASAP Double SNAP program exploded into over $200,000 in redeemed Double Snap benefits and over $400,000 in additional sales for farmers. The number of SNAP users at the market tripled, and then doubled again the next year.

The early results proved that we were improving the diets of at-risk households and making healthy food more affordable and accessible, and at the same time helping our local farmers who were struggling. The fact that we now had proof that the program worked allowed Charlie Jackson and ASAP to quickly reach out to other generous organizations and grant funders to grow the program. ASAP was able to quickly expand the program to 8 other farmers markets across Western North Carolina. The sales to SNAP users tripled in the first year, and then doubled again in the second.

After so much inner turmoil from the pandemic, as I stood there watching busses pull up throughout the day and unloading people who, some for the first time in their lives went to market, I felt good. I had a renewed sense of hope about humankind and felt less worried about the pandemic and our future.

The Covid-19 pandemic suddenly left us with a motivated group of radicals with nothing to do.

Social distancing took the wind out of our sails as a rebel organization. There would be no senseless acts of protest. No picket lines. No handcuffing to fenceposts. No arrests. Other more immediate concerns became more important. People were getting laid off and some were getting hungry, while farmers were growing food with nowhere to sell it. For years, local restaurants had been a key customer group for our local growers, and now they were closed down.

My little band of poets and artists and growers were getting antsy. We needed to do something. Anything. This viral disaster could be the impetus to change the food system. It could be the catalyst for change that created a more resilient and self-reliant community, perhaps even a more self-sufficient society, and one that might become less dependent on foreign nations. As we all sat at home, isolated, I thought we might be squandering an opportunity to teach ourselves and others a valuable lesson on self-reliance—a chance to bounce forward.

Many people were just now becoming aware of the insane risks that come from becoming dependent on far-away places for critical drugs and medical supplies. And now they might understand how important it is to retain our own food sovereignty. This could be our big chance to change things, I thought. Maybe people have finally had enough of the modern food era that started with the TV dinner in the 1950's. Maybe they would realize that it's time that we moved on. The modern era of industrialized agriculture was destroying the land and the waterways, that was clear, and perhaps people were starting to recognize that industrial food just isn't all that satisfying or fulfilling anyway. It seemed to me that the combined effects of Covid and climate change could be the knock on the head that launch us into a postmodern era; a post-industrial food era, where things might be less concentrated and fairer to farmers.

For some time now it seemed to me that the world was already changing, and it was moving way beyond solar panels and electric vehicles. It was moving toward sustainability, sustainability with far less reliance on fossil fuels and limited resources. And soon people won't be just demanding paper straws—they're going to want answers to some serious questions, like where did this come from? How was this grown? What is its real cost, including to the environment? How long can this go on? Our kids and grandkids are already asking these questions for us.

But at the time, in the midst of the pandemic, I wasn't sure where to turn next. I felt I needed some spiritual guidance, so I called on my spiritual mentor, Lewis Mumford. He saw me pull up to the house and came out to his front porch. I stood at a distance just off the porch and asked him, straight up, "What do you think will happen? And what do we do now?"

"I'm not sure what to tell you Robert, but now is not the time for protests and revolution. Now is the time for righteous acts." I stood there looking at him, trying to understand what he might have meant by that.

"In the end," said Mumford, "we'll all be judged not by what we believe or say, but by our work. Show people the way by your acts and what you do." I stood still, silent.

"Just do what you can, Robert. That's all," Mumford said. "Grow more food if you can."

And suddenly I was reminded of a book that I had read long ago, back in college; Voltaire's work titled *Candide*. The main character suffers one calamitous event after another, going from rags to riches and back again, and finally ending up poor, on small farm in a foreign country. After all the terrible suffering and hardship that he endures, he asks himself and others, is it all for the better or for the worse? Will things always work out to the best possible outcome?

A wise man, a farmer, gives him the answer, "Just cultivate your garden."

That was all I could do—work the farm. Who knows how things will turn out, or if there is some divine providence that will guide us through it all and to the best possible outcome, so stop worrying about it? All we could do, all we should do, was stop asking unknowable questions and tend to our own garden—accept our lot and do what we can do in the moment.

It was no longer necessary to lead people to some distant Eden, some self-sustaining Utopia or illusory Promised Land. I realized that the most heroic action was to inhabit the place fully and at once, and to offer simple acts of kindness when the opportunities came and when things were in season.

Besides, as Voltaire points out, work in the garden keeps at bay three great evils: boredom, vice and need. And to that I would add a fourth: fear. And a fifth: dependence. Farming is an existence preferable by far to that of kings, who are often betrayed and murdered, said Voltaire.

I am familiar with another story related to Voltaire. Benjamin Franklin met with Voltaire on a trip to France to negotiate its assistance in the American Revolution. The meeting was greatly promoted in the newspapers and billed as a meeting of two of the greatest living minds on earth—the literary sage of France meets the backwoods philosopher from America. Franklin played that role perfectly. French aristocratic ladies loved him and started wearing their hair 'a la Franklin', wrapped in a manner resembling the coonskin hat he would often wear to social events.

I looked up at Mumford in his customary flannel shirt and nylon basketball shorts and thought that no one would ever try to imitate that look. But I was grateful for his homespun advice. We had no idea how long this pandemic would last, or how bad it would get. We could not gather; we could not protest—but we could grow food. We quickly purchased more seeds and transplants and cultivated the ground to plant it all in the late Spring of 2020. We would show the way, and lead by example, to a more resilient future.

As Mumford said that day, it is not what you know or believe or say, it is what you do that matters in this world, and that alone will have lasting impact. We, the food fighters of Western North Carolina, determined at this most perilous hour, as the entire world economy was shutting down, to plant as much seed and grow as much food as we possibly could, and that was all that mattered. That turned out to be our ultimate act of radicalism—a move toward self-reliance and self-provisioning.

How Bad Did It Get?

In the depths of the pandemic, I made a few phone calls to see how this thing was affecting other local farms and food organizations. First, I called my dairy farmer friend and neighbor Lynn Bonham to see how she was doing.

"We're not affected by it yet," she said. "The milk processor is still taking what we can deliver. But I heard milk prices are going to hit the floor after this thing passes. Don't know why that would happen. The people who buy futures, I guess. Don't really understand it."

Like most farmers, Lynn was at the mercy of something she really didn't understand and had no way of responding or planning for it—the whims of the markets.

"I'm thinking I need to set aside more land for growing more vegetables," I told her. "Maybe taking part of the hay field to grow a few more things, like corn and beans. What do you think, Lynn?" I asked her.

"I was thinking the same thing. Maybe we should grow as much as we can, so we don't have to count on the stores so much."

"You have a drill seeder, don't you? Could I borrow that? I'm thinking of letting Melissa do her thing for the CSA, but I think maybe I ought to plant some row crops and grow some bulk food, if I can," I said.

"I have a small two row seeder you can borrow," she answered. "That ought to work good for what you're talking about. It'll plant sweet corn, and I think your beans too. You going to grow bush beans or string beans?"

"I'm thinking string beans, although that's a lot more work stringing 'em up."

"I don't like bush beans that much. I prefer string beans too. Don't blame you."

"Where do you get your seed from, Southern States?" I asked.

"I get my beans from Southern States, and my sweet corn from Valley Ag. I don't know why I go to two places, but I've known them both for years and years and they're all friends of mine. So, I just split up the business and try to help them both out, especially now."

Lynn was tending to her own farm, and in doing that, she helped others. Maybe Providence isn't out there guiding us to a better place, I thought, but our actions will guide us there, if we just do what we can do, and try to do the right thing.

Lynn came out OK, but millions of gallons of milk were dumped on the ground at farms across the country when Covid shut down or slowed down large milk processors and farmers had nowhere to send their raw milk. You can't stop milking a cow, they need to be milked every day, twice a day, or problems can set in for the cow.

One of the reasons Lynn didn't experience disastrous implications like many other dairy farmers was because we still have a regional milk processor in Asheville called Milkco. There used to be hundreds of dairy farms spread out across Buncombe County (now there's just two), and in the 1950's there were 22 milk-bottling plants in Western North Carolina. Now Milkco is the only milk bottling company left in the entire region. It's located in West Asheville, not that far from Firestorm Books as it turns out.

Milkco employs about 250 people at the plant, which makes it one of the larger employers in the county, and they process a whopping one million gallons of raw milk every week. Most of that raw milk supply comes from local farms within a 150-mile radius of Milkco's facility. It's a hold-out in a dairy business that has been decimated by consolidation in recent years.

Milkco President Keith Collins told me that there's been a slight uptick in milk consumption over the recent pandemic months, which may be related to more people eating at home and drinking milk with a meal, versus a soda, a glass of wine, or a beer at a restaurant. It takes a confident man to order a chocolate milk in a restaurant. I know because I do it all the time. But I ask for it in a dirty glass just in case anyone wants to question my manliness.

While most dairy farmers across the country have one massive corporation to send all their milk to, thank goodness, I thought, Asheville still has a local milk processor called Milkco where a farmer can still bring her raw milk. It relates back to the regional strength that we've been talking about.

Regional strength and resilience come from the conscious breaking down of larger national structures into smaller and more manageable local ones, along with the understanding of place—our place. Regionalism is not a political movement toward separatism. We are all proud Americans. But we do need to build self-reliance with the understanding that we are a unique and valuable region with our own strengths and capacities. We can feed ourselves and become less dependent on things from far-away places. Milkco represents that for me.

I called Lee Warren at Organic Growers School to get her take on things. Fortunately, the coronavirus shutdown happened just after their big Spring Conference, the biggest event and source of revenue in the year for that non-profit. Financially they would be OK. Like everyone else, they were all working from home now and using Zoom for meetings.

Mumford and Voltaire's advice to "stop being paralyzed by questions and just tend your garden" was still fresh in my mind, and I remembered how 'Victory Gardens' had once fed millions of people. In my father's generation, at a very scary time during World War II, as much as half the fruits and vegetables consumed in the United States came from local gardens that popped up in parks, vacant lots and backyards. Known as Victory Gardens, they helped reduce the pressure on the food supply brought on by the war. A big part of our rebel strategy at the School of Postmodern Activities became teaching people how to grow more food at home.

"Now would be a good time to bring back Victory Gardens, don't you think?" I asked Lee.

"You're right. Big time," she said. "And we need to set up new systems for people to buy from local farmers. Some growers are setting up roadside stands. The farmers markets are still up in the air at the moment. And of course, restaurants aren't buying anything right now."

"We're trying to drive more people to the web site" Lee continued. "There's some good info on starting a home garden on the site now. We want to start weekly email blasts to suggest and help, like, 'this week plant this.'"

"Great idea," I said. "Speaking of planting, I'm thinking about planting some row crops, like potatoes, corn and beans. Maybe plant a few other things."

"I think it's a good idea, Robert. I'm afraid we're going to need a lot of food to feed some hungry people. Do you need any help?"

"Maybe," I replied, "I was going to ask you that. Can I tap into your network? Not sure if we can pay them, or what we can pay, but if MANNA or someone gets a grant, they might be able to buy what we can grow, and your helpers would get paid from that. But no guarantees right now. Do you think you can find a few people?"

"Let me check into it and get back to you," said Lee.

I realized that OGS had done more to prepare us for this battle that we were now facing than just about anyone else.

Organic Growers School had taught thousands of people how to grow, process, and store food over the past 30 years.

Just about anyone can join in the fight for food security, I thought, and Victory Gardens gave us a darn good example to follow. With young men leaving the farm to fight in the war effort during World War I and World War II, many nations feared that there wouldn't be enough farmers and food producers left to feed the population. Commercial crops were diverted to feeding soldiers overseas, and food rationing that began in the Spring of 1942 became another incentive to get Americans to grow some of their own food in backyard gardens and plots of land wherever they could find it.

The US Department of Agriculture and other organizations printed instructional gardening pamphlets and even issued shovels and other gardening tools. Gardening radio shows encouraged gardeners with helpful tips on growing vegetables. Posters popped up everywhere with slogans like "Our food is fighting", "Grow your own, can your own" and "Sow the seeds of Victory!"

Victory gardens kept Americans fed at home by producing over 40%, and by some accounts almost half, the fruits and vegetables consumed in the United States towards the end of WWII.[161] Having more food grown locally in neighborhoods also reduced the need for trucks, transportation, and fuel that could be redirected to the war effort and transporting valuable military equipment and supplies. Victory Gardens have already shown us that we can become a nation of gardeners and local food producers again if we had to.

The Victory Garden movement also united and energized the home-front and gave people feelings of empowerment at a fearful time. I remembered Lee's mention of those studies showing that growing your own food has psychological benefits, and creates feelings of self-reliance, confidence, and community strength. We needed that.

With people laid off or out of work by COVID, home gardens did start popping up in neighborhoods around the country. Perhaps the fear of food shortages or the fear of going into a grocery store also gave people an incentive to grow some of their own food at home. Record sales of gardening books, tools and supplies were registered at the major home and garden centers.

After Lee and Lynn both showed their support of the idea to grow some row crops at Creekside, I started to think about putting the plan into action. I would need seed, and so I called my buddy Levi over at Southern States to check on seed availability and asked how things were going there. He said they had a run on feed, but everything else was pretty normal for this time of year. Spring planting time is always crazy. And it appeared that farmers hadn't stopped or slowed down, which was a good sign.

"Had a run on feed, huh? Why is that do you think?"

"I don't know for sure," said Levy. "I think a lot of farmers just wanted to stockpile it in case there's a 'shelter in place' message from the governor. They didn't want to be caught short. Of course, we'll be able to stay open since we're an essential service for food and farmers and all. I'm not worried about that."

Levi had the seed that I needed in stock. After that call, I gave my farmer neighbor Jason Davis a call to see what this pandemic was doing to his business and crop planning. Jason is one of the biggest farmers in the county, and he farms about 1500 acres of land conventionally, some that he owns but mostly land that he leases from neighbors.

Unlike most of the small growers and farmers in the area growing organically on five acres or less, Jason is a big-time farmer with big equipment like large tractors and combine harvesters. He grows some grains like corn, but also more labor-intensive crops like tomatoes and strawberries.

"I'm hoping this passes quickly," Jason said. "We need our Mexican migrant worker force, and right now they've stopped processing H2A applications for temporary farm worker visas. And of course, the border with Mexico has been closed. If they don't change things quick, farms around here will be hurting real soon and our vegetable supply in this country will be severely impacted."

"Wow—that could lead to some serious food shortages this summer and fall. The administration has to see this, right?"

"I think they see it and will have to do something fast. These are essential workers for sure. They plant and pick our food."

Recent research had shown that the food system cannot withstand a 10% labor shortage for more than a few months, and a 25% reduction in labor would cause a 49% reduction in food production. Labor shortages, the study noted, could be between 20% to 40% in the next severe pandemic, which could devastate the food system.

Worse yet, news reports were already showing how many migrant workers were getting sick. Many migrant workers lived together in cramped, temporary housing, and they drove to the fields in tightly packed vans and busses. Workers in the fields of Mexico and Central America were also getting sick. The pandemic looked like it was starting to affect food labor and so our food supply.

"Do you have any other concerns? I guess social distancing isn't really a problem on the farm, right? Most of your workers will be safe, I mean a guy on a tractor out in a field. And workers can always stay a few rows apart. But is anything else concerning you?"

"No, not really. I think there will be enough supply of seeds and fertilizers and pesticides and things like that. Fuel shouldn't be a problem. Mostly just the workers. We're in real trouble without them. It's been a struggle for the past couple of years to get enough workers anyway and we don't need anything compounding that problem."

"What about demand for your products? Restaurants are shut down, but people will still have to eat so business at grocery stores should go up, which would make up most of the difference, right?"

"We may see a downturn in consumption of vegetables. A lot of people may just stock up on frozen burgers and mac 'n cheese. I don't know. We might also see a surge in demand after this passes and more people start canning and storing their own vegetables. I don't know."

That made a lot of sense. I wouldn't doubt that there would be a surge in the purchase of mason jars and canning equipment after this. I asked another question.

"I'm thinking about planting some row crops in my upper pasture. Maybe some beans, potatoes and corn, just in case. Might need the food in a few months. What do you think?"

"Might not be a bad idea," said Jason.

"I'm just not sure what kind of equipment I'm going to need. I'd be growing this conventionally. Do you have a potato mounder? I might need to borrow it."

"Sure you can. You'll also need a lay-off plow, and I got a couple of those here. You're welcome to it."

"I appreciate any advice you can give, I mean, if I do this," I said. "I'm kind of flying blind here. But I just don't want to have any regrets in a few months if we needed the food and I didn't do anything about it now. Hopefully it won't be needed, but I have to make a decision and spend some money now if I'm going to do it. I need to buy seed and get the ground ready."

"Well, I'll be here if you need me," said Jason. "And I'll stop by when I'm over your way to check in on you."

I remember thinking how grateful I was for all those people like Jason and others working across the food supply chain to ensure that our food is planted, harvested, and processed, and those others that were making sure our grocery shelves are stocked and food was available to people—and at no small risk to themselves. It took selfless sacrifice, hard work and some personal risk to ensure the continuity of our food system during the pandemic. If our food supply broke down, this pandemic would move from a crisis to a catastrophe. I think I just really started to appreciate the people working across the food system a little more.

That was it then. I had no reason not to try it, other than a little work and a few thousand dollars invested in seeds and soil amendments. The only question that remained was how deep and how big? I could grow one acre or ten acres. I needed the hay field to grow hay for the cattle for winter, but we all had to get through the summer and fall first. And I would likely be able to buy hay from other farms if I needed it the next winter anyway.

Calories Are What Count

I decided we would plant eight acres of corn and about 4 acres of potatoes. Why did I choose to grow corn and potatoes? Because I ran the numbers—and in the end, calories are what counts. Calories matter because every one of us needs about one million of them every year. They certainly aren't the only thing we need; we also need vitamins and minerals, fats and protein. But if we don't have those 1 million calories for energy, other needs start to fade into the background.

In the vegetable kingdom, both corn and potatoes are very high calorie foods. Corn gets a bad rap all the time because of the high fructose corn syrup used in many processed foods and soft drinks, and that's true, it can be made into cheap sugar. But corn is also a great source of good calories, and if you use the metric "calories per acre," corn ranks highest in crop yields.

Corn has been an especially important plant in North America for a very long time, having been a staple crop for indigenous people since it was first domesticated in the Americas thousands of years ago.

In 2018, the average corn yield in the United States was 171 bushels per acre for corn. The world record is 503 bushels, set by a farmer in Valdosta, Ga. Each bushel weighs 56 pounds and each pound of corn yields about 1,566 calories. That means corn averages roughly 15 million calories per acre, so theoretically, each acre would provide the annual caloric intake for about 15 people.

This estimate is related to field corn, or dent corn, which is dried before processing. Sweet corn and popcorn are different varieties, grown for much more limited uses, and have slightly lower yields. But with some easy math I could quickly determine that my eight acres of corn could feed roughly 120 people their caloric requirements for a full year (eight acres times fifteen people per acre).

By contrast, wheat comes in at about 4 million calories per acre, and soybeans at 6 million. Rice is also very high-yielding, at 11 million calories per acre. Beans are high in protein and calories, but they're very labor intensive to string up, and even bush beans are hard to harvest by hand. We just didn't have the labor, so I gave up on planting beans.

The other vegetables we were already growing for the CSA, while much more nutritious than corn, are far less calorie and energy dense. Broccoli yields about 2.5 million calories per acre, and spinach is under 2 million. We all need those vegetables, but we get our full days' worth of vitamins and nutrition from them in a fraction of the 2,000 calories that we need for energy every day. That leaves plenty of room for inexpensive, easily grown calories that aren't as nutrient-dense, like corn and potatoes.

Potatoes are one of the few crops that can rival corn because they also yield about 15 million calories per acre. Five acres of potatoes would yield enough calories to feed another 80 people. Together, we could grow enough corn and potatoes to support the caloric needs of roughly 200 people for a year; or 400 people for six months. We had about 100 chickens that gave us about 80 to 90 eggs per day in the summer for a good protein source. We could also butcher a cow occasionally for about 600 pounds of protein. It started to look like we might be able to feed most of the people in Walnut Cove, if we had to, and if I didn't screw it all up.

There might be a lot more than 400 people living in Walnut Cove, I thought, as you go further up the mountain. I never actually took a census or counted homes, and you can't see most of the houses in the woods. A cove is like a valley that doesn't go anywhere because mountains close it off at one end. It's a valley with mountains on three sides, often with one way in and out. In our case, that was Avery Creek Road. My farm sits on a hilltop, and I can see the circle of mountains and hillsides that make up the cove and that held within its mountain walls most of the residents that made up what I considered to be my neighborhood.

Perhaps we couldn't feed everyone, but at least it gave me a target to shoot for. We couldn't feed the world, but maybe we could feed these people right here, if we had to. And I could put a face on it, my neighbor's face, and a specific geographic location, the valley and the hills surrounding my farm.

It was still early June, a bit late to be planting, when food fighters led by Butch showed up at the farm and we planted corn and potatoes, and then we planted some more. Butch borrowed Mumford's old 1942 International Harvester and the mounder attachment to hill the rows for potatoes. That was after I got the ground ready and cultivated with my big tractor. Then we borrowed Lynn's seed drill and planted rows of corn. The whole process went fast without much trouble.

If anyone asked me that spring what they should grow at home, I suggested they try planting beans, corn and squash (the three sisters), and potatoes, like the Native North and South Americans did. Then plant whatever else you want.

MANNA in Covid

Calling and checking in with all these people was reminding me how powerful my community was, so I called my friend Chad Conaty from MANNA FoodBank to see how they were doing in this pandemic. News reports were already talking about how food banks were starting to get overwhelmed by mid-March 2020. What made things particularly difficult was that large groups of older, retired people, who were regular volunteers at MANNA, stopped coming to volunteer because of the health risks for them. Fifty percent of the volunteer force who sort and pack the food were 55 and older, and MANNA couldn't see putting them at risk either.

Entire church groups and youth groups who would normally show up for regular service had to stop coming. Meanwhile, other organizations, like Habitat for Humanity, were getting shut down and many of those groups and volunteers came over to MANNA to help out. Some people just need to serve.

Chad set up a meeting at my farm as demand at MANNA was skyrocketing. He invited a couple other people from the organization, including the director of sourcing. We were coming together to discuss what the farm might grow just for MANNA. We had been donating food to MANNA every year, but Chad wanted to know if there was something else that we might be able to grow in bulk just for them. He brought a list of what they needed and what their clients were asking for at the food banks. Collards and mustard greens were first on the list. Hey, we're in North Carolina.

"We could also use peppers and red potatoes if you can grow them," Chad said.

I said that I didn't know about the collards and mustard greens, but we might have some corn and potatoes. I said that I would keep them posted when things were ready for harvest, but I couldn't really commit because I hadn't done this before, and I wasn't sure how the crops would come out.

MANNA Foodbank got slammed by COVID. The number of households coming to them for food assistance doubled over pre-pandemic levels. The need for food increased more than 60% since the start of the pandemic. And when you consider that one in five children in Western North Carolina lived in a food-insecure household even before the pandemic hit, you can better understand the numbers and the need.

From April 2020 through April 2021 MANNA provided over 25.6 million meals to residents in Western North Carolina. That's about 65,000 meals per day, and they still did that after losing a big part of their volunteer labor base because of COVID risk to older folks. Other groups, including members of the national guard, stepped up to fill the boxes and distribute the food.

We started to have more meetings at the farm to formulate the crop plan and figure out how to implement it with projected labor needs, and I started to realize that I had more of a support network than I thought. I started to realize that we had already created this hub where people could come together, talk, plan, share ideas and learn from each other. And we were dramatically increasing the amount of food that the farm produced, and the larger community was starting to grow a lot more food in backyards and community gardens. It looked like we were starting to 'bounce forward', something Laura Lengnick was talking about.

Early in the pandemic, while I was freaking out about the coming zombie apocalypse, George Wiley's army of pollical activists were bogging down in the trenches. But in the Spring of 2020, we started to figure things out.

The pandemic lock-down enveloped the world by mid-2020, and the food fighters, led by people like George Wiley, came up with a plan that included two priorities: Grow as much food as possible and teach people to grow some of their own food in their own backyards and community gardens. The goal was hundreds of Victory Gardens across the region, each one a little rebel base of help and resistance.

We organized and started giving in-person but socially

distanced outdoor gardening classes. We also directed people to the best books and gardening channels on YouTube. We printed and distributed pamphlets with simple gardening tips and other info on where to purchase seeds and transplants.

We dug up old WWI and WWII Victory Garden posters from the internet and digitally modified them to include some additional messaging. We were a subversive organization after all—what did you expect? We liked the old, retro look of the posters, but if a poster said, "Dig For Victory!" we changed it to say, "Dig For Food Sovereignty!" and "Dig For Climate!" If it showed a picture of a farm basket and said, "Fill It!" we added text at the bottom "Without all the Chemicals!" If it said, "Grow More Food" we added "Stop Corporate Concentration". Why not add a little revolutionary messaging while we were at it, what the heck?

Sometimes we would just erase the old text entirely and add our own subversive message like "Shop at a Farmers Market" or "Eat a Plant Based Diet" or "Join the Women's Land Army" or whatever we wanted. One said, "For a happy, healthy life, Be a Farmer." I don't know how many people we convinced to change careers because of a poster but it sure looked cool, with a drawing of a girl from 1944 standing on a hill holding a pitchfork. The editing software was so simple even I could do it. You can view some of our posters at EatYourView.com in the Gallery tab. Print them up if you want. Staple one up to a telephone pole. Be a radical.

Jerry, my printer and insurgent at Whole Foods, printed up the full-size Victory Garden posters and we hung them up around Asheville or gave them away. Jerry wisely added the web site addresses where people could find more information about starting their own Victory Garden. He still shopped at Whole Foods, by the way, but always looked a little more closely at the packaging and never forgets to bring his reading glasses. If he can tell that it came from China or somewhere else far away, he puts it back on the shelf, and sometimes calls me about it.

We gave away or loaned out equipment and tools like shovels and hoes from the farm. Sometimes we would run the tractor down the road to till up a neighbor's yard. I had a friend who owned City Bakery in Asheville who really started feeling the pinch when local restaurants closed down because a lot of his business came from baking fresh bread for those restaurants, including his own sandwich shops. So, we offered and took orders from our CSA members for City Bakery bread, and CSA members could pick up fresh baked bread during the weekly vegetable pick up, which became a limited contact, Covid-safe, drive thru process.

We sent another cow off to the butcher and offered meat to our members. We worked a deal with a small, local creamery to distribute dairy products to our members, including locally produced butter, cheese, milk and cream products. And we started distributing some produce from other farms to our CSA members and at the market to cover the things we didn't grow ourselves. We were setting up new distribution channels for food—an entirely new food system. Covid was helping us to build our own local food distribution network. We were aggregating food, collecting it from multiple producers, sorting it and distributing it. It was small scale, but it was an entirely new business model that supported several businesses. We weren't just bouncing back from Covid, we were bouncing forward.

While we were at it, we started mobilizing radical food fighters in the fields. We were growing more food at the farm in bulk than we ever had, and some of our food fighters began helping with the chickens and raising a few hogs for pork.

There was always help needed pulling weeds and watering plants, and there was always someone working in the trenches.

Many food fighters also started helping at other farms so those farmers could stay afloat. Other fighters with digital media experience started helping farmers by promoting their produce on social media and building Instagram accounts or internet stores. An entire network of people with different occupational experiences became food fighters, at a time when it was needed most.

We started distributing the ASAP Local Food Guide and directing people to the on-line version through social media so they could find places where they could purchase food directly from other farmers, whether that was through roadside stands or new online shopping sites. That put more of the retail dollars into the farmers pockets, and not just the wholesale dollars that they used to get from restaurants and grocers. Some of the food fighters were helping to make the Asheville City Market and other farmers markets compliant with social distancing rules by volunteering to direct traffic and customer flow, and by encouraging attendance through their own networks and social media accounts.

We increased the number of CSA shares and maxed out our CSA membership, and we brought more food to the farmers market than ever before, which meant we were feeding more people directly from our farm, in addition to the row crops we planted.

While we were struggling to get more plants in and out of the ground, we were building overall resilience as a community. We promoted our Eat Your View web site through signage and social media and distributed hundreds of bumper stickers with the web site address. We pushed links to Organic Growers School for on-line gardening classes and farming information, and to the ASAP local food guide with its own links to find a CSA membership, farm stands and nearby farmer's market. Links on top of links in a growing network.

Several organizations started producing short cooking videos to teach people how to cook quick and easy healthy meals at home, and other short videos to teach kids about healthy food and where it comes from. We added links to more videos about canning and storing food. And as often as we could, we promoted the local dairy processor, the local flour mill, local meat producers, and of course, local farmers. The pandemic became the disrupter that helped us bounce forward with new ties and networks that made our community and our region stronger, and we discovered community assets like people, equipment, and infrastructures that we never knew we had.

CHAPTER ELEVEN

HARVEST

When it came time to harvest the row crops of corn and potatoes, a small army of food fighters showed up to help pick and pack tons of food.

Over the summer and fall of 2020 there were some food shortages, but the farmers, distributors, wholesalers, grocery stores and grocery workers stepped up and kept the distribution channels open and functioning, which was a great relief. None of the weak links in the food system broke. And because the system held, our row crops weren't needed to feed all the residents of Walnut Cove and the surrounding neighborhood, as I had feared, but demand was way up at food banks because so many people were out of work.

The food fighters came to the rescue. They did the hard work of walking the rows to harvest potatoes and corn by hand and then box them up and walk those boxes back to the truck parked in the field. Even with all of the help it took a several days of strenuous work.

The rebel guitar players, the artists and tree huggers, the socialists and beatnik poets, the small farmers and backyard growers, the lady who runs the farmers market and some of the people who go to the market, they were the ones who showed up when it mattered.

These people who serve other people in time of need, like those who volunteer at MANNA FoodBank, they are society's back up plan. When people lost jobs and hunger set in, the question wasn't "What's our back-up plan?", because there wasn't any back up plan. The real question was, "Who's our back-up plan?" Whenever society fails to protect the most vulnerable among us, the question is always, who will step up? When the system breaks down or doesn't work, and people need a helping hand, it is always those volunteers who serve others that fill in the gaps and make a community stronger and more resilient.

Throughout this time, I kept asking myself, why do people do this stuff? What makes them volunteer to work in the fields or serve at a food kitchen? Why are they so willing to serve others and working so hard to right a wrong? What made them food fighters? It was a diverse group from diverse backgrounds to be certain, and no two people were the same. But I had been around the Food Fighters long enough to identify a few key values and character traits that they all shared to one degree or another.

The Food Fighters and the Core Human Strengths

Maybe this question kept coming up for me because there's no profit in it, and it goes against my own capitalist pig-dog tendencies. I don't know. I just really wanted to understand these people.

Who are these people that fight injustice at great personal cost and hardship, and why do they do it? What are the character traits that describe a good and virtuous person? How do we identify a decent human being, and how do we define strength of character?

It may not always be easy to identify a human virtue or character strength until you get to know someone, and I believe it is sometimes easier to spot a character flaw, the opposite of a given strength. We seem quicker to point out the flaws than the strengths anyway.

These are the values and strengths that make a movement and help to spur social change. Without them, nothing happens. I describe them here because I have a hunch that these are the traits that defined members in our own movement. They also happen to be the core values that underly a healthy democracy, and I believe they should be considered when entering a voting booth. I also believe that these are the things that keep evil and chaos at bay in society.

We all know and can recognize these traits innately, but it is research in the field of positive psychology that gives us many of the terms and definitions I've chosen to share here.[162] In order to remember them, I created an acronym using the first letter of each trait to spell the word 'justice', which is the first strength in the list.

The food fighters believed in JUSTICE, which includes fairness and doing what is right based on moral reasoning. They believed that every human being has a right to eat, no matter what their circumstances, and many also believed that it wasn't right or just when a few powerful people take control of the food system, because that is a form of tyranny. The opposite of justice or fairness as a character trait might be called selfishness, egotism, self-centeredness, meanness, prejudice, and cruelty.

The food fighters valued UNDERSTANDING, wisdom and knowledge, and they had a love of science and learning. This also includes the traits of creativity, curiosity, and open-mindedness. The food fighters weren't all looking to find some fantasized utopia. They listened to the climatologists and the soil scientists. They based decisions on scientific evidence and fact. The opposite is described with words like ignorance, misguided, delusional, or an inability to see and understand things from different points of view.

The food fighters searched for SPIRITUALITY and transcendence, which includes the ability to find deeper meaning, to transcend, to sense awe and the sublime, to look beyond your own self-interest and with some deeper experience or reality. It is the ability to sense awe and wonder in art or the natural world, and it usually manifests in deep connections with nature and the environment. It also includes traits such as Appreciation of Beauty, Gratitude, Hope, and Humor. The opposite would be people who seem shallow, trivial, oblivious, crude, and banal; they miss the meaning and experience of life entirely.

The food fighters practiced TEMPERANCE, or the ability to temper one's feelings, and it includes prudence, self-regulation, and self-control. This virtue protects us (often from ourselves and excessive behavior). It helps us to look out for our "future selves" and keeps us from regret. It also includes the traits of humility and modesty, forgiveness and mercy. The opposite is rash behavior, over-reacting, gluttony, excessive greed, addiction, perversion, rage, arrogance, hate and other uncontrolled emotions, primarily due to a lack of self-control. Most food fighters tempered their desires and needs for things, lived simply and were satisfied with their situation. It was temperance and patience that kept many of us from turning into an angry mob and running down the street. Temperance also includes the concept of moderation. Everything in moderation, as the saying goes, even the beer.

The food fighters loved INDEPENDENCE and self-reliance, which includes a strong work ethic, persistence, and determination. It means 'pulling your weight' and working to provide for your family. Many food fighters worked hard in the fields and gardens for their own self provisioning. The opposite would be described as sloth, laziness, or dependence on others for basic needs.

The food fighters often expressed COURAGE and bravery, and the closely related traits of perseverance (to endure suffering and hardship), honesty and integrity. The opposite is cowardice, overwhelming and uncontrolled fear, and dishonesty. It takes courage to stand up for what you believe in. Farmers by nature of their occupation must have courage because they risk it all, every year, when they till and plant the ground, fully knowing that pests and the weather might ruin them.

It is interesting to know that you can strengthen all of these human virtues with a little practice and exercise, like strengthening a muscle in your arm. Push past your comfort level, and little by little you build that strength. Thus, small acts of bravery, like sending an email to your congressman or starting a community garden, builds the virtue of courage.

The food fighters fought for EQUALITY because they believed in humanity, or the sameness of all human beings, and it includes love, kindness and relationships, and an ability to connect with others. It also includes empathy and an ability to put yourself in someone else's shoes, to understand the human condition. It includes a belief in the fair and equal treatment of others. The opposite is expressed as shallowness, racism, self-interest, petty self-concern, hate, and an inability to connect with others and humanity[163]

I believe that these are the core human virtues in all humankind. Take it for what it's worth, but I believe that many of these core human strengths are what drive people to work in the fields and urban gardens and at the food kitchens. And while not everyone has all the key character strengths or traits described above in the same measure, everyone has some key strengths, at least one or two of them, that help to define their character.

For example, as I got to know the kid with the blonde dreadlocks who I first encountered at Firestorm Books accessing free internet, I was able to identify two key strengths from the above list. In him, I discovered the key traits of courage and spirituality. He was fearless and he lived for transcendent moments on mountain tops. He lost out on temperance because he smoked way too much pot and partied until two in the morning most nights. But he had these key redeeming qualities and strengths, as all the food fighters did.

Here's the important thing. Doing what we know is right affects our self-esteem and happiness, as we discussed earlier. Feelings of self-respect and 'life satisfaction' come from the willful pursuit of morally praiseworthy activities. And human dignity comes with the respect of nature and all its creatures.

Many of the food fighters were pot smokers and some heavy drinkers and they didn't all fit into the accepted norms of our capitalistic modern society in the way they looked, dressed, and often acted. Most couldn't sit in a cubicle all day, and needed to be outdoors as much as possible, and they didn't buy a lot of unnecessary stuff to support America's GDP. But they had human strengths that make them invaluable in our postmodern world, and they would perhaps lead us all to our salvation because they defined many of the values that are at the root of sustainable living and positive human behavior.

Will Change Come?

The chilling effects of the Covid-19 crises became the twist in the plot that forced our radical movement to change course and to see a different path. The revolution turned from one of angry protest into acts of love and kindness, as we began to focus our energies on the critical need of feeding the hungry and helping small farmers produce and distribute more food within the community. This was the work of creating an entirely new food system, based on aggregating food from various producers and distributing it in a food system based on local ownership and fair, democratic governance. It would become a model for a much larger regional system of food production and distribution, a microcosm of the larger macrocosm that was needed if we were ever going to take back control of our food, sequester carbon at scale, and limit the effects of climate change.

Prior to the pandemic all I kept thinking about was how we might change a system so firmly entrenched by powerful multinational corporations and big money and asking myself scary questions like—is an uprising or the threat of radical revolution the only course of action that will wake people up? My head was filled with research and outrage about the industrialized, global food web and the innate risks and problems that it creates for the health of people and the planet. I wanted people to get jolted out of everyday complacency and see the food world as it really is; a risky and dangerous place where very few people control what we're all having for dinner, at the great peril of our soils, waterways, insects, and wildlife.

In a small way, I got what I wanted. Covid-19 revealed the vulnerabilities in our food system that in good times went unnoticed. The shockwaves of a meat plant shutdown exposed some of the weak links in our food chain that left many grocery store shelves empty of staple products like meat, eggs, and milk, if only for a short time. The industrialized system that made the abundance of the American supermarket possible now seemed questionable, if not completely misguided. This was a warning—one of those small "shocks" that Laura Lengnick often talked about that might be a necessary knock on the head. And let's not forget that the industrialized food system was easily linked to the chronic diseases that made us all unhealthier and more vulnerable to Covid-19 in the first place.

More people now, including some politicians, are beginning to realize the necessity to decentralize the entire system. We can no longer depend on a few centralized, massive facilities for concentrated mass production. We need hundreds or thousands of food processors spread out across the country so that the closure or disruption at one facility will not cause havoc for millions of people. And relevant to all of it is a recent statement by President Joe Biden to a group of farmer representatives; "Capitalism without competition is not capitalism. It's exploitation." People are starting to listen and understand.

The food fighters were forced to set up an entirely new food aggregation and distribution system that was not tied to the global food supply chain. With time and a lot more work, we could build the infrastructure for a more solid regional plan that could become a model for other communities and regions to follow. It was becoming clear to me that what was needed was a regionally based food system that focuses on local farms and local food processors, and one that is not completely dependent on long-distance transportation or large multinationals. If we could grind wheat and make bread or pasta at some size and scale, we could do anything.

Our disrupter rebels simply refused to trade resilience and

self-reliance for efficiency and price. They dared to imagine how different things might be if there were still tens of thousands of chicken and pig farmers bringing their animals to thousands of regional slaughterhouses spread out across the United States, like in previous decades. They dared to imagine hundreds of flour mills grinding wheat, and thousands of regional 'mom and pop' producers of things like bread and pasta.

Another future outbreak or crisis would barely disturb the system because of its innate redundancy across the country. Meat would probably be a little more expensive, but the system would be one thousand times more resilient, making a complete breakdown in the national supply chain a non-issue, and at the same time spreading out the profits and wealth among the local and regional communities where it can circle around a few more times. While the food chain was buckling under the pandemic, our rebel heroes worked hard to prove that local food systems, with more work and improvement can be incredibly resilient under the strain.

Will the pandemic become a catalyst for deindustrializing and decentralizing the American food system, breaking up the meat oligopoly and pushing for policies and action that might sacrifice some degree of efficiency in favor of much greater resilience?

A lot of the groundwork has already been laid. There are currently more than 10,000 farmers markets in the U.S, up from just 1700 two decades ago, and many already offer local meats, cheese and other dairy products, grains and rice, canned and baked goods. Tens of thousands of Community Supported Agriculture (CSA) programs now exist around the world, while there were almost none just a decade ago. The National Restaurant Association says that Farm to Table is now the #1 restaurant trend in America. There is a growing awareness to the perils of high sugar, high fat, high calorie processed foods and the companies who make them.

The movement already stood on firm, cultivated ground. The global pandemic only brought a deeper meaning and a sense of urgency to it. We must redefine the nature of food security and move from a global and national system to multiple regionally based systems where there is redundancy built into the system.

I remember again that time as a child driving down that road with my father and counting the bugs that hit the windshield, and the memory of that strange Jackson Pollack painting splattered across the glass in bright greens, reds and yellows is burned deep into my mind but has taken on a different meaning for me now. The memory paints a vivid picture of the stark loss of biodiversity on this planet since my childhood.

Forgetting for the moment about the thousands of species of plants and animals that are already gone or near extinction, the simple fact that there are 45% fewer insects in North America now than in the 1960's, including many that we depend on to pollinate our crops, is truly difficult to comprehend. That there are 30% fewer birds flying over our heads than there were the 1970's is completely unsettling to me. The loss of biodiversity on this planet has been catastrophic, and so much of it is closely related to our chemically intensive, industrial-scale agricultural system that has been taken over by a very few powerful men.

There is an oligarchy of massive corporations that grab most of the profit in the food economy. They squeeze profits out of farmers and consumers and dump the costs of environmental damage on the rest of us and future generations. They also dump the true costs of their inputs, like subsidized corn and soybeans, on the U.S. taxpayer. Large multinationals control a food system that is keeping farmers on the edge of solvency while it destroys our soils and ecosystems.

We cannot assume that a company focused on profits for shareholders will concern itself with the complexities of nature and its ecosystems, or with the environmental damage that they leave behind. But as informed consumers, our shared human responsibility, shared values, and collective conscience will call us to recognize the need for changes in production and consumption.

Never in history have human beings faced such serious threats to our food security, including a terrible loss of biodiversity, global desertification, significant loss of topsoil, climate change and massive concentration of power in the food supply. We lose over one ton of topsoil for every ton of corn we pull off the land; four tons per acre on average per year, and we know this cannot go on. We have 60 years of topsoil left, says the U.N., or just 60 harvests.

But there are tools within capitalism to fix our problems. We can invest public and private funds into smart solutions, like regenerative agriculture, which improve our soils and farmer yields. Consumer education will also lead us to a more sustainable future because we can all easily vote with our dollars. The only question is this: can we influence General Mills, or even Exxon, to source more sustainably? Can companies like Exxon require their suppliers, the ethanol refineries and the farmers who supply them, to use cover crops when producing the corn for ethanol? That simple question can create a choice for consumers about which corner gas station they choose to pull into. And can we someday choose to purchase meat from cattle that, if not pasture raised, are at least fed corn grown with regenerative practices like cover crops and reduced chemical applications? I think the answer is yes, and I believe consumers will soon demand that choice.

We must make our peace with the biosphere. That requires building closer ties between people and regenerative, sustainable food production—relationships that are good for the health of human beings and the environment. It also requires building closer relationships between communities and local, sustainable food sources.

The solutions to our problems, I believe, mostly involve impact investing and consumer education. Wall Street investment in farmland is not a good idea. Public and private investments in tools for regenerative agriculture are a good idea for farmer incomes, consumers, and the planet. Links to more information about regenerative agriculture can be found on my website at www.roberteturner.com. The 'e' stands for Emmett. Don't laugh.

Let's not forget that regenerative agriculture is the most cost-effective solution that we have to pull excess carbon from the atmosphere and store it in the ground. It is the key to atmospheric carbon mitigation and climate change. Regenerative agriculture can capture and store over one ton of carbon per acre, per year. Building up soil organic matter can increase carbon sequestration and reduce overall greenhouse gasses.

Increasing solar function and carbon storage, increasing soil organic matter, mycorrhizal fungi, and soil microbes, all through regenerative practices, will reduce soil erosion and allow our soils to become more resilient to the threats of climate change, including drought and flood. We achieve that with multi-species cover crops, no till and limited till planting, crop rotations, reduced chemical applications, and organic practices. Regenerative agriculture also supports the necessary biodiversity, including bugs, birds, plants and animals. We must move away from a corn economy, get animals out of CAFO's and back on pasture, and produce food closer to where it's consumed using regenerative farming practices.

There you have it. I've beaten it all into your head several times, and now you probably know more about farming and food than most of your friends and neighbors. The good news is that you can enlist their help using simple tools within capitalism. Encourage your friends to buy local and convince your grocer and favorite restaurants to carry local foods. Buy grass fed beef when you can. Go to the farmers market. Join a Community Supported Agriculture (CSA) program. Vote, and call your congressman or congresswomen. Influence corporations with your purchases and consider sending them an email once in a while.

Small civic organizations are the School of Democracy, including things like a food bank, a farmers market, a garden club, a CSA, a community garden, or an Organic Growers School. This is where it all starts. This is where change begins and spreads. Change happens when people come together.

Sometimes disruption can be a good thing because it can help to bring change. It was the fall of tobacco that helped expand a local, healthy food movement, and a more resilient community in Asheville, through the work of ASAP and other farmers and organizations in this region where I live. The demise of tobacco added greatly to our food sovereignty, food security, and community resilience. Disruption of a powerful industry (like big tobacco) gave us the ability to adapt and change, to become stronger and more self-reliant.

But the fall of big tobacco didn't come without a fight. The lies, deceit and corruption were all there. The false 'research' and 'scientific studies' funded by the tobacco companies, the flat out lies to congress from tobacco company CEO's, the company infiltration of scientific and public organizations, the corporate spies; we now know full well the whole sordid story. That same game-plan is working now in the processed food industry and the industrial agriculture system that supports it.

I want to take those lessons learned from the fall of big tobacco and the Covid pandemic and bring them to the Midwestern corn belt. If electric vehicles are going to drive corn farmers to the brink of mass disruption, I want the food fighters, with their experiences of success, to be there ahead of time to see if we can help others prepare for it. And more importantly, to see if we could use this coming disruption as a catalyst for change in growing practices. Could we convince farmers to use more regenerative farming practices that might turn some part of the corn belt, like Central Illinois, into a giant carbon sink? Many farmers were already using no-till methods there, but less than 6% were using cover crops. Could we get them to start using cover crops and then rotate the cash crops into something other than just corn and soybeans. Could we help them build up the soil, and eventually reduce or eliminate chemical applications, while increasing their profits? Research has shown that regenerative practices can do all these things.

Ottawa, Illinois

I don't want to spoil the next book for you, so I'll just describe my first day in Ottawa, Illinois.

If you placed a pin on a map in the exact geographic center of the corn belt, you'd land pretty darn close to Ottawa, a small town about two hours west of Chicago. Ottawa, Illinois, population 19,000, is a nice little Midwestern town with clean streets and no shops boarded up downtown; all the shops appeared to be full of small mom and pop businesses that have been able to hold on even after Walmart came to town.

The town is an island in the sea of corn, and I felt it best to keep the "mass disruption ahead from electric vehicles" thing under my hat when I first visited Ottawa. I didn't want to panic anyone or set off any unnecessary alarms. But while 40% of the national corn crop goes to ethanol production as a gasoline additive, in LaSalle County, where Ottawa is located, it's half (51%). I didn't know what was going to happen, but I just knew from business experience that there aren't many industries that can handle a big drop in demand like that without some disruption and heartache.

I knew that I needed to find some rebel food fighters in the local community, and right away I could see that there was hope for this. As I walked out of my first meeting at the Ottawa Chamber of Commerce in an upstairs office of a downtown building, I could see, just down the street, a craft brewery and restaurant called The Lone Buffalo. That was a very good sign. Local, craft beer was obviously important to these people, as I stood there and watched several people come and go from the business. The popularity of micro-breweries and locally brewed beer can be the catalyst for change in the local food scene, and I find that very appropriate. It's a sign from heaven, because as Ben Franklin said, "Beer is proof that God loves us and wants us to be happy." There are now thousands of micro-breweries across the United States. He's sending us a sign. The time is now.

Local beer can be an important spark for a broader, thriving local food scene, but I also see it as a form of social conditioning. Take a sip of local beer, your brain is rewarded, and you think "local is good." Take another sip, think "local is nice." Repeat again and again. It sinks in. "Local, Good". I haven't had time to conduct a formal experiment on this hypothesis yet, other than on myself, but I think the idea is just as good as my 'bugs on windshield' experiment, and I know where I can easily get volunteers for the local beer study.

As I turned away from the micro-brewery and walked in the opposite direction to my car parked on the main street, literally next door to the Chamber of Commerce office, I noticed the most peculiar and positive sign of all; a crazy, unexpected business that stopped me in my tracks.

The store was called "Rocks, Soul and Love". What the heck is this, I thought, smack dab in the middle of the conservative corn belt? It was a rock and crystal store, with definite spiritual and metaphysical undertones. Crystal necklaces, crystal charms, colorful rocks and various minerals, incense, and oils, all displayed in the front window. "What the heck is this?" I said again to myself out loud. Do radicals live here? Is it possible that revolutionary insurgents occupy this space? I could use these people. I need these people.

I walked in and quickly noticed a wall of mason jars with a sign that read "Mother Earth's Medicine Chest" and jars labeled with various medicinal herbs. This is something that you would expect to find in progressive, liberal Asheville, not Midwestern corn country. There were signs for "Sacred Eclipse

Yoga" and "Titanium Quartz Healing Crystals" and a class on the "Reiki Spiritual Sprouting Process," whatever that is.

Then I saw her. A pretty blond standing behind the counter with short, cropped hair, and many piercings and tattoos. That was my girl! I knew it right off. I couldn't believe my luck! This would be my rebel base and recruitment center!

Her name was Ari (of course) and she was just like that girl Audrey, the flowerchild I met behind the counter at that anti-capitalist bookstore in Asheville called Firestorm Books; young, positive, content, and hopeful, like someone who believes there is more to this world than meets the eye.

After some small talk about crystals, I told her why I was in town, working on a local food campaign (I may have used the word revolution) and she immediately volunteered to help. She said that she used to be a vegan, but not so much anymore, and she fully understood the problems of the average American diet and that she and her friends were "big advocates for the environment and organic, sustainable food." How about that. Just dumb luck on my part. I didn't go searching her out, but I found her on the first day in town.

And I wondered, which came first, the micro-brewery or the healing crystal store? Did the local beer cause an 'awakening' in some of the people, and so the crystal shop opened, or was it the other way around?

I signed Ari up to this local food campaign, we exchanged phone numbers and emails, and she would reach out to her friends to get them involved. Here was a cluster of underground food radicals living in a conservative, Midwestern town in the heart of the corn belt. It was a very positive, progressive sign, but I think you'll find that everywhere, mostly among young people, but not always, lying dormant like a seed that just needs to be watered.

Ottawa and LaSalle County was for me a test. It was a test to see if it was possible to turn things around; to turn a conservative, monocropping, soil eroding, chemical spraying, tractor riding group of people into regenerative, climate solution pioneers that also fed people. And I knew that there was enough good dirt left, if we had the systems and distribution channels in place, to help feed a large city like Chicago.

But that's for our next story. What I've learned from this one is that they were all food fighters. The artists and poets and writers and carpenters. The waitress from the small diner. The activist mother of three. There were the farmers of course, but also many others involved in the food industry, including chefs and grocery store clerks and stock personnel. People from the local Women's March movement also joined our cause because food touches everyone. They were all food fighters.

Our network had grown from the first small group of radicals to show up at the first meeting, to an army of radical believers. We found our place and took our stand. The old red schoolhouse was not simply a rebel base for a subversive, revolutionary counterculture, it became a hub for something much more powerful. We were like hungry people, who tried to show other hungry people where we had found bread. And at the end of life, like the end of a day on the farm, you dust off the dirt and debris and you must ask, was it good? How have I done. Did I plant the seeds of good or evil? Did I tend my garden well?

At the School of Postmodern Activities, that one-room shack on Avery Creek Road in the heart of Appalachia, happiness comes to people joining together to share and celebrate food. To just be there in the present, to hear the warm chatter in the background like the crackling of wood in a fireplace, the high- and low-pitched voices of several conversations going on at each table, the smell of pork and potatoes permeating the room, to see and feel these things is to know community, and that is all that matters. And outside the windows, looking out into the green pasture where cows grazed peacefully, and further up the hill where the corn waved in a soft breeze. And further up and out over the rolling hills spread wide and then flattening out into the piedmont and down to the sea. To be mindful of these things is to know happiness. This is our place. This is our region, our culture, our heritage, and our children's future.

On fields of tall grass, I steer my tractor and crest a small hill, and then slide down the other side. I see the wind as it blows over the tops of the tall grass in successive waves. With a side cutter, I leave a wake of fallen grass behind me, and I know my purpose. I have no great unfulfilled needs or desires. I carry no jealousies or malice toward others. I tend my garden and my pasture, and hope to feed a few people from my effort, and that is all I need to do.

AFTERWORD

HOW TO ORGANIZE YOUR OWN REBEL FOOD FIGHTERS

Asheville has a lot of food fighters now. It became a leader in regional food security, food sovereignty and community resilience because we had a head start with the fall of tobacco and because we have two outstanding organizations, among many, that showed us the way. Here's my short list to building a stronger regional food system, with a lot more information on the web sites listed below, including www.eatyourview.com.

- Grow your own food if you can. The simplest place for anyone to start is to grow a couple tomato plants on your deck or in a kitchen window. That, hopefully, starts a lifelong learning curve about food production. Then start a garden and share the produce. Tell your friends and neighbors how you did it and encourage them to start their own garden. Start your own Victory Garden and learn how to can some produce for the winter, and you'll be well on your way to some self-reliance and food sovereignty. Congratulations! Great first step. Remember, it doesn't have to be everything you eat, but just providing some of your own sustenance is very rewarding on multiple levels.

- Go to the farmers market and get your friends to go with you. That is probably the simplest and most important thing you can do for food sovereignty in your area. Besides, it's a fun way to spend a morning and a great social experience. Farmers love to talk about how they grew their produce and how to cook it. You'll get some great food tips.

- Learn about soil health. Organize a community viewing of the documentary "Kiss the Ground", one of the best documentaries about soil and regenerative farming. Go one step further by taking the Kiss the Ground advocacy course.

- Research your current resource base and regional food capabilities. ASAP offers a lot of help here. https://asapconnections.org/consulting-by-asap/. There's also a great template to follow for gathering and organizing a community food snapshot available from an organization called Community Food Strategies at their website https://communityfoodstrategies.org.

- Begin to organize. Start by organizing your own 'food-fighters'. Get together with friends and neighbors to talk about some of the things you can do together to build the local food system, like how you can help to get the word out about the local farmers market and CSA programs. How can you encourage attendance at the market or help a farmer sell CSA shares? You can host a small farm to table meal with your close friends and neighbors featuring food you grew yourself or purchased locally from a farm or farmer's market. All movements start at the grassroots with meetings and get-togethers just like this.

- Get your friends and neighbors to start asking for more local food at your favorite restaurants and grocers. This alone can have a big impact on local farmers. Always encourage and thank your grocer or chef for carrying local food when you see it in a store or on a menu—tell the waiter to tell the chef. He'll appreciate it because he had to go out of his way to order and buy local, and he'll be glad to know someone notices and cares and appreciates his extra effort.

- Support or create a Double SNAP program. I believe that the single greatest thing that any food fighter can do is to make certain that your local farmers market accepts SNAP benefits (food stamps) and to begin a program to fund something like the ASAP Double SNAP program. Remember, the program does two wonderful things with the same dollar—it supports healthier eating habits at low-income households, and so improves community health, and it supports local farms and farmers. The Double SNAP program works, and we've been able to prove that in Asheville. It draws more people to the market and improves healthy eating habits in a more equitable food system.

- Want to take it to the next level? Try building two key organizations like Appalachian Sustainable Agriculture Project (ASAP) and Organic Growers School (OGS) in your region, if you don't already have something like them. Organizations like these will give you a huge leap forward in regional food security; one for farmer training in sustainable growing practices and the other for the marketing and promotion of the goods that local farmers produce and that will help to support them financially. If a database of local farms and food sources doesn't exist in your area, start a local food guide and create a local food brand. Both of these organizations offer terrific web sites that can become your guide to establishing this necessary infrastructure in your area. Both can also do some consulting for your local government or non-profit organization. Visit www.organicgrowersschool.org and www.asapconnections.org

We must all strive toward breaking the chains of corporate concentration and dominance in the food system, and the other systems prevalent in our modern world that support it. This may become the epic battle of our postmodern world, a battle between the spiritual and material world, between human virtue and our own selfish inclinations. But I believe we can as a society move from fear and anger to wisdom and understanding, toward courage, and finally transcendence—to a closer, spiritual connection to food and the living planet. This is the battle we are fighting in a postmodern world. Start by tending your own garden, and let it become a connection point for others and all the future food fighters that may come and be touched by it.

ENDNOTES

1   To view the ten companies and the brands that they own, see the Oxfam graphic at www.eaty-ourview.com/whylocal

2   For a summary of the CDC report, see: "Now, 2 Out of Every 5 Americans Expected to Develop Type 2 Diabetes During Their Lifetime," Centers for Disease Control and Prevention, published November 2014, https://4282524b-11a6-4da2-a01c-e0c5b893f09.filesusr.com/ugd/547c18_03324ae2f6d2416fac0656a48b0d9f89.pdf

For the full report: Dr. Edward W. Gregg, et al., "Trends in Lifetime Risk and Years of Life Lost Due to Diabetes in the USA, 1985-2011: a Modelling Study," *The Lancet – Diabetes and Endocrinology* (November 2014): 867-874, https://www.sciencedirect.com/science/article/abs/pii/S2213858714701615

3   "U.S. Imports of Fresh Fruit and Vegetable," Rural Migration News, University of California Davis, published February 24, 2021, https://migration.ucdavis.edu/rmn/blog/post/?id=2569 . See also: "U.S. Aquaculture," NOAA Fisheries, last updated July 8, 2021, https://www.fisheries.noaa.gov/national/aquaculture/us-aquaculture

4   "California Agricultural Production Statistics," California Department of Food and Agriculture, 2022, https://www.cdfa.ca.gov/Statistics/

5   Laura Reiley, "Meat Processing Plants Are Closing Due to COVID-19 Outbreaks. Beef Shortfalls May Follow," *Washington Post*, April 16, 2020, https://www.washingtonpost.com/business/2020/04/16/meat-processing-plants-are-closing-due-covid-19-outbreaks-beef-shortfalls-may-follow/

6   My education on consolidation in the food industry was greatly influenced by OCM, their publications, and weekly newsletter. Angela Huffman, Joe Maxwell, and Andres Salerno. "Consolidation, Globalization, and the American Family Farm", policy brief from the Office of Competitive Markets (OCM), August 2017. Can be viewed here at: https://competitivemarkets.com/wp-content/uploads/2017/08/Consolidation-Globalization-and-the-American-Family-Farm.pdf Report references: Midwest Center for Investigative Reporting. Agricultural Foreign Investment Disclosure Act Database. Available at http://apps.investigatemidwest.org/afida/. Accessed August 2017. See also: Nathan Halverson, "How China purchased a prime cut of America's pork industry," Reveal News, January 24, 2015, https://www.revealnews.org/article/how-china-purchased-a-prime-cut-of-americas-pork-industry/

7   David Karp, "Most of America's Fruit Is Now Imported. Is That a Bad Thing?," *New York Times*, published March 13, 2018, https://www.nytimes.com/2018/03/13/dining/fruit-vegetables-imports.html. See also: "Yes, More of Your Fruits and Veggies Are from Overseas," Diego Mendoza-Moyers, published April 12, 2019, https://www.timesunion.com/business/article/Yes-more-of-the-fruits-and-vegetables-you-re-13762595.php

8   Some estimates put California fruit and vegetable production at 70% of the total U.S. production – "The States Producing the Most Fruits and Vegetables," Tulsa World, published December 10, 2021, https://tulsaworld.com/lifestyles/the-states-producing-the-most-fruits-and-vegetables/collection_73374d96-1b2b-5ccb-ab7d-afca4c80fa41.html#1 . See also: "California Agricultural Production Statistics," California Department of Food and Agriculture, 2022, https://www.cdfa.ca.gov/Statistics/

9   3.34 billion pounds of imported beef and veal (2020) divided by U.S. population (329M) = 10 pounds per person. For imports, see: "U.S. Total Beef and Veal Imports and Exports 2006-2022," M. Shahbandeh, published February

10   Congress repealed COOL labeling regulations in 2015, but new legislation will be proposed in 2022 to reinstate mandatory COOL (mCool) regulations.

11   Agustin Escobar, Philip Martin, and Omar Stabridis, "Farm Labor and Mexico's Export Produce Industry (Wilson Center, 2019), https://www.wilsoncenter.org/sites/default/files/media/uploads/documents/mexico%20farm%20book_V2.pdf

12   Carlos Ballesteros, "Mexican Cartels Used Government Data to Kidnap and Extort Avocado Farmers," *News Week*, October 30, 2017, https://www.newsweek.com/cartels-kidnap-avocado-farmers-696301

13   "The Farmworker Wage Gap Continued in 2020," Daniel Costa, published July 20, 2021, https://www.epi.org/blog/the-farmworker-wage-gap-continued-in-2020-farmworkers-and-h-2a-workers-earned-very-low-wages-during-the-pandemic-even-compared-with-other-low-wage-workers/

14   "What Is the Average Hourly Wage in the U.S.?," Indeed Editorial Team, published March 30, 2021, https://www.indeed.com/career-advice/pay-salary/average-hourly-wage-in-us Chart cited: "Table B-3," U.S. Bureau of Labor Statistics, last modified February 4, 2022, https://www.bls.gov/news.release/empsit.t19.htm

15   Information related to U.S. farm production can be found in summary charts produced by the U.S. Department of Agriculture: "Ag and Food Statistics – Charting the Essentials," U.S. Department of Agriculture Economic Research Service, published February 2020, https://www.ers.usda.gov/webdocs/publications/96957/ap-083.pdf?v=7732.7

16   Eliza Barclay, "Your Grandparents Spent More of Their Money on Food Than You Do," *NPR*, March 2, 2015, https://www.npr.org/sections/thesalt/2015/03/02/389578089/your-grandparents-spent-more-of-their-money-on-food-than-you-do

17   There are many excellent accounts of the collapse of ancient societies related to soil degradation, including the early publication: Dr. Walter Clay Lowdermilk, *Conquest of the Land Through 7000 Years – Personal Report of a Study in 1938 and 1939* (U.S. Department of Agriculture, 2014). See also: breakdown on Dr. Lowdermilk's findings: "Walter Lowdermilk's Journey: Forester to Land Conservationist," Douglas Helms, reprinted from *Environmental Review 8* (1984): 132-145, United States Department of Agriculture, https://www.nrcs.usda.gov/wps/portal/nrcs/detail/national/about/history/?cid=nrcs143_021442

18   Chris Arsenault, "Only 60 Years of Farming Left If Soil Degradation Continues", Scientific American and Reuters, December 5, 2014. Based on United Nations - Food and Agriculture Organization (FAO) Report, https://www.scientificamerican.com/article/only-60-years-of-farming-left-if-soil-degradation-continues/#:~:text=ROME%20(Thomson%20Reuters%20Foundation)%20%2D,UN%20official%20said%20on%20Friday.&text=Soils%20play%20a%20key%20role,filtering%20water%2C%20the%20FAO%20reported.

19   My understanding and interpretation of regenerative agriculture was greatly influenced by several scientists, researchers, and growers. A recent publication of influence: Charles Massy, *Call of the Reed Warbler* (Chelsea Green Publishing, 2018).

20   For a wonderful description of the early spice traders, see Giles Milton's book *Nathaniel's Nutmeg.* Penguin Books, 2000

21   Kathryn Lipton, William Edmondson and Alden Manchester, The Food and Fiber System: Contributing to U.S. and World Economies, Agricultural Information Bulletin No. 742, July 1998 (Washington, D.C.: USDA ERS).

22   Tom Philpott, *Perilous Bounty* (Bloomsbury Publishing, 2020). An insightful account of labor and California food production can be found in Philpott's excellent book.

23   Bill Gates, *How to Avoid a Climate Disaster* (Alfred A. Knopf, 2021).

24   The EPA estimates agricultures contribution to greenhouse gas emissions at 24% (vs. my estimate of 25-30%) but does not include transportation of inputs or outputs. The report does include some charts that break greenhouse emissions down by country here: "Global Greenhouse Gas Emissions Data," U.S. Environmental Protection Agency, last modified October 26, 2021, https://www.epa.gov/ghgemissions/global-greenhouse-gas-emissions-data

25   For an excellent discussion on the water crisis in California, and problems related to soil erosion in the Midwest: Tom Philpott, *Perilous Bounty* (Bloomsbury Publishing, 2020).

26   "California's Central Valley: Producing America's Fruits and Vegetables," House Committee on Natural Resources, published February 5, 2014 https://republicans-naturalresources.house.gov/newsroom/documentsingle.aspx?DocumentID=368934

27   "One-Third of Farmland in the U.S. Corn Belt Has Lost Its Topsoil," Yale Environment 360, published February 18, 2021, https://e360.yale.edu/digest/one-third-of-farmland-in-the-u-s-corn-belt-has-lost-its-topsoil

28   Ibid

29   "Farmers' Suicides in India," Wikipedia, last modified February 8, 2022, https://en.wikipedia.org/wiki/Farmers%27_suicides_in_India

30   Katie Wedell, Lucille Sherman, and Sky Chadde, "Midwest Farmers Face a Crisis. Hundreds Are Dying by Suicide," *USA Today News*, last modified March 9, 2020, https://www.usatoday.com/in-depth/news/investigations/2020/03/09/climate-tariffs-debt-and-isolation-drive-some-farmers-suicide/4955865002/

31   "Can $1 Billion Really Fix a Meat Industry Dominated by Just Four Companies?," Jessica Fu, published January 5, 2022, https://thecounter.org/big-four-meatpackers-antitrust-consolidation/

32   "The Impact of Coronavirus COVID-19 on U.S. Meat and Livestock Markets," Joseph Balagtas and Joseph Cooper, published March 2021, https://www.usda.gov/sites/default/files/documents/covid-impact-livestock-markets.pdf

33   For seeds and chemicals, see: "A Fair Deal for Farmers," Caius Z. Willingham and Andy Green, published May 7, 2019, https://www.americanprogress.org/article/fair-deal-farmers/ . For corn and soybeans, see: "Cereal Secrets: the World's Largest Grain Traders and Global Agriculture," Sophia Murphy, David Burch, and Jennifer Clapp, published August 2012, https://www-cdn.oxfam.org/s3fs-public/file_attachments/rr-cereal-secrets-grain-traders-agriculture-30082012-en_4.pdf

34   Breakdown of clients/lobbyists lobbying the U.S. Department of Agriculture: "Agency Profile: Department of Agriculture," published 2019, https://www.opensecrets.org/federal-lobbying/agencies/summary?cycle=2019&id=023 . See also breakdown of lobbyist spending in U.S. for agribusiness: "Sector Profile: Agribusiness," published 2019, https://www.opensecrets.org/federal-lobbying/sectors/summary?cycle=2019&id=A . See also: Vincent H. Smith, "Farm-Sector Spending on Federal Campaign Contributions and Lobbying Expenditures: Evidence from 2003 to 2020," *American Enterprise Institute*, published December 7, 2021, https://www.aei.org/research-products/report/farm-sector-spending-on-federal-campaign-contributions-and-lobbying-expenditures-evidence-from-2003-to-2020/

35   An insightful description of societies control by elites can be found here: Daron Acemoglu and James Robinson, *Why Nation's Fail* (Crown Business, 2012).

36   "Cattle Ranching's Impact on the Rainforest," Mongabay, July 22, 2012, https://rainforests.mongabay.com/0812.htm

37   "Good Practices Compendium on Combating Corruption in the Response to COVID-19," United Nations Office on Drugs and Crime, October 16, 2020, https://www.unodc.org/pdf/corruption/G20_Compendium_COVID-19_FINAL.pdf

38   For maps of locations of cartels, see: "Mapping the Presence of Mexican Cartels in Central America," Paris Martinez, July 2, 2013, https://insightcrime.org/news/analysis/map-of-mexican-cartel-presence-in-central-america/

39   Dave Goulson, "Insect Declines and Why They Matter," *The Wildlife Trusts*, 2021, https://www.somersetwildlife.org/sites/default/files/2019-11/FULL%20AFI%20REPORT%20WEB1_1.pdf. See also: "More Than 50% of Insects Have Disappeared Since 1970, An Ecologist Warns – Even More Evidence of an 'Insect Apocalypse'," Aylin Woodward, November 14, 2019, https://www.businessinsider.com/insect-apocalypse-ecosystem-collapse-food-insecurity-2019-11 . See also: Stephen Leahy, "Insect 'Apocalypse' in U.S. Driven by 50x Increase in Toxic Pesticides," *National Geographic*, August 6, 2019, https://www.nationalgeographic.com/environment/article/insect-apocalypse-under-way-toxic-pesticides-agriculture . See also: Francisco Sánchez-Bayo and Kris A.G. Wyckhuys, "Worldwide Decline of the Entomofauna: a Review of Its Drivers," *Science Direct* (April 2019): 8-27, https://www.sciencedirect.com/science/article/abs/pii/S0006320718313636

40   Gustave Axelson, "Nearly 30% of Birds in U.S., Canada Have Vanished Since 1970," Cornell University, Cornell Chronicle, September 2019, https://news.cornell.edu/stories/2019/09/nearly-30-birds-us-canada-have-vanished-1970 . See also: Elizabeth Pennisi, "Three Billion North American Birds Have Vanished Since 1970," *Science Journal*, September 19, 2019, https://www.science.org/content/article/three-billion-north-american-birds-have-vanished-1970-surveys-show . See also: Kenneth V. Rosenberg, et al., "Decline of the North American Avifauna," *Science Journal*, September 19, 2019, https://www.science.org/doi/10.1126/science.aaw1313

41   "National Geographic: Insect 'Apocalypse' in U.S. Driven by 50x Increase in Toxic Pesticides," Laurel Hopwood, Sierra Club Grassroots Network, August 7, 2019, https://content.sierraclub.org/grassrootsnetwork/team-news/2019/08/national-geographic-insect-apocalypse-us-driven-50x-increase-toxic-pesticides

42   Stephen Leahy, "Insect 'Apocalypse' in U.S. Driven by 50x Increase in Toxic Pesticides," *National Geographic*, August 6, 2019, https://www.nationalgeographic.com/environment/article/insect-apocalypse-under-way-toxic-pesticides-agriculture

43   My understanding and interpretation of soil and pests was greatly influenced by soil scientist and resilience expert Laura Lengnick. Recent publication: Laura Lengnick, *Resilient Agriculture: Cultivating Food Systems for a Changing Climate* (New Society Publishers, second edition, 2022).

44   Ibid

45   Adrea X Silva et al., "Insecticide Resistance Mechanisms in the Green Peach Aphid Myzus Persicae (Hemiptera: Aphididae) I: a Transcriptomic Survey," *National Center for Biotechnology Information* (June 2012), https://pubmed.ncbi.nlm.nih.gov/22685538/ . See also: "Green Peach Aphid," John L. Capinera, University of Florida Entomology and Nematology, last modified June 2017, last reviewed June 2020, https://entnemdept.ufl.edu/creatures/veg/aphid/green_peach_aphid.htm

46   See www.eatyourview.com/publications for recent articles.

47   "General Motors to Start Selling Only Electric Vehicles by 2035," Charles Digges, Published February 3, 2021, https://bellona.org/news/climate-change/2021-02-general-motors-to-start-selling-only-electric-vehicles-by-2035

48   "Ethanol Market is Disturbing to American Farmers. and Now There's COVID-19," Carson Vaughan, Published March 30, 2020, https://www.agriculture.com/news/business/ethanol-market-is-disturbing-as-hell-to-american-farmers-and-now-there-s-covid-19

49   "Production of corn for grain in the U.S. from 2001 to 2021". Statista. M. Shahbandeh, Jan 14, 2022, https://www.statista.com/statistics/190871/corn-for-grain-production-in-the-us-since-2000/. Information on corn production can also be found from the USDA Agriculture Research Service at - https://www.ars.usda.gov

50   "How Planting Crops Used to Feed Livestock is Contributing to Habitat Destruction," Arianna Pittman, 2021, https://www.onegreenplanet.org/environment/livestock-feed-and-habitat-destruction/

51   "Corn and Feeder Cattle Prices," Josh Maples, Mississippi State University, June 18, 2018, https://blogs.extension.msstate.edu/agecon/2018/06/18/corn-and-feeder-cattle-prices/ . See also: Gary Schnitkey, Nick Paulson, and Krista Swanson, "2022 Break-Even Prices for Corn and Soybeans," *Department of Agricultural and Consumer Economics*, University of Illinois at Urbana-Champaign (December 2021): *farmdoc daily* (11):168, https://farmdocdaily.illinois.edu/2021/12/2022-break-even-prices-for-corn-and-soybeans.html

52   "Corn 2019 Export Highlights," U.S. Department of Agriculture – Foreign Agricultural Service, https://www.fas.usda.gov/corn-2019-export-highlights . See also: "Feedgrains Sector at a Glance," U.S. Department of Agriculture Economic Research Service, last modified June 28, 2021, https://www.ers.usda.gov/topics/crops/corn-and-other-feedgrains/feedgrains-sector-at-a-glance/

53   Elizabeth Becker, "U.S. Corn Subsidies Said to Damage Mexico," *New York Times*, August 27, 2003, https://www.nytimes.com/2003/08/27/business/us-corn-subsidies-said-to-damage-mexico.html

54   An inspiring account for the fall of tobacco and rise of vegetable production in Appalachia can be found on the Appalachian Sustainable Agriculture Project (ASAP) web site at www.asapconnections.org.

55   For an overview on the subject, watch the insightful documentary: *Kiss the Ground*, directed by Joshua Tickell and Rebecca Harrell Tickell (Benenson Productions, 2020), Netflix.

56   Laura Lengnick, *Resilient Agriculture: Cultivating Food Systems for a Changing Climate* (New Society Publishers, second edition 2022). See also: "What is a Carbon Sink?," ClientEarth Communications, published December 22, 2020, https://www.clientearth.org/latest/latest-updates/stories/what-is-a-carbon-sink/ . See also: "Is Carbon the 'Crop' of the Future?," Paul Schattenberg, AgriLife Today, published May 27, 2021, https://agrilifetoday.tamu.edu/2021/05/27/is-carbon-the-crop-of-the-future/

57   See Oxfam graphic at www.eatyourview/whylocal

58   For an excellent overview about food imports, see New York Times article here: David Karp, "Most of America's Fruit Is Now Imported. Is That a Bad Thing?," *New York Times*, March 13, 2018, https://www.nytimes.com/2018/03/13/dining/fruit-vegetables-imports.html

59   The first and best account of the perils of modern agriculture can be found in: Michael Pollan, *The Omnivore's Dilemma* (Penguin Books, 2007). Like many writers, farmers, and eaters, Pollan influenced my understanding about food and farming.

60   See recent CDC report on diabetes here: Dr. Edward W. Gregg, et al., "Trends in Lifetime Risk and Years of Life Lost Due to Diabetes in the USA, 1985-2011: a Modelling Study," *The Lancet – Diabetes and Endocrinology* (November 2014): 867-874, https://www.sciencedirect.com/science/article/abs/pii/S2213858714701615

61   Lisa Held, "Just a Few Companies Control the Meat Industry. Can a New Approach to Monopolies Level the Playing Field?," Civil Eats, July 14, 2021, https://civileats.com/2021/07/14/just-a-few-companies-control-the-meat-industry-can-a-new-approach-to-monopolies-level-the-playing-field/

62   Over 95% of food consumed in Iowa comes from outside the state: "Iowa Food and Farm Facts," Iowa State University Extension and Outreach, published November 2016, https://www.extension. iastate.edu/ffed/wp-content/uploads/2018/04/IowaFoodandFarmFacts-2018-1.pdf

63   Almost half net income on the farm comes from taxpayer subsidies: "Examining America's Farm Subsidy Problem," Scott Lincicome, CATO Institute, published December 18, 2020, https://www. cato.org/commentary/examining-americas-farm-subsidy-problem

64   "Assets, Debt, and Wealth," U.S. Department of Agriculture Economic Research Service, published February 4, 2022, https://www.ers.usda.gov/topics/farm-economy/farm-sector-income-finances/assets-debt-and-wealth/ . Read a story about a farm owning family in Wisconsin: Alana Semuels, "They're Trying to Wipe Us Off the Map. Small American Farmers Are Nearing Extinction," Time, published November 27, 2019, https://time.com/5736789/small-american-farmers-debt-crisis-extinction/

65   "Assets, Debt, and Wealth," U.S. Department of Agriculture Economic Research Service, February 4, 2022.

66   Inspirational publication for generations of writers and farmers: Wendell Berry, Bringing it to the Table (Counterpoint, 2009).

67   Dr. Edward W. Gregg, et al., "Trends in Lifetime Risk and Years of Life Lost Due to Diabetes in the USA, 1985-2011: a Modelling Study," The Lancet – Diabetes and Endocrinology (November 2014): 867-874, https://www.sciencedirect.com/science/article/abs/pii/S2213858714701615

68   To learn about the agrihood community, see: https://www.creeksidefarmwc.com/

69   Robert Turner, Carrots Don't Grow on Trees: Building Sustainable and Resilient Communities (Discovery Books, 2019). See also: www.eatyourview.com

70   For an excellent overview on the loss of topsoil: Melissa D. Ho, "Soil Erosion and Degradation," World Wildlife, last modified 2022, https://www.worldwildlife.org/threats/soil-erosion-and-degradation

71   Many companies like Kellogg's and General Mills are starting to listen to their customers and looking to improve the environmental impacts of their business. See for example: General Mills, Global Responsibility Report, 2019 which can be downloaded at: https://globalresponsibility.generalmills.com/2019/HTML1/default.htm

72   An inciteful description of farm bill policy can be found here: Daryll E. Ray, et all, "Rethinking U.S. Agricultural Policy: Changing Course to Secure Farmer Livelihoods Worldwide," Agricultural Policy Analysis Center, The University of Tennessee, 2003.

73   Several US Senators and Congressman, including Corey Booker, are backing legislature for 2022 that will help to diversify the food system.

74   An excellent description of regionalism, or bioregionalism, can be found here: Kirkpatrick Sale, Dwellers in the Land: The Bioregional Vision (University of Georgia Press, 1991).

75   "Soil Health Nuggets – There Are Some Amazing Things Going on Underground," United States Department of Agriculture, https://www.nrcs.usda.gov/Internet/FSE_DOCUMENTS/stelprdb1101660.pdf

76   Hannah Ritchie and Max Roser, "Fertilizers," Our World in Data, original publication 2013, https://ourworldindata.org/fertilizers#citation

77   "Glyphosate Herbicide Found in Many Midwestern Streams, Antibiotics not Common," United States Geological Survey, last modified April 16, 2019, https://toxics.usgs.gov/highlights/glyphosate02.html

78   Patricia Cohen, "Roundup Maker to Pay $10 Billion to Settle Cancer Suits," New York Times, June 24, 2020, https://www.nytimes.com/2020/06/24/business/roundup-settlement-lawsuits.html

79   RJ Rickson, LK Deeks, et al., "Input Constraints to Food Production: The Impact of Soil Degradation," Springer Link (March 16, 2015): 351-364, https://link.springer.com/article/10.1007/s12571-015-0437-x . See also: Stacey Noel, et al., Economics of Land Degradation Initiative: Report for Policy and Decision Makers (The Economics of Land Degradation, 2015), https://www.eld-initiative.org/fileadmin/pdf/ELD-pm-report_05_web_300dpi.pdf

80   A stunning video of the timelapse map can be found at: Bill Putman and NASA Goddard, "NASA | A Year in the Life of Earth's CO2," published November 17, 2014, video, https://www.youtube.com/watch?v=x1Sg_mFa0r04

81   For a list of classes offered at Organic Growers School, visit www.organicgrowersschool.org/events

82   "Iowa Food and Farm Facts," Iowa State University, Extension and Outreach, published November 2016, https://www.extension.iastate.edu/ffed/wp-content/uploads/2018/04/IowaFoodandFarm-Facts-2018-1.pdf

83   "Cattle Prices Falling," Idaho Farm Bureau Federation, published March 17, 2020, https://www.idahofb.org/news-room/posts/cattle-prices-falling/ . See also: "Why Beef Prices Are Up and Cattle Prices Are Down," Brett Crosby, published April 2, 2020, https://www.beefmagazine.com/marketing/why-beef-prices-are-and-cattle-prices-are-down See also: Balagtas, Joseph, and Joseph Cooper. "The Impact of Coronavirus COVID-19 on U.S. Meat and Livestock Markets," March 2021, https://www.usda.gov/sites/default/files/documents/covid-impact-livestock-markets.pdf.

84   Christine Hauser, "Nearly 2 Million Chickens Killed as Poultry Workers Are Sidelined," New York Times, published April 28, 2020, https://www.nytimes.com/2020/04/28/us/coronavirus-chicken-poultry-farm-workers.html Also: Corkery, Michael, and David Yaffe-Bellany. "Dumped Milk, Smashed Eggs, Plowed Vegetables: Food Waste of the Pandemic," The New York Times, April 11, 2020, https://www.nytimes.com/2020/04/11/business/coronavirus-destroying-food.html.

85   Jennifer Dempsey, Julia Freedgood, Mitch Hunter, and Ann Sorensen. "Farms Under Threat: The State of the States," American Farmland Trust, May 13, 2020, https://farmland.org/project/farms-under-threat/.

86   Joey Pitchford, "Farmland under threat part 1: What is the issue?" N.C. Department of Agriculture and Consumer Services, June 24, 2020, http://info.ncagr.gov/blog/2020/06/24/farmland-under-threat-part-1-what-is-the-issue/

87   Kathleen Kassel, and Anikka Martin. "Ag and Food Sectors and The Economy," USDA Economic Research Service, December 27, 2021, https://www.ers.usda.gov/data-products/ag-and-food-statistics-charting-the-essentials/ag-and-food-sectors-and-the-economy/#:~:text=What%20is%20agriculture's%20share%20of,about%200.6%20percent%20of%20GDP

88   Christopher Peterson, and Martin E.P. Seligman. Character Strengths and Virtues: A Handbook and Classification. Oxford, UK: Oxford University Press, 2004. My understanding and interpretation of good citizenship, and all human virtues and character strengths, was greatly influenced by this textbook.

89   Nathan Halverson, "How China purchased a prime cut of America's pork industry," Reveal News, January 24, 2015, https://revealnews.org/article/how-china-purchased-a-prime-cut-of-americas-pork-industry/.

90   For a good expose on the corruption at JBS, see this story in The Bureau of Investigative Journalism: Campos, André, Alexandra Heal, Diego Junqueira, Lucy Michaels, Dom Phillips, Claire Smyth, Andrew Wasley, and Rory Winters. "JBS: The Brazilian butchers who took over the world," The Bureau of Investigative Journalism, July 2, 2019, https://www.thebureauinvestigates.com/stories/2019-07-02/jbs-brazilian-butchers-took-over-the-world.

91   Angela Huffman, Joe Maxwell, and Andres Salerno. "Consolidation, Globalization, and the American Family Farm", policy brief from the Office of Competitive Markets (OCM), August 2017. My education on consolidation in the food industry was greatly influenced by OCM. Can be viewed here at: https://competitivemarkets.com/wp-content/uploads/2017/08/Consolidation-Globalization-and-the-American-Family-Farm.pdf

92   View the corporate ownership chart at www.eatyourview.com/whylocal

93   Ross Lukas, "Down on the Farm," The Oakland Institute, February 18, 2014. An excellent account of Wall Street's takeover of farmland can be found in this report which can be downloaded at: https://www.oaklandinstitute.org/down-on-the-farm. Also see Thapar, Neil. "The Future of Farmland (Part 1): The New Land Grab," Sustainable Economics Law Center, June 15, 2017, https://www.theselc.org/reit_blog_part_1.

94   Sophie Ackoff, Andrew Bahrenburg, and Lindsey Lusher Shute. "An Aging Farm Population," Building a Future With Farmers II: Results and Recommendations from the National Young Farmer Survey, November 2017. https://www.youngfarmers.org/wp-content/uploads/2018/02/NYFC-Report-2017.pdf

95   Katy Keiffer, "Who really owns American farmland?" The Counter, updated July, 2017 https://thecounter.org/who-really-owns-american-farmland/

96   Daniel Bigelow, Allison Borchers, and Todd Hubbs. "U.S. Farmland Ownership, Tenure, and Transfer," USDA Economic Research Service, August 2016, https://www.ers.usda.gov/webdocs/publications/74672/eib-161.pdf

97 Ross Lukas, "Down on the Farm," The Oakland Institute, February 18, 2014, https://www.oaklandinstitute.org/down-on-the-farm

98 Anne Barnard, "New York's $226 Billion Pension Fund Is Dropping Fossil Fuel Stocks", New York Times, Updated Aug. 11, 2021, https://www.nytimes.com/2020/12/09/nyregion/new-york-pension-fossil-fuels.html

99 United States Department of Agriculture. Selected Charts from Ag and Food Statistics, Charting the Essentials, February 2020," February 2020, https://www.ers.usda.gov/webdocs/publications/96957/ap-083.pdf?v=7732.7

100 "Increased corporate concentration and the influence of market power," Barclays, March 26, 2019. My understanding of the risks of corporate concentration were greatly influenced by this Barclays report found here at: https://www.cib.barclays/content/dam/barclaysmicrosites/ibpublic/documents/our-insights/MarketPower/Barclays-ImpactSeries5-MarketPower_final_2.4MB.pdf .

101 USDA National Agriculture Statistics Service. "Beginning Farmers - Characteristics of Farmers by Years on Current Farm," June, 2014, https://www.nass.usda.gov/Publications/Highlights/2014/Beginning_Farmers/index.php.

102 Parker, Suzi. "How Poultry Producers are Ravaging the Rural South," Grist, February 22, 2006, https://grist.org/article/parker1/.

103 Nina Lakhani, "'They rake in profits – everyone else suffers': US workers lose out as big chicken gets bigger," The Guardian, August 11, 2021, https://www.theguardian.com/environment/2021/aug/11/tyson-chicken-indsutry-arkansas-poultry-monopoly.

104 "Increased corporate concentration and the influence of market power," Barclays. March 26, 2019, https://www.cib.barclays/content/dam/barclaysmicrosites/ibpublic/documents/our-insights/MarketPower/Barclays-ImpactSeries5-MarketPower_final_2.4MB.pdf

105 Hope Kirwan, "Wisconsin Lost Record-Breaking Percent of Dairy Farms In 2018," Wisconsin Public Radio NPR, December 17, 2018, https://www.wpr.org/wisconsin-lost-record-breaking-percent-dairy-farms-2018. See also https://www.agweb.com/news/livestock/dairy/wisconsin-loses-818-dairies-2019-largest-decline-state-history

106 The Environmental Working Group. "USDA subsidies in the United States totaled $424.4 billion from 1995-2020," June 30, 2020, https://farm.ewg.org/progdetail.php?fips=00000&page=conc&progcode=total.

107 Congressional Research Service. "Foreign Farmland Ownership in the United States," November 18, 2021 https://crsreports.congress.gov/product/pdf/IF/IF11977#:~:text=USDA%20reports%20foreign%20persons%20and,acres%20per%20year%20since%202015.

108 USDA Farm Service Agency. "Foreign Holdings of U.S Agricultural Lands," December 31, 2014, https://www.fsa.usda.gov/Assets/USDA-FSA-Public/usdafiles/EPAS/PDF/afida2014report.pdf. See also: USDA Farm Service Agency. "Foreign Ownership of U.S. Agricultural Lands," February 28, 2004, https://www.fsa.usda.gov/Assets/USDA-FSA-Public/usdafiles/EPAS/PDF/022804_foreign_owner.pdf.

109 Edward Wong, "One-Fifth of China's Farmland Is Polluted, State Study Finds," The New York Times, April 17, 2014, https://www.nytimes.com/2014/04/18/world/asia/one-fifth-of-chinas-farmland-is-polluted-state-report-finds.html.

110 Institute on Taxation and Economic Policy. "60 Fortune 500 Companies Avoided All Federal Income Tax in 2018 Under New Tax Law," April 11, 2019, https://itep.org/60-fortune-500-companies-avoided-all-federal-income-tax-in-2018-under-new-tax-law/.

111 Jayson Beckman, Jennifer Ifft, Todd Kuethe, Mitchell Morehart, Cynthia Nickerson, and Ryan Williams. "Trends in U.S. Farmland Values and Ownership," United States Department of Agriculture, February, 2012, https://www.ers.usda.gov/webdocs/publications/44656/16748_eib92_2_.pdf.

112 USDA Economic Research Service, "U.S. Farmland Ownership, Tenure, and Transfer." August 2016, https://www.ers.usda.gov/webdocs/publications/74672/eib-161.pdf?v=9137.4

113 American Farmland Trust, "Farms Under Threat: The State of America's Farmland." Report Update, April 2020 Download it here at: https://s30428.pcdn.co/wp-content/uploads/sites/2/2020/05/AFT_FUT_SAF_2020final.pdf.

114 Martin Seligman, et al. *Character Strengths and Virtues*

115 Bill Gates, *How to Avoid a Climate Disaster*, Knopf, 2021. I'm using Bill Gates numbers here because he has more money and people than me to gather the research and the data. If you were a scientist and Bill Gates was on the phone, wouldn't you take the call? He probably wants to donate some money. The total 50 gigatons and agricultures percentage contribution can be confirmed by this report from the UN Food and Ag Organization here at: https://www.fao.org/news/story/en/item/197623/icode/#:~:text=Total%20emissions%20from%20global%20livestock,analysis%20and%20improved%20data%20sets

116 Ibid. More wisdom from farmer Bill.

117 My education and understanding of carbon and soil was greatly influenced by a soil advocacy course offered by the Kiss the Ground organization. www.kisstheground.com

118 Steven Wallander, David Smith, Maria Bowman, and Roger Claassen. "Cover Crop Trends, Programs, and Practices in the United States," USDA Economic Research Service, February 2021

119 Bill Gates, *How to Avoid a Climate Disaster*, Knopf, 2021. See also: https://www.fao.org/news/story/en/item/197623/icode/#:~:text=Total%20emissions%20from%20global%20livestock,analysis%20and%20improved%20data%20sets

120 Tom Philpott, *Perilous Bounty: The Looming Collapse of American Farming and How We Can Prevent It*. London, UK: Bloomsbury Publishing, 2020. Philpott gives an excellent description on the looming water crisis in the west.

121 A. Park Williams, et al, "Rapid intensification of the emerging southwestern North American megadrought in 2020–2021" Nature Climate Change.

122 Reuters. "Weather woes hit French vineyards: wine production seen falling this year," July 19, 2019, https://www.reuters.com/article/us-france-wine-idUKKCN1UE1JE.

123 Sylvia Neeley, *A Concise History of the French Revolution*. Lanham, MD: Rowman & Littlefield Publishers, 2007.

124 Daren Acemoglu and James A. Robinson. *Why Nations Fail*. New York: Crown Business, 2012. An excellent description of how elites in societies through time have captured wealth and power, which eventually leads to failed nations.

125 Ibid

126 My understanding and interpretation of political power and elitism was greatly influenced by four authors, beginning with the two previously mentioned, Daren Acemoglu and James Robinson and their brilliant work *Why Nations Fail* (Crown Business, 2012); Jared Diamond for *Collapse* (Penguin Books, 2005) and other related works; and Francis Fukuyama for his excellent books *The Origin of Political Order* and *Political Order and Political Decay* (Farrar, Strauss, and Giroux, 2015).

127 U.S.D.A. Economic Research Service

128 David Karp, "Most of America's Fruit Is Now Imported. Is That a Bad Thing?" The New York Times, March 13, 2018, https://www.nytimes.com/2018/03/13/dining/fruit-vegetables-imports.html. See also: https://www.timesunion.com/business/article/Yes-more-of-the-fruits-and-vegetables-you-re-13762595.php

129 "Iowa Food and Farm Facts," Iowa State University, Extension and Outreach, published November 2016, https://www.extension.iastate.edu/ffed/wp-content/uploads/2018/04/IowaFoodandFarm-Facts-2018-1.pdf

130 A. Harold Achicanoy, Anne D. Bjorkman, Nora P. Castañeda-Álvarez, Hannes Dempewolf, Johannes M. M. Engels, Ximena Flores-Palacios, Luigi Guarino, et al. "Origins of food crops connect countries worldwide," The Royal Society Publishing, June 15, 2016, https://royalsocietypublishing.org/doi/10.1098/rspb.2016.0792.

131 Chris McGreal, "How America's food Giants Swallowed Family Farms," The Guardian, March 9, 2019, https://www.theguardian.com/environment/2019/mar/09/american-food-giants-swallow-the-family-farms-iowa. See also: https://downloads.usda.library.cornell.edu/usda-esmis/files/b5644r52v/jd473028z/7w62fc23r/SlauOverview-10-27-2016.pdf. See also: https://www.meatinstitute.org/index.php?ht=d/sp/i/47465/pid/47465

132 United States Department of Agriculture. "Overview of the United States Slaughter Industry," October 27, 2016, https://downloads.usda.library.cornell.edu/usda-esmis/files/b5644r52v/jd473028z/7w62fc23r/SlauOverview-10-27-2016.pdf. See also: https://www.nytimes.com/2020/04/18/business/coronavirus-meat-slaughterhouses.html

133 Bee Wilson, *The Way We Eat Now*. Basic Books, 2019. An excellent account of the current food culture.

134 United States Food and Drug Administration. "GMO Crops, Animal Food, and Beyond", Updated 09/28/2020. https://www.fda.gov/food/agricultural-biotechnology/gmo-crops-animal-food-and-beyond

135 "Efforts to Address Seasonal Agricultural Import Competition in the NAFTA Renegotiation", Congressional Research Service, 2017

136 An excellent summary of some of the more crazy examples of world food trade, with plenty of links to direct sources, can be found here at: "Just How Insane is Trade These Days?", Local Futures, Economics of Happiness, and can be accessed here at: https://www.localfutures.org/wp-content/uploads/Insane-Trade-Factsheet-Final.pdf

137 Ibid

138 USDA. Selected Charts from Ag and Food Statistics, Charting the Essentials, February 2020

139 For current beef export data, see United States Department of Agriculture. "Livestock and Poultry: World Markets and Trade," January 12, 2022, https://apps.fas.usda.gov/psdonline/circulars/livestock_poultry.pdf

140 For demographics and dangerous working conditions in the meat packing industry, see this excellent article: Dollar T. Nathan, and Angela Stuesse. "Who are America's Meat and Poultry Workers?" Economic Policy Institute, September 24, 2020, https://www.epi.org/blog/meat-and-poultry-worker-demographics/.

141 USDA Food Safety Inspection Service, "Evaluation of HACCP Inspection Models Project for Market Hogs" https://www.fsis.usda.gov/sites/default/files/media_file/2020-10/Evaluation-HIMP-Market-Hogs.pdf

142 "Feeding The World: Think U.S. Agriculture Will End World Hunger? Think Again.", Environmental Working Group report, updated October 5, 2016, https://www.ewg.org/research/feeding-world

143 Ibid

144 Glenn Rifkin, "Making a Profit and a Difference," The New York Times, October 5, 2006, https://www.nytimes.com/2006/10/05/business/making-a-profit-and-a-difference.html.

145 U.S. Food and Drug Administration. "Food Facts: How to Cut Food Waste and Maintain Food Safety," November, 2019. https://www.fda.gov/food/consumers/how-cut-food-waste-and-maintain-food-safety. See also: https://www.fao.org/food-loss-and-food-waste/flw-data and more here at : https://www.pbs.org/newshour/show/americans-waste-up-to-40-percent-of-the-food-they-produce#:~:text=In%20the%20U.S.%2C%20up%20to,food%20that%20never%20gets%20eaten.

146 United States Environmental Protection Agency. "Sources of Greenhouse Gas Emissions," 2019, https://www.epa.gov/ghgemissions/sources-greenhouse-gas-emissions#agriculture. Also United Nations. "Food systems account for over one-third of global greenhouse gas emissions," March 9, 2021, https://news.un.org/en/story/2021/03/1086822.

147 Water Footprint Calculator. "Food's Big Water Footprint," April 25, 2020, https://www.watercalculator.org/footprint/foods-big-water-footprint/.

148 U.S. Department of Agriculture. "Why should we care about food waste?" https://www.usda.gov/foodlossandwaste/why . For more on food waste, see EPA report here: https://www.epa.gov/sustainable-management-food/sustainable-management-food-basics

149 According to the United Nations, annual crop loss is around 40%. Here at: https://news.un.org/en/story/2021/06/1093202#:~:text=Some%2040%20per%20cent%20of,main%20drivers%20of%20biodiversity%20loss. See also: "The Future of Food and Agriculture: Trends and Challenges," Food and Agriculture Organization of the United Nations, 2017, https://www.fao.org/3/i6583e/i6583e.pdf.

150 For a good overview on pesticide use, see "Pesticides in Our Food System", Foodprint. Last updated: 2/08/21, https://foodprint.org/issues/pesticides/

151 For a terrific summary of USDA statistics, see the charts here at USDA Economic Research Survey. "Ag and Food Statistics: Charting the Essentials," February 2020, https://www.ers.usda.gov/webdocs/publications/96957/ap-083.pdf?v=7732.7. See page 7 of report for percent cotton exported.

152 Stephen Leahy, "Insect 'apocalypse' in U.S. driven by 50x increase in toxic pesticides", National Geographic, August 6, 2019 https://www.nationalgeographic.com/environment/article/insect-apocalypse-under-way-toxic-pesticides-agriculture

153 Safe Drinking Water Foundation. "Pesticides and Water Pollution," January 23, 2017, https:// www.safewater.org/fact-sheets-1/2017/1/23/pesticides.

154 Dave Goulson, "Insect Declines and Why They Matter," The Wildlife Trusts, 2021. https:// www.somersetwildlife.org/sites/default/files/2019-11/FULL%20AFI%20REPORT%20WEB1 1. pdf. See also Business Insider report at: https://www.businessinsider.com/insect-apocalypse-ecosys-tem-collapse-food-insecurity-2019-11. See also: https://www.nationalgeographic.com/environment/article/insect-apocalypse-under-way-toxic-pesticides-agriculture and https://www.sciencedirect.com/science/article/abs/pii/S0006320718313636

155 Adrion R., Jeffrey, Nick M. Haddad, Leslie Ries, Tyson Wepprich, and Jerome Wiedmann. "Butterfly abundance declines over 20 years of systematic monitoring in Ohio, USA," July 9, 2019, https://journals.plos.org/plosone/article?id=10.1371/journal.pone.0216270.

156 Francisco Sánchez-Bayo and Kris A.G. Wyckhuys. "Worldwide decline of the entomofauna: A review of its drivers," Biological Conservation, Volume 232, April 2019, https://www.sciencedirect.com/science/article/pii/S0006320718313636.

157 Daniel Raichel and Dr. Jennifer Sass. "Bigger Than Bees: How Neonics Contaminate Water, Threaten Ecosystems, And Cause Human Health Concerns In New York". The Natural Resources Defense Council, January 2020. https://www.nrdc.org/sites/default/files/bigger-than-bees-neonics-new-york-report.pdf

158 I'm using Michael Pollan's numbers here from *Omnivore's Dilemma.*

159 Laura Lengnick, *Resilient Agriculture: Cultivating Food Systems for a Changing Climate.* Gabriola, BC, Canada: New Society Publishers, second edition 2022.

160 NASA "The Effects of Climate Change", 2022 https://climate.nasa.gov/effects/

161 Laura Schumm, "America's Patriotic Victory Gardens: During both World Wars, America's agricultural production became a powerful military tool," History, August 31, 2018, https://www.history.com/news/americas-patriotic-victory-gardens. See also: https://www.compostingcouncil.org/page/VictoryGardens

162 Peterson and Seligman, et all. *Classification of Character Strengths and Virtues.* Includes six core strengths: Wisdom and Knowledge; Courage; Humanity; Justice; Temperance; and Transcendence. I added Industry to that list, and present them in a different order, sometimes using a different term as a heading, such as "Understanding" or "Spirituality" to help with the acronym of JUSTICE so that the core virtues may be easily remembered.

163 Peterson and Seligman, et all. *Classification of Character Strengths and Virtues*